History from Crime

Selections from *Quaderni Storici*

Edward Muir and Guido Ruggiero, Series Editors

Sex and Gender in Historical Perspective
Microhistory and the Lost Peoples of Europe
History from Crime

History from Crime

Edited by Edward Muir and Guido Ruggiero

Translated by Corrada Biazzo Curry,
Margaret A. Gallucci, and Mary M. Gallucci

The Johns Hopkins University Press
Baltimore and London

The Johns Hopkins University Press
2715 North Charles Street
Baltimore, Maryland 21218-4319
The Johns Hopkins Press Ltd., London

Library of Congress Cataloging-in-Publication Data
History from crime / edited by Edward Muir and Guido Ruggiero ; translated by
    Corrada Biazzo Curry, Margaret A. Gallucci, and Mary M. Gallucci.
        p.   cm.—(Selections from Quaderni storici)
    Translated from Italian.
    Includes index.
    ISBN 0-8018-4732-X (hc : acid-free paper).—ISBN 0-8018-4733-8 (p. : acid-free
paper)
    1. Crime—Europe—History.   2. Criminal registers—Europe—History.
3. Europe—Historiography.   4. History—Methodology.   I. Muir, Edward,
1946–   . II. Ruggiero, Guido, 1944–   .   III. Series.
HV6937.A22   1994
364.94—dc20   93-32009

A catalog record of this book is available from the British Library.

ঽ Contents

❧ Introduction: The Crime of History

by Edward Muir and Guido Ruggiero

History begins where justice ends. Long after the judge finishes a case and sends its record off to gather dust in the archives, a historian reclaims it for his or her own purposes. Few concern themselves so long after the crime with the contested issues of guilt or innocence, since the value of criminal records for history is not so much what they uncover about a particular crime as what they reveal about otherwise invisible or opaque realms of human experience. Nevertheless, it has long been fashionable to compare historical and judicial methods, typically by assigning to the historian a judicial role such as witness, detective, or judge. The comparison is obviously a metaphoric one, useful to the degree that it illuminates something about historical practice. It might be especially illuminating, however, to play with the metaphor by suspending the flattering comparisons. Consider what might be unmasked by seeing the historian as criminal, historical practice as a kind of crime.

What crimes do historians commit? They might best be seen as thieves, as persons who practice a form of grave robbing. Renaissance grave robbers carried off bodies to sell to physicians for dissections, and historians also appropriate and dismember the past, absconding with the words of others to make their own classifications and to write new narratives. Even more than the inquisitors and judges of the criminal record, historians are likely to suborn witnesses, depriving them of their own integrity; at the worst they are even forced to answer historians' questions with words spoken in answer to other questions. From a slightly different perspective influenced by Foucault, the crime of history, like that of medicine, might be seen as originating in its construction as a discipline. Fulfilling the demands of their discipline, historians justify their little thefts, unveiling past derelictions and expropriating judicial secrets.

Despite their pilferings, historians must retain certain obligations to their victims, obligations that stretch beyond the workings of justice. A crime is a moment when a culture fails in its own terms, a moment when microsystems challenge macrosystems of power and values. Criminal justice attempts to reassert or even establish macrosystems by classifying the actors in an event according to a schema of roles: there are perpetrators, victims, accusers, witnesses, friends, enemies, police, jailers, judges, executioners, and lawgivers. Although historians so often masquerade as participants in the judicial process, they cannot passively accept the schema of roles and results assigned by the dominating ideology of the criminal justice system. Instead they must seek to discover opportunities in a disturbing moment of the past to identify other ideologies, values, and lives often masked or obliterated by the hegemonic vision of criminal records. Thus, even as he snitches on the dead, the historian's fundamental obligation is to respect them in their own terms rather than in those of the judicial record that brings their experiences to view.

Historians find in criminal records an alluring venue from which they can perpetrate their own crimes because the misdeeds of the past generated a body of texts that reveal otherwise unspoken cultural assumptions, that give voice to the illiterate, that disclose the discontinuities of the society, that generate little dramas about human conflicts and dilemmas, that resurrect the otherwise hidden life of the street, gaming hall, counterfeiter's workshop, priest's bedroom, and prison cell. The multiple and overlapping texts describe events from different points of view and often report the actual words spoken centuries ago. The marvelous mine of judicial documents gives up many kinds of riches: legal traditions, denunciations, jurisdictional and definitional disputes, criminal investigations, depositions, incarceration lists, accounts of torture sessions, material evidence, legal and institutional maneuverings, trials, sentences, appeals, punishments, and classifications of certain persons as members of a criminal class. Each level offers different possibilities for the writing of history.

The most beguiling possibilities take the reader far beyond the crime itself into the social and cultural worlds revealed through the criminal record. The texts that lead into these worlds present historians with distinctive problems. First, each text is, by definition, biased and approximate. Not only do witnesses and those giving depositions characteristically tell lies that they hope will sound truthful, the judicial process itself limits what can be asked, what can be answered, what can be admitted as evidence, what can be considered in a verdict. Often silences are as revealing as any words in the recorded dialogue. For example, in Giovanna Fiume's article "The Old Vinegar Lady," published in this volume, some of the defendants are strangely silent in the record because they were freed from the inquisitorial dialogue by external political influence and eventually exempted from punishment. Evidently criminal records can never be simple windows into the past; rather, they are highly crafted images fashioned in accord with legal procedures, statutes, precedents, and the cultural and power dynamics of the past.

Second, judicial texts serve as scripts in a theater of authority. Everyone who speaks during a criminal procedure does so under the constraints of authority, which means that all speech has been conditioned by threats of punishment, the fear of torture, the influence of well-connected persons, and the need of the regime to make criminal sentences exemplary. Historians have long recognized that court cases generate evidence that has been polluted by authority. One response favored in recent years has been to treat criminal records as dialogues in which as much attention is paid to questions asked as answers given, and special note is made of moments when defendant and judge misunderstand each other. A crucial factor that qualifies the dialogic model is that the interchange between a judge or inquisitor and a defendant or witness is imbalanced, especially since only one party has the power to coerce and the command of all the information. Nevertheless, the witness's opportunity to fashion evidence was certainly no small thing, especially if unchecked by others.

Third, such texts are always multivocal. Legal procedures tend to privilege certain voices over others, but historians need to retain some sense of the multiplicity of voices and avoid slipping into the role of retrospective judges who render verdicts by deciding who is telling the truth. When Sabina Loriga in "A Secret to Kill the King" uncovers accusations that inmates in the state prisons were sticking pins into magical dolls to kill the king, she worries less about the truth of the denunciation than the social atmosphere in which the accusations took place. Respecting diversity, however, does not mean that all interpretations are equally valid. The documents limit possibilities as well as break down the notion of unitary truth. In the criminal records each voice narrates its own story, which defines the event that has taken place and establishes how it is to be interpreted. Faced with proliferating stories, historians typically piece together yet another version, written according to the rhetorical canons of modern scholarship in an act that implicates them along with the criminal justice system in the process of defining roles. In recognizing their work as theft and accepting the irony of their narrations, however, historians have not despaired, and many have reveled in the possibilities of new interpretations.

Historians have understood criminality in many ways: breaking a law sets apart certain actions as a special kind of event, which can disrupt some social solidarities and create others; crimes exercise power in ways that reveal social hierarchies and fields of disempowerment; they communicate values, especially contested ones; and they generate symbols for social relationships. No matter how he or she interprets them, however, no matter how solid the evidence, no matter how just the judicial decision, the historian must treat the crime itself as a provisional and open-ended example of a social interaction situated in a particular time and place. In addition, the authorities' classifications of crimes mean that criminal records appear in series: individual rapes, murders, and thefts are revealed to the historian as part of a series of incidents categorized under the same statutory rubric. These series of criminal records have led some historians to analyze similar crimes in aggregate form, as Oscar Di Simplicio does here for cases involving clerical morals, Andrea Zorzi for incidents of official corruption, Angelo Torre for examples of feuding violence, and Edoardo Grendi for samples of counterfeiting. Others have ignored the preestablished series of the criminal records and extracted individual cases, following the names of participants and actors through a variety of sources.

A common trait of the essays in this volume is that they use a particular crime merely as the point of departure for investigating society and culture from the various perspectives that the records of crime provide. The essays break down into two areas, those that use crime to study cultural patterns and those devoted to uncovering political and economic structures. Thus the first three essays—Silvano Cavazza's "Double Death: Resurrection and Baptism in a Seventeenth-Century Rite," Oscar Di Simplicio's "Perpetuas: The Women Who Kept Priests, Siena 1600–1800," and Giovanna Fiume's "The Old Vinegar Lady or the Judicial Modernization of the Crime of Witchcraft"— can be read largely as exciting contributions to the new cultural history. Sabina Loriga's essay, the fourth in this volume, "A Secret to

Kill the King: Magic and Protection in Piedmont in the Eighteenth Century," swings from culture to politics and therefore provides a transition to the second section, which deals primarily with the latter issue. The next three essays—Andrea Zorzi's "The Florentines and Their Public Offices in the Early Fifteenth Century: Competition, Abuses of Power, and Unlawful Acts," Angelo Torre's "Feuding, Factions, and Parties: The Redefinition of Politics in the Imperial Fiefs of Langhe in the Seventeenth and Eighteenth Centuries," and Edoardo Grendi's "Counterfeit Coins and Monetary Exchange Structures in the Republic of Genoa during the Sixteenth and Seventeenth Centuries"—focus on politics and to a lesser extent economics, but they provide a rather unusual and decidedly stimulating perspective of both. Finally, the last essay of the volume, Ingeborg Walter's "A Dream of Infanticide in *Fin de Siècle* Vienna," takes the idea of crime to its outer limits by discussing the representations of a dream of a crime that was never actually committed. Walter's analysis of a dream of an imagined crime brings together all the rich possibilities explored by the other essays and suggested by the records of crime, powerfully illustrating how society's construction of criminality helps to fashion individual psyches.

Silvano Cavazza begins the volume with death, and a particularly disturbing form of death at that: the death of unbaptized babies. Theologians had long held that infants who died without the benefit of baptism were damned without hope of salvation, but the logic of that position, which can be traced back to Saint Augustine, faced resistance when it began to be pressed on the laity, who were uncertain about maintaining doctrinal purity when aggrieved by the death of a child. Thus, in the little mountain village of Trava in Friuli in northeastern Italy the problem of unbaptized dead babies was rectified by a ceremony that seemed miraculously to resurrect the dead for a short time so that they could be baptized, be reburied in holy ground, and merit salvation.

Fra Antonio Dall'Occhio, who was concerned about the legitimacy of the ceremony and the miraculous rebirths, began an investigation aimed at proving the heretical nature of these practices and ending the abuse of the sacrament. Ultimately his investigation failed because he faced powerful interests in the vicinity who profited from the "resurrections" and the shrine that had grown up around them and also because the double deaths met significant spiritual needs of the peasants in the region, who were deeply disturbed by the Augustinian view of the damnation of unbaptized infants.

This seemingly marginal incident grows under Cavazza's historical cultivation into a powerful study of the influence of theological traditions on popular culture across much of Europe in the early modern period. Tracing the "miracle" of infant resurrection, Cavazza explains it as a popular reaction to the coercive impulse of the early modern church, which was anxious to disseminate a more theologically correct vision of the sacraments and especially baptism. That reaction reveals an impressive popular commitment to spirituality and reveals the vitality of popular Christian values across rural Europe.

Historians are already deeply involved in studying the popular world we have lost, not as a curiosity, but as a rich and evocative culture or series of cultures that interacted with high culture. Cavazza demonstrates that the peasants' concern for dead infants (along with more recognized desires for familial reintegration through the burial of unbaptized babies in consecrated ground) was significant enough that many people were willing to travel long distances and pay a considerable sum to secure the momentary resurrection of a dead child to enable baptism. He also suggestively reconsiders folk beliefs about the spirits of unbaptized dead to conclude that fear as well as love played an important role in seeking out miracles that would allow unbaptized infants to rest in peace.

Cavazza's close analysis of an obscure crime in an isolated mountain valley of Friuli provides a richly revealing portrait of the meaning of death and the power of love and fear among peasants in the early modern period. Yet in the end, this article may make its most useful contribution to the history of fear. For in many ways the post-Tridentine church advanced into rural Europe with a bureaucracy and system of sacramental ritual aimed at ordering life and overcoming fear. Baptism was one key to that program. It incorporated Christians into a religious community—in fact, baptism was the ultimate binding tie of community—and it opened the doors to a sacramental and confessional system that potentially had the power to sustain the community and to triumph over death. The church's stress on baptism as a sacrament that overcame death created in its very success, however, a new series of fears and reinforced deep uncertainties in ways that ironically sustained pseudomiracles and an elaborate folk culture.

Oscar Di Simplicio's "Perpetuas: The Women Who Kept Priests" is on the surface a much more traditional look at the range of crimes associated with priests who kept female servants in and around Siena in the seventeenth and eighteenth centuries. A rough statistical profile broken down by century and location (rural versus urban) provides the broad frame of the analysis, but the crime data have been enriched by tracing the tracks left in the documents by names much in the manner of microhistory. Most important, however, Di Simplicio, like Cavazza, employs a study of seemingly insignificant little crimes to recapture a world dense with significations both for contemporaries and for the modern historian. Thus these crimes reveal how some female servants could become masters of the parish and even control access to the sacred; how the categories of widow, wife, and spinster worked for practical purposes, such as getting a job as a servant, or for broader concerns, such as maintaining honor; how the ideal of a companionate heterosexual relationship was both recognized and rejected by the church; and how ideas about gender constructed the public self of lower-class women.

This article also demonstrates how understanding microsystems of power has at times the potential to redimension in significant ways our understanding of macrosystems, for to a great extent the church was an economic and bureaucratic organization based on a macrosystem of benefices granted to support the clergy and their ecclesiastical functions. Many of the little crimes illuminated by Di Simplicio show how that macrosystem could be directed by the strategies of relatively humble local priests and their servants. The church was a force in local life in the early modern period in many ways, but here crime shows a host of relationships that may well have been more important for the church and its interaction with society than has been realized. One theme among many which seems particularly interesting and worthy of further research, although Di Simplicio does not stress it, is the way in which alliances between priests and local women had the potential both to integrate a priest in his community and to give women a role in the church and its functions. Was there in the local parishes a previously unnoticed female presence that was curtailed only by eliminating the abuses of the perpetua system?

The cultural and practical significances of the classification of crimes are a central theme in Giovanna Fiume's "The Old Vinegar Lady." A failure to understand a change in the classification led the old vinegar lady, Giovanna Bonanno, to misread events, a misapprehension that resulted in her execution. Her misreading hinged on a transition in the way magic and witchcraft were perceived by elites across the eighteenth century. Fiume shows that in the early part of the century both were dismissed by elites as folk superstitions of no particular power or significance and thus did not warrant serious punishment. Bonanno and many of her peers were by the late century perfectly aware of how this attitude had been reflected in the dismissive way the authorities treated accusations of witchcraft and magical practice. As a result, she was prepared to play the role of the witch as others before her had done to escape serious punishment. She fully expected the authorities to denigrate the power of her magic, exculpating her of any criminal responsibility for her deeds.

In a cruel irony, however, which highlights the complexity of micro-strategies of power in the context of crime, Bonanno did not realize that the changing perceptions of crime had moved on to her disadvantage. As a result the claim of witchcraft which would have once freed her had been refitted into a new schema of scientific criminology. Now her magical vinegar cure was identified as a lethal poison, a label that transformed her from a deluded old lady who thought she was a witch to the archetype of the secret female poisoner who had lurked in the fears of men for centuries. Playing on this paradox, Fiume cleverly constructs a powerful microstudy that builds out from the uncertainty about what is real and what is illusory in trials, using that uncertainty about truth to reveal meaning rather than hide it. Rather than being daunted by the fact that the trial proceedings can be read in more than one way (as either magic or poisoning at the simplest level), she actually accepts and uses the ambiguity in the texts to take us deeper into the issues and the conflicting cultures that are revealed in them. Here we are in a world where trials may be read as theater, where judges, accusers, and accused follow and improvise within the limits of cultural scripts, scripts that can be and are briefly illuminated by a close analysis of a series of related crimes.

From Fiume's article one also obtains a clear sense of the highly problematic yet significant relationship between law, criminal practice, and perceptions both judicial and lay—in many ways Bonanno's perceptions of her situation were legally current (as a confused old witch she should have been treated leniently), procedurally correct (as a witch her self-demeaning confession should have ended the investigation), but culturally wrong (she was executed as a poisoner). From another perspective Bonanno's trial was more than a procedure designed to determine whether or not she had committed a crime: it was also a kind of cultural workshop in which perceptions of order and community were measured and fashioned. Terror was central to this process, as Fiume shows by analyzing the unnecessary torture of the seventy-five-year-old vinegar lady. While torture was not necessary to prove her guilt—Bonanno in her innocent cleverness had more than admitted her guilt—Fiume argues that authorities nonetheless employed the pain and terror of torture to empower the symbols the trial was promulgating. In much the same vein her ceremonial punishment underlined that magic was now murder: the cultural workshop of pain and death was attempting to "reorder" society, culture, and public perceptions. Fiume has given us a fine example of how crime documentation often depicts with striking clarity particularly poignant (or brutal) moments of the process of social and cultural fashioning and refashioning which is at the heart of modern society.

Sabina Loriga's "A Secret to Kill the King: Magic and Protection in Piedmont in the Eighteenth Century" parallels Fiume's analysis of the role of witchcraft accusations in the enlightened eighteenth century. Loriga, however, does not emphasize the dichotomy between high and low culture as much as Fiume does; rather, she sees the accusations as part of what might be called the "culture of the everyday," a set of beliefs sustained across class lines. In these Piedmontese cases, inmates in prisons and charitable hospitals, those "total institutions" that regulated the entire lives of their charges, accused others of making magical dolls to kill members of the royal family. Although beliefs in the efficacy of magic may have declined among intellectuals and officials, accusations such as these struck at the very heart of the dynamics of power and could not be ignored by magistrates who would have scoffed at more traditional witchcraft denunciations emanating from the tensions of village life.

By focusing on the accusers rather than the defendants or the judges, Loriga reveals how marginal persons can be quite clever manipulators of the political system, employing in this case frightful allegations in order to improve their own situation as inmates in a public institution for the poor. The sophistication of the accusers constitutes a telling example of the "weapons of the weak" in an early modern society. Recognizing how the state has taken complete control of, and indeed responsibility for, the bodies of many of the weak, the accusers have reversed the trajectory of power by conjuring magical control over the body of the prince. In addition, Loriga has shown that rather than being isolated from daily life, total institutions were completely integrated into society and the state, a theme echoed in Grendi's study of counterfeiting. Even a starving, abused, and abandoned wife had a card to play to draw the king's attention to her plight.

Sabina Loriga's Piedmontese study also demonstrates how popular magical beliefs could enter into the workings of the Savoyard monarchy at a moment of dynastic crisis. In a more direct fashion, Andrea Zorzi's examination of allegations of official corruption in early fifteenth-century Florence, Angelo Torre's analysis of feuding in the imperial fiefs of Langhe, and Edoardo Grendi's consideration of the relationship between counterfeiting and monetary exchanges in Genoa destructure the self-presentations of *ancien régime* states.

Like Loriga, Zorzi concentrates on the significance of accusations of criminal conduct. In "The Florentines and Their Public Offices in the Early Fifteenth Century," he shows how accusing someone of official corruption was a form of political competition during the decades of oligarchic closure before the Medici takeover of the Florentine republic. Zorzi notes that the teleology behind moralistic charges of public corruption was, in fact, constructed out of the struggle for power, prestige, and profit. The moral dimension of the state, which was particularly ambiguous for the merchant republic of Florence, so lacking in a charismatic prince and traditions of aristocratic honor, made public offices an especially contested ground. In addition to the inevitable tussle for power, every public official faced a great deal of ambiguity over the proper values appropriate to his duties. Zorzi points to a characteristic double standard in the advice Paolo da Certaldo gave to his son: avoid accepting gifts while in office but be sure to give them; that is, owe nothing to others but try to make others indebted to you. Zorzi's view of civic morality as a political construct that served private ends provides a useful corrective to the historians of humanism who have isolated this period as particularly crucial in the evolution of an ideology of civic patriotism.

Far more radical in destructuring government is Angelo Torre's brilliant and complex article, "Feuding, Factions, and Parties." By looking through the multiple refractions of feuds, Torre reveals the almost complete plasticity of all social and political institutions: family, clan, community, youth abbey, seigneurial class, and even the royal bureaucracy. In the context of a feud every social group is a temporary alliance of convenience and every action has many potential meanings, a situation that opens the door for creative and multiple interpretations such as Torre provides. A judicial record only begins to yield meaning when the names of persons contained in it are identified and their reputed actions compared with other reported actions. Thus, Torre demonstrates how the kidnapping of a young woman can be both a rape and a competitive move for advantage, a crime and a political act. From Torre's point of view, feuding could generate all aspects of community life: godparentage, confraternity rituals, charitable contributions, the collection of taxes, office holding, commerce, smuggling, and political affiliations. Most important of all was criminal justice, which was merely one more card in a lethal game to win local power and influence. Neither regal justice nor the monarchy itself stood above these deeply entrenched mountain valley conflicts; rather, they were deeply implicated in them. The state was not so much an antagonist of private feuds as an extension of them. Zorzi's study turns the very notion of state justice on its head: judicial practice was merely a facet of crime, which was less a kind of pathology than the very stuff of everyday life.

In Edoardo Grendi's "Counterfeit Coins and Monetary Exchange Structures in the Republic of Genoa during the Sixteenth and Seventeenth Centuries," microhistorical analysis is used to challenge macrohistorical concepts about the nature of the state and the operations of monetary exchange markets. By examining a series of cases of counterfeiting, Grendi situates the exchange of coins in what he calls the "social culture of money," which reveals a widespread collective consciousness of the individuality of each coin, evaluated not just by its face value but also by its color, appearance, and weight. At all social levels, people understood the relative value of coinages and were knowledgeable about recognizing, passing, and making false or clipped coins. Far from being an aberrant criminal activity, counterfeiting was completely integrated into the normal operations of smuggling, seigneurial minting privileges, alchemy, and foreign trade. Goldsmiths, soldiers, convicts serving on galleys, bankers, wholesalers, grain merchants, butchers, millers, and especially priests specialized in counterfeit and coin-clipping operations.

At the higher social levels and in the relations between states, arbitrage between different monetary exchange markets was a normal way of doing business in which passing adulterated coins played a systematic part. Aristocrats and public officials employed their authority to gain advantages in this exchange market. Seen from Grendi's perspective, the state did not so much guarantee the purity and intrinsic value of coins as it acted as a vast alchemical enterprise. The desire of so many monarchs in Renaissance Europe to patronize the best alchemists merely reflects the fact that alchemy was one of the higher forms of counterfeiting. The idea of criminal counterfeiting, thus, can only be understood as an aspect of market exchange mechanisms. In attempting to monopolize or at least manipulate coinages, early modern governments tried to classify their competition as criminals. Grendi's analysis shows how official arbitrage practices undermine the symbolic claims of the state which made counterfeiting a crime of lese majesty.

The final article, Ingeborg Walter's "A Dream of Infanticide in *Fin de Siècle* Vienna," offers as its subject neither defendant nor judge nor even a disputed action but only the dream of a crime. In the dream of infanticide the process of criminalizing certain kinds of behavior which began with the Renaissance state has become an attribute of modern neurosis. Freud's patient, Mr. E., commits no felony but has so internalized the paradigm of criminality that he dreams that he has; in effect, he criminalizes his own sexual behavior. The external constraints on behavior which the *ancien régime* states attempted to inculcate through judicial punishments have been internalized by Mr. E., who needed Dr. Freud's help to untie his internalized bonds. Walter's article raises the question of what is the object in historical study. Is it the idea of infanticide, the dream about it, Mr. E.'s version of the dream, Dr. Freud's first or second account of Mr. E.'s version, Freud's analysis of Mr. E., the known facts about Mr. E.'s life, the culture of *fin de siècle* Vienna, or the paradigm of criminality itself?

Questions about the object of study persist in any historical account based on criminal records. The historians in this collection have struggled to avoid either being implicated in the judicial process itself or submitting themselves to the dreams of the states that invented the idea of crime, criminals, a criminal class, criminal desires, and criminal dreams. In so doing they have selected a variety of objects to study from the judicial record: defendants, accusers, political figures surrounding the cases, all the names mentioned in the documents, the social groups charged with criminal conduct, and the mere idea of crime. Their answers show that it matters not so much who is studied as how the study is undertaken. By concentrating so precisely on the process of analysis, these historians have shown how fruitful the enterprise can be.

History from Crime

1 ৡ Double Death: Resurrection and Baptism in a Seventeenth-Century Rite

by Silvano Cavazza

In November 1681, Fra Antonio Dall'Occhio, who had already served four years as priest of the tribunal of the Holy Office of Udine, with jurisdiction over the patriarchate of Aquileia and the neighboring diocese of Concordia, opened a new dossier with this annotation:

> The Dominican officer and vicar of this Holy Office in San Daniele, Girolamo Maria, has several times warned me orally that in the village of Trava, above Tolmezzo on the way to Carnia, there are some wicked women who for many years, with the consent of the parish priest, have abused the sacrament of baptism and, taking advantage of the ignorance of the faithful, pretend to resuscitate the dead. These women are brought the babies who came out of their mothers' wombs dead, and they display them before the altar of the Madonna and have the Holy Mass celebrated. Saying particular prayers, all of a sudden they shout that the Madonna has performed a miracle, that the baby has given signs of life, opened an eye, shed a tear, moved an arm, urinated; and immediately with the water they have ready they baptize it; then, having baptized it, they say that it again has returned to death and they bury it, taking so much from the baby's parents, or, to be more accurate, from the parents of the corpse that emerged inanimate from the maternal womb.[1]

This was undoubtedly a significant enough charge that the Holy Office could not ignore it; and that was even more true when the

---

"La doppia morte: Resurrezione e battesimo in un rito del Seicento," *Quaderni storici* 50 (1982): 551–82. Translated by Mary M. Gallucci.

following May the same Dominican from San Daniele added, this time in writing, new and disquieting particulars on this "most significant abuse." At the little sanctuary in a very isolated high valley of the Tagliamento, those who were coming to see the miracle came not only from the surrounding localities but also from the plains, from Cadore, and from Comelico. "This great miracle is so well known, long standing and regular," continued the friar, "and so successful, that among the great number who happen to go there for such an affair, who come by the hundreds in a few months and sometimes more in one day only, not even one of those disgraced things remains without being revived (as they say) and in consequence all are baptised." Along with his own report he enclosed in the letter some written forms, evidently confiscated from parents involved, in which the notary of Trava had attested to the resurrection, which occurred with great solemnity, listing the signs of life and the names of the witnesses who saw them and specifying especially the administration of the baptism, which immediately followed.[2]

From his very first notes it is evident that the inquisitor of Udine gave no credence whatsoever to these beliefs; nevertheless, he endeavored to gather as complete documentation as possible on the subject, consulting his rural collaborators and the parish priests who were more directly involved. Only after three and a half years of investigation did he send a detailed report to his direct superiors—the Congregation of the Holy Office in Rome. Their reply, on June 9, 1685, was laconic yet exhaustive: "These my most eminent colleagues, the most illustrious Cardinals and Inquisitors General. . ." wrote Cardinal Cybo in the name of the entire Congregation, "have commanded that you effect the removal of similar abuses by those means that your prudence will judge most opportune."[3] Even before the answer from Rome, in January 1683, the inquisitorial vicar of San Daniele had begun the first trial, involving a farmer from Teor (a village of lower Friuli, about one hundred kilometers south of Trava) who had been stopped while on his way to the sanctuary with the remains of a stillborn son.[4] From 1683 until 1686 the Dominicans of San Daniele, whose monastery served as the seat of the vicarial tribunal of the Holy Office for the area, investigated nine other members of the faithful who had confessed to having brought dead infants to Trava or who had been surprised while doing so. Each immediately recognized their error and submitted to the spiritual punishments assigned, which were, in reality, quite light, declaring their own good faith and full obedience to the teachings of the church.[5]

In Udine, however, Dall'Occhio had to proceed more cautiously: he fully approved of the actions of the vicar of San Daniele and thus followed them carefully, even suggesting the questions to be asked of those being investigated as well as a precise form for registering their answers.[6] At the same time, he continued to collect information about the alleged resurrections. Thus eventually the file "False Resurrections of Babies Who Came out of the Maternal Womb Dead," which he had begun in 1681 with the notes referred to earlier, became a large dossier of more than one hundred pages, which should be read along with the reports of the investigations of San Daniele, filed separately in the series of the Acta Sancti Officii. Strangely, however, all this material did not lead to any trials directly, nor were those who early on appeared to be genuinely responsible for the abuses and irregularities committed at Trava ever prosecuted. From 1682, the inquisitor had statements and information that made it evident that the chaplain of the locality, Don Giovanni Beorchia, as well as the notary Giovanni Lischiutta had fully encouraged the behavior of the two women, the former by celebrating Mass for the souls of babies, the latter by drawing up certificates of the resurrection and baptism, and both had been rewarded for their services. To Dall'Occhio it appeared unacceptable that "such great abuses, such false resurrections, such impious operations, such ill-got gain" would be endorsed by members of the clergy. Already in 1683 he wrote very explicitly: "The parish priest himself and how many other priests know about these false operations and they participate in them positively, not only permitting them, but celebrating the Holy Mass for them; they have no more faith than infidels and render themselves gravely suspicious of heresy."[7] Nevertheless, even backed by the favorable opinion of the Roman Congregation, he was unable to take any measures against these two characters.

The protagonists, in effect, had a certain support and protection in Udine, even if they resided in one of the most inaccessible and secluded areas of Friuli. Trava was a hamlet so tiny (at the beginning of the century it contained no more than fifty families) that it did not even constitute a parish by itself, depending, along with other localities, on the parish of Invillino, four miles from the valley. In the middle of the small village, however, there stood next to the Church of San Leonardo the only prominent building, the stone palace of the Beorchia, a large and wealthy family, bolstered by an ancient and indisputable authority.[8] It was one of the Beorchia, in 1657, who had bequeathed a sum of money so that a small church would be built at the threshold of the village, in honor of the Madonna of Carmelo. In 1659 the notary Giovanni Lischiutta—the same person noted earlier and related to Beorchia through his wife—redacted the relevant documents and sent them, in the name of "this commune and people of Trava," to the Patriarchal Court, which immediately consented to the founding of the sanctuary. At that time the curate of the village was Don Michele Beorchia; his brother Francesco was elected by his fellow citizens to be chaplain of the new church. In 1675, with the death of his brother, Don Francesco succeeded to the benefice of San Leonardo, and the chaplaincy of the sanctuary was assigned to a non-family member; but this newcomer had a much reduced salary, and, his protests notwithstanding, he could not even gain access to the documents relative to his church, since Beorchia had taken them with him.[9]

It is easy to see in this the desire not to entrust the delicate question of miracles to such uncertain hands. In fact, it had been Michele Beorchia himself who had recorded the first miraculous events in 1659, the exact same year as the founding of the sanctuary.[10] In the beginning, however, the clergy of the area had shown serious doubts about the matter, so much so that in 1663 the parish priest of Invillino had written to the authorities of the Curia to inform them about what was happening and to complain about the behavior of the clerics of Trava, "particularly concerning the *putti* who were baptized."[11] In the same year the Holy Office itself became involved in the question, though from a rather different perspective. A bricklayer from Portis, "to unburden his own conscience, to obviate the dishonor done to God, to his Holy Mother, and to the Saints," had denounced the parish priest of Venzone, a respected man of great culture (he had studied with the Jesuits of Graz), for reservations that he expressed publicly about the miracles worked by the Madonna of Trava: "These miracles have gained the reputation," the man declared in his deposition, "that they revive unbaptized babies, about 150 in total, until they are baptized, on account of which one sees a great rush to the Madonna."[12] This denunciation was not investigated; but it is significant that in this case neither the patriarch nor the Holy Office had taken a position on the issue. Thus, it was a local power long established which Dall'Occhio attempted to take on about twenty years later; and it was no accident that Giovanni Beorchia, chaplain of Trava at the time of the investigation and cousin or nephew of the two priests mentioned earlier, knew how to parry successfully each threat.

In 1684 the records of the pastoral visit carried out in this area make no mention of the resurrections and the attendant baptismal rites, although the inquisitor had already publicly raised the question two years before.[13] In 1686, however, Monsignor Celso of Prampero, vicar general of the diocese, personally examined the problem and decreed in an official act that the only manifest irregularity in those actions was the administration of the sacrament by two women while a priest was present.[14] It was an implicit recognition of the validity of the miracles, and from then on Beorchia himself baptized the tiny bodies brought to him, even drawing up a regular certificate (the old notary Lischiutta must have died at the beginning of that year) in which he declared with great solemnity that he had completed the ceremony "with the authority of the most illustrious and most reverend Signor Count Celso of Prampero, most worthy vicar general of Aquileia."[15]

Dall'Occhio must have been aware then that part of the Friulian clergy was hostile to his initiative to impose order on the affairs of Trava. The patriarchal vicar's position, though evidently indirect and a rather ambiguous, was probably merely the conclusion of a series of maneuvers and compromises, which are rather difficult to retrace through official documents. It is clear, however, that the inquisitor at the end of 1687, after having written up his conclusions in a long report, abandoned the investigation he had begun six years earlier. Perhaps he believed he had done his duty, or perhaps he was only following that "prudent course" advised by the Congregation of the Holy Office already in 1685. He did, however, continue to gather and to preserve carefully the documents that were sent to him on the subject, especially from the Dominicans of San Daniele, who had consistently been very supportive of his investigation. In October 1691, one of these friars, whose ministry took him to the interior of Carnia, was still sending alarming news to Udine: "I have been informed by many people," he wrote, "about the bringing of babies who died without baptism to the Madonna of Trava. One person told me that last year more than one hundred of them were brought, and if this thing continues as now, Your Most Reverend Father will see that to impose a remedy on them will need a higher power than mine."[16] This is the last document collected in the file "False Resurrections"; two years later Dall'Occhio left Friuli, and neither the Holy Office nor the ecclesiastical authorities ever occupied themselves with the miracles of Trava again, at least as far as can be known from official acts. The rite continued to be both clandestine and known to all; and this circumstance must certainly not have displeased those who favored it.

   🖜 In the course of his investigation, Dall'Occhio did not limit himself to reconstructing the events surrounding the "miracles" of Trava: in the voluminous notes he left on the subject there is also a sincere effort to understand the phenomenon better. To denounce the irregularities and confusion of the notary and chaplain was, in effect, not enough to solve the problem; by now the faith in the miracles was deeply rooted in the people, and one could not doubt the honesty of the intentions of those who went to the sanctuary.

The official reports of the trials of San Daniele show very clearly that the rite was already considered a time-honored tradition: "I, Zuanne Zuanello," declared the first of those examined on January 27, 1683, "having heard tell seven years ago that the Madonna of Trava worked many miracles, and especially resuscitating dead babies so that they could be baptized, when a dead child was born to me, even though I knew that they died again soon after baptism, I set off on foot to bring it to the aforementioned Madonna, believing it could be baptized." To the peasant of Teor it appeared natural to face a long trip, during the most difficult season, if that could serve to save the soul of his child. To the insinuating questions of the inquisitor (Had he acted for money? Didn't he know that such actions required "always the tacit invocation of the demon"?) he answered with great dignity: "I acted as I said above, because I believed by this that I was saving a soul, nor would I ever had done it if I had known that it was a sin." Moreover, one of his neighbors had done the same thing several years ago as well as many others.[17]

The reference to neighbors and to members of his own family, who in the past had gone to Trava to ask for a similar grace, was common to almost all those investigated in San Daniele. The outcome of such pilgrimages was generally given as certain: all of the newborns had been resuscitated for enough time to administer baptism. Andrea Pinzan, tried in February of the same year, admitted this explicitly, responding to a precise question of the inquisitor: "All of those who were brought have shown signs of life I have heard."[18]

Andrea Pinzan, who appeared spontaneously before the inquisitor to confess that he had brought stillborn twins to Trava the year before, gave a fairly precise summary of the rite that took place. It had been a very simple ceremony, dignified, free from theatrical moments during its long unfolding. The two women had the little casket with the two tiny corpses placed in the middle of the church, in such a way that all present could see them.

> Then they placed themselves on either side of the dead creatures and kneeling with rosaries in their hands they prayed, as did the people around them also, and they remained like this in prayer for the space of four hours. Then, suddenly the surrounding people were told by the two women that the babies were both sweating and it appeared that they really were sweating, and even more, that they were opening and closing their eyes. These signs lasted until each function was completed. As soon as these signs appeared, the more important of the two women took from behind the altar a bowl with holy water and with the aspergillum she sprinkled some water in the face of each creature, saying certain words which meant that she was baptizing them. Afterward we left the church together with the babies dead as before, and after digging a grave, we buried them; in fact, while digging the grave we could hardly find the space in which to bury them, for the terrain was full of small coffins. Finally the same women locked the church and I gave twelve soldi to the principal one and eight to her companion, and having given them something to eat and drink at the hosteria, I departed and returned to my house in San Daniele.[19]

During the celebration of the rite the chaplain of Trava stayed carefully apart. And before going up to the sanctuary from the village, Pinzan had arranged with him the celebration of the Mass for the two infants, giving him twenty-five soldi; afterward the priest had disappeared with some excuse, so that he could not say if the former had actually celebrated the Mass. For the entire ceremony the only protagonists were the two women: they had guided the prayers of those present, reciting the rosary; they had first discerned the signs of life in the tiny bodies and then baptized them. On this point the inquisitor insisted with a particular care, and Pinzan knew how to give precise answers:

> Asked, "How long had those women said those dead babies had shown signs of life?" he replied: "As soon as they saw them sweat, which was three hours after the prayer." Asked, "Did both women say they saw signs of life or just one of them?" he answered: "The principal one was the first to inform the surrounding people and

then even the companion went about saying: 'Look how they sweat.' " Asked "Then it was those women who baptized them?" he replied: "They were there waiting almost one hour, showing how they were sweating and then they seemed dry, opening and then closing their eyes." Asked "Which of the women baptized the children?" he answered: "The principal woman was the one who baptized them and the other one was still praying."

But had he really seen signs of life, the Dominican pressed. He had no doubts in this regard: "I saw with my own eyes the sweating and the opening of the eyes."[20] Francesco Cossat, tried in 1685, also admitted that the two women were the ones who first indicated the signs of life in the baby, but he immediately clarified that all present had recognized them; he himself could still describe them minutely, although he was speaking about an event that had occurred five years earlier: "The signs, then, were that at first it soiled itself a little from behind, then it urinated two or three drops, then it opened one of its hands, that is the left one, then it opened an eye, and having done that, it was baptized by those women."[21]

Dall'Occhio surely had all of these testimonies before him when in his long summation he sought to bring together all his arguments against the faith placed in the miracle. Many declared that they had witnessed this phenomenon, he wrote, but on closer examination the two women were the only ones each time who pointed out the signs of life in the babies: it was they who unfailingly convinced the others present. But it was only a form of collective delusion: "No one could actually verify having seen those supposed signs, for actually one has it according to the reports that no one ever saw such signs. But they have believed and supported this, because those two women said it and supported it. And if someone thought they had seen the signs, it must have been actually an illusion caused by a strong imagination, or an intense desire to see them: but in fact that person had not seen them."

So, only the two women had recognized the signs of the miracle: "Two women only had said this, whose word, both given the nature of their sex and for other reasons, would always be suspicious." God would never entrust the proof of such a great occurrence to such untenable witnesses, or, to say it more frankly: "with only the evidence of two females, who do not have any other goal for their fake resurrections beyond personal gain, and given the notary and the celebrant, the whole thing was more likely to move God to be indignant rather than work miracles."

Besides the inadequacy of the witnesses, there were other aspects of the miracles of Trava which made them hard to believe. Was it possible, Dall'Occhio asked himself, that, among all the babies resuscitated, none remained alive after the baptism? Or that the Virgin, after having obtained from her Son the grace for the resurrections, could not have interceded occasionally so that the newborns would be restored to their parents rather than die—a miracle certainly no greater than the former but perhaps more gratifying and human in consequence? But that never occurred. This was a decisive argument for viewing the resurrections of Trava as quite different from the miracles that the Holy Scriptures attributed to Christ and to the prophets: there, in fact, people were always recalled to life in a nonephemeral way. Thus it was not valid to use such examples to defend the supposed miracles at the sanctuary in Carnia. And then, why should the grace of eternal salvation for the babies, who otherwise would have been deprived of it, be asked for in such a complicated and difficult manner? The parents could have obtained a similar benefit praying in their home if they had faith in divine mercy. Instead it seemed that only the invocations of the two women worked infallibly. This, observed Dall'Occhio with sarcasm, meant thinking that God had established the condemnation of those who died without baptism "not with ultimate and definitive judgment, but only *ad tempus*, only until, that is, it pleased him to be prayed to by those women for their salvation." Instead Divine Law was inflexible and just, and it never unwisely changed its rules. It was a truism of faith that babies born without baptism "[were] all excluded from that Blessed Kingdom and [were] condemned eternally by God to the punishment of damnation, which consist[ed] in the exclusion from His Kingdom." It would have been improbable and impious that God would have so many thousands of babies die without the sacrament, "in order to have them then resuscitated so that they could be baptized, when no such necessity for doing it ha[d] appeared and when according to common and ordinary law one should not interfere with such things that cause the death of so many babies without baptism."[22]

Once the miracle was denounced as unreal, the entire ceremony of Trava became merely an abuse of the sacrament of baptism, for which the two women, the babies' parents, and all those who participated were responsible. Dall'Occhio had written at the beginning of 1683 that one could not, in fact, baptize the dead, "no more than a piece of wood, a stone, let's even say a dog, a hare; things that are, that is, incapable of baptism," The priest who sinned most gravely was he who celebrated "the Holy Mass for condemned souls such as those of the babies born dead from maternal wombs, because those souls had already been marked out for Hell and the punishment of damnation."[23] For the same reason the tiny corpses should not have been buried in a consecrated place: the inquisitor insisted on this point right up to the last instructions he gave on the subject in 1687.[24] At that point, just before abandoning the investigation, he also believed that he had found in the canons a precedent that demonstrated that the rite was to be considered not merely abusive but definitely heretical:

> From these abuses there are born grave suspicions of heresy in those women, and even more grave in that lord chaplain of Trava, who ex officio is able to and must prevent and block these abuses. He instead permits them and consents to them, showing in this way that he believes it is licit to baptize the dead. This was the opinion of Cataphrygians, Marcionites, and Montanists, condemned as heretical in the Third Council of Carthage in Article 6, where they were reported as saying that 'to baptize the dead so that the dead one may have his future, a live person is baptized for the dead one,' in such a way that having baptized a live baby, these heretics were asserting that such a baptism helped the one who died without baptism.[25]

This was probably the inquisitor's response to the authority that Beorchia had arrogated to baptize the tiny bodies himself, on the basis of the document of the patriarchal vicar. The reference to the ancient heresy appears, however, rather weak, and Dall'Occhio did not emphasize it much. In general he preferred to condemn simply "the error, the deception, the weakness and the blindness" of the parents who relied on the supposed miracles, "allowing themselves foolishly and obstinately to believe that their dead babies were reborn, got baptized, died, and their souls went to Paradise, while actually they were already destined by God for the pain of damnation in Hell."[26] More than a doctrinal error, these cases involved the desperate love of fathers and mothers. Even the inquisitor had to notice this, notwithstanding the intransigence of his vision as a theologian and canonist.

❧ In the seventeenth century, the belief in temporary resurrections was not limited to the mountains of Friuli. Dall'Occhio learned that until midcentury the faithful of Carnia and of Cadore had gone to ask for the same miracle at the sanctuary of Maria Luggau in Carinthia, in the valley of the Gail, just over the divide of the Alps. This was the northernmost border of the Patriarchate of Aquileia, and German territory, even if it was related to Carnia by ancient ties and relationships. The Servite friars of that sanctuary commonly baptized and buried babies who were brought to them "because in reality it was a miracle," an informer reported in 1684. This, however, was the sole report because by then pilgrimages from the Italian side had ceased, for people were finding the same grace at the Madonna of Trava as at that distant sanctuary.[27] Dall'Occhio did not delve too closely into this report, although the sanctuary fell, at least formally, under the jurisdiction of the Holy Office of Aquileia. Perhaps, if he had investigated there too, he would have realized that in reality Maria Luggau and Trava represented merely the eastern manifestations of a belief that was well established in Europe, in a vast territory that in the seventeenth century swung without interruption from Flanders and Brabant to Provence, reaching eastward through the Alpine and pre-Alpine regions, from Savoy to Franche-Comté and on to areas of Switzerland and the southern Tyrol, including branches in Italy, in the high valleys of the Adige and Piave.[28]

The evidence for these miracles, or at least for belief in them, comes to us from a remarkable series of sources, each quite different: synodal statutes (especially in France); the acts of pastoral visits; the "memoirs" of sanctuaries and convents; and for certain locales even detailed lists of the revived babies, along with the names and addresses of the parents, or of certificates of baptism like those left at Trava by Giovanni Lischiutta.[29] Besides this only minimally studied documentary material, there exist more or less detailed references by various writers of the seventeenth and eighteenth centuries; the chronicles of cities and provinces; the lives and feasts of local saints and of the Madonna. Even in the seventeenth century, a work appeared which provided a fairly complete view of the phenomenon's diffusion: the monumental *Atlas Marianus* by the Bavarian Jesuit Wilhelm Gumppenberg, published in 1657 and thereafter reprinted and translated several times, which recorded the miracles of some twelve hundred Marian sanctuaries scattered about the world. In this massive collection, no fewer than twelve sanctuaries were mentioned where temporary resurrections had occurred: Maria Luggau, already discussed; three others from the diocese of Trento; and eight more from Flanders and Brabant.[30] Various local traditions were, however, even richer, and churches where it was possible to find the miracle could be quite numerous even within a limited area. In 1635, Martin Lhermite, the historian of the saints of the Vallone region of Flanders, reported that resurrections took place in at least eight different churches in the area between Lille and Douai alone; concerning the number of miracles, he wrote, "Their number is infinite."[31]

In French-speaking lands, however, the belief appears to have been more diffuse and of greater antiquity than elsewhere: the records go back to the beginning of the fifteenth century, and in Savoy perhaps even to the mid-fourteenth century.[32] The miracle was usually attributed to the Madonna but occasionally also to local, highly venerated saints, such as Claudio di Combat at Besançon, Leonizio in Muri (in Switzerland, near Lucerne), or Modesto at Aldeno in the Trentino.[33] In some cases the grace was said to come from the intercession of people who were not even officially recognized by the church. The veneration at the tomb of Philippe de Chantemilan in Vienne, a pious woman of the populace (d. 1451), is a good example. Fifty-six miracles were registered there between 1453 and 1480, about one-third of which were temporary resurrections.[34] On the other hand, a similar miracle was attributed to Saint Francis de Sales by his first biographer while he was still alive.[35]

Aside from these local variations, in the various records the miracle always preserved the same structure and development encountered at Trava. The story Gumppenberg reports of the first miracle worked by the Madonna of Alsenberg, in Brabant, serves as a good example:

> A dead baby, taken directly from its mother's womb to its tomb, after having been buried for fifty-four hours, was finally, at the prayers of the aggrieved mother, disinterred, and, in the presence of sage witnesses, entrusted and offered up to the Virgin of Alsenberg. Soon, from the infant's umbilical cord, a half libra of blood gushed forth; he moved his tongue and opened his eyes; after he was purged with regenerative waters, he lived on for the space of sixteen hours and then once more he died. This miracle was examined in the usual manner and approved on the nineteenth day of April, 1473.[36]

The confirmation of the miracle by a notary or other public authority was another constant, especially after the middle of the sixteenth century. Some documents on the subject, redacted at Fayl-Billot in Alta Marna, were published in 1657; they differ from similar statements at Trava only in the language. Both the former and the latter contain information about the parents, a list of the signs of life, and the names of the witnesses and of those who did the baptism (these latter, in French localities, swore solemnly to the validity of their actions).[37] Significantly, virtually wherever the belief was found, the clergy usually had a quite marginal role in the ceremony. The priest of the church, for example, consented to placing the small body on the altar, he celebrated the Mass, and he sometimes drew up the certificate of baptism. But it was hardly ever the priest who confirmed the vital signs or administered the sacrament; for these essential functions those of simple faith were in charge, women more often than men, who served for long periods and, in some cases, declared that their responsibilities had been delegated to them officially by their communities.[38]

Concerning the statistics of the miracles, the sources, rich in details about other aspects, often appear reticent or vague. In records from the fifteenth century a central element was the exceptional character of the phenomenon; even if about thirty resurrections in fewer than thirty years were attributed to Philippe of Chantemilan and at Notre Dame de la Grace in Caëstre, Flanders, Gumppenberg recorded nine miracles between 1494 and 1496.[39] A century later, the situation had changed dramatically: at Notre Dame de Loos, near Lille, thirteen miracles of this type were confirmed in 1591–92 alone.[40] At Spor, in the Trentino, Gumppenberg again reported: "An authenticated document sent by the most excellent Bishop and Prince of Trent, Carlo Madruzzo, declares that in the years 1652, 1653, 1654 twenty-five babies were recalled to life and baptized."[41]

When one moves from the official documents, or at least from those sanctioned by the church, to the notarial acts redacted merely for the benefit of the parents concerned, the data become even more impressive. At the sanctuary of Notre Dame la Blanche, at Faverney in Franche-Comté, the documents from the end of the sixteenth century report 489 resurrections in twenty-five years.[42] At Fayl-Billot, eleven confirmations of miracles have been found for one span of only four months, from May 2 to September 5, 1657. It seems that, at a certain point, all of the little corpses brought to those sanctuaries showed signs of life and got baptized. Such a supposition is strongly supported each time testimony is available from the faithful, as was the case with Andrea Pinzan at Trava. And even in the Trentino there is an analogous testimony. In 1708, in the course of a pastoral visit, a man testified who was one of two who commonly presided over the ceremony of bringing dead infants to the altar of San Modesto. To the precise question "Did every child in the above manner displayed and observed show the said signs?" (that is, signs of life), he answered with confidence: "I have always observed in all [of them] some sign of life, conceded to them by God through the intercession of the Saint."[43]

In such circumstances, the miracle obviously lost its characteristics of a supernatural and unexpected event, a sign of the inscrutable will of God. It still remained clearly an exceptional occurrence, which, however, occurred infallibly when predetermined forms were followed: the pilgrimage to the sanctuary with the body of the dead baby, the collective prayers, the intention to save a soul from eternal condemnation. Such certainty about the concession of the grace sought is often attributed to a more general attitude in the peasant world toward miracles, and not without reason. But it should be remembered that across the seventeenth century belief in temporary resurrections had the approval of even authoritative writers, from the university world and official ecclesiastical culture. In 1605, for example, Justus Lipsius, a distinguished Flemish philologist and philosopher, published a short Latin work in which he exalted the miracles of the Madonna of Halle, near Brussels. In this treatise, when he began to write about dead babies and of mothers first suffering and then joyful about those miraculously saved souls, the old humanist actually changed from prose to lyric meter to express more adequately the emotions of the faithful.[44] Three years later, in a distant part of Europe, Eustachio Rudio, professor at Padua, in his massive five-volume *Ars medica*, reported on the resurrections of Luggau, affirming that he had observed them with his own eyes.[45] Gumppenberg's already discussed book, widely read and reprinted, brought the reports of such miracles past midcentury. As late as 1680, the Theatine Giovanni Battista Bagatta, in the *Admiranda orbis Christiani*, a massive catalogue of miraculous events from all times and places, assembled as a work of apologetics, mentioned with great reverence the temporary resurrections, dedicating to them an appendix at the end of his work, the *Admiranda perennia circa resurrectionem mortuorum*, as well as various allusions throughout the text. The Theatine referred to Gumppenberg often, as well as to other contemporary writers, but he also used patristic and medieval sources. The validity of the miracle was thus strengthened by its connection to an ancient and uninterrupted tradition.[46]

Toward the end of the seventeenth century, however, a vigorous opposition led by several noted French authors began to develop. The first was probably Jean Baptiste Thiers in his *Traité des superstitions qui regardent les sacrements*, published in 1679 and reprinted several times. This writer, like Dall'Occhio, spoke of the abuse of baptism and of the heresy of Cataphrygians and Marcionites; but more important, he cited, often verbatim, a long series of decisions by the French episcopate which disavowed the supposed resurrections and explicitly prohibited the rites connected to them. The list began with the rulings of the bishop of Langres promulgated in 1452 and renewed in 1479 by his successor; this was followed by the synodal decrees of Sens in 1524, of Lyons in 1557 and 1566, of Bescançon in 1592 and 1656, of Toul in 1658 and 1670.[47] Thiers did not enjoy a reputation for being especially orthodox, and, in fact, the *Traité* was condemned; but fifteen years later the same opposition to the miracles was expressed by the Dominican Noel Alexandre, a theologian who always enjoyed a large following and full approval in official circles. In his great *Theologia dogmatica et moralis secundum ordinem Catechismi Tridentini* (1694), he decreed unequivocally: "Infants who are born dead must not be baptized or taken to any holy place where simple and superstitious women give them some movement, or some heat, or other signs of life."

Alexandre also cited in confirmation of his judgment the earlier synodal rulings, first those of Langres, where the apparent signs of life were explained away by such things as the warmth of the wax and of the people who crowded about the inanimate bodies.[48] The learned Benedictine and historian Jean Mabillon also referred at the time to those documents, in his *Epistola de cultu sanctorum ignotorum* of 1698, in which he attacked this and other equally abusive practices originating from a false conception of miracles and the cult of saints.[49]

The synodal provisions cited in great numbers by these authors were valid only in the dioceses where they had been proclaimed, and even there, one is inclined to think, they had little impact. In general, however, the ecclesiastical authorities demonstrated an uncertain, if not contradictory, attitude toward the miracle; in contrast with the explicit condemnations of certain bishops there was often silence, caution, and sometimes the open patronage of others. A synod that met at Cambrai in 1631, for example, noted the irregularity of the phenomenon, but instead of prohibiting the display of the infants in church, it forbade only that the resurrections be greeted with the sound of bells or that they be spoken of as miracles; the synod tolerated, in substance, the ceremony, as long as it did not stir up any clamor.[50] In Trent, Bishop Carlo Emanuele Madruzzo (d. 1658) had gathered reports on and confirmation of the diffusion of the belief in his diocese; but instead of combating it, he transmitted that material to Gumppenberg—as noted—openly displaying his consent. In 1707, the episcopal visitors who investigated the miracles of San Modesto at Aldeno still did not order the parish priest to stop the rite; they merely indicated that the two men in charge there should be better prepared, so that they would not commit errors in judging the vital signs or in giving baptisms; they also ordered that no one profit in any way from the ceremony, "to remove any shadow of self-interest from the administration of the said sacrament." Only in 1731, and with greater force in 1749, did the episcopal authorities of Trent take official measures to repress the phenomenon.[51] By then, however, the Roman Curia had also expressed its opinion about the resurrections, not as earlier in reserved communications, but in public documents valid for all Catholic countries. A great clamor had been stirred up by the fact that in the Marian sanctuary at Ursberg, in Swabia (a part of the old convent of Premonstratensian monks), dead babies had been baptized who had given the by now familiar uncertain and ephemeral signs of life. In the area the miracle must not have been known earlier, because the Congregation of the Holy Office became directly involved in the matter and condemned wholesale the behavior of the Bavarian monks in six different judgments from 1729 to 1751. Pope Benedict XIV himself finally prohibited the ceremony as an abuse in the collection of instructions *De synodo diocesana* of 1755, citing, besides the events of Ursberg, the testimony of Thiers, of Bagatta, and of Alexandre.[52]

≈ Before the papal condemnation, however, belief in temporary resurrections had been widespread among the faithful, not only in mountainous and isolated regions, such as Savoy, Franche-Comté or Carnia, but also in very civilized areas such as Flanders, the countryside around Paris, and commercial centers like Marseilles.[53] The reasons for this diffusion, however, are not immediately evident. Theological difficulties aside, the miracle always concluded painfully. It never restored the babies to their families but accorded merely a brief respite from death, for the time necessary to carry out a baptism.[54] These events, then, eschewing human emotional weaknesses, appeared to turn on an orthodox conception of the sacrament directed toward exalting its promise of salvation solemnly and firmly against the eternal damnation of the unforgiven, a fate more terrible than natural death. In the seventeenth century, in fact, some writers accepted this vision without qualms and even noted a patristic text that seemed to justify it fully. Saint Augustine was the first to speak of a temporary resurrection in a late sermon.[55] A woman of Uzalis, near Hippo, had appealed to the reliquary of the protomartyr Stefano so that the soul of her son, who had died without baptism, would be saved. Her prayers were answered: the baby was resurrected for the time necessary to receive baptism and immediately afterward died, as a Christian worthy of heavenly glory. In those years Augustine was busy in the long struggle against the Pelagians, who denied the consequences of original sin; thus, the miracle served to make clear the absolute necessity of baptism, without which there was no salvation, not even for an infant entirely free of personal sin.[56]

But the reference to the Augustinian text seems to have been made largely to justify a widely diffused belief that was by then uncontestable. It seems, in fact, that the Augustinian text did not have much of a following in patristic and medieval literature, which did, however, acknowledge numerous miracles worked through baptism, a major instrument of thaumaturgic activities. There was very little mention of temporary resurrections for approximately ten centuries, at least in the Christian tradition of continental Europe. In the *Leggenda aurea* of Jacopo da Varazze, for example, there is only one episode that might be construed in terms of the topos resurrection-baptism-death, the famous episode of Trajan's salvation. But it is difficult to connect this with the beliefs about the resurrection of dead babies, both because of the exceptional nature of the person and Jacopo's emphasis on the unique nature of the story he was telling.[57] It is telling that in the same work, when the miracles of Saint Stephen are described, they are always simply resurrections, even though Augustine is cited explicitly as his source.[58] Even if caution is advisable, it seems a likely hypothesis that temporary resurrections were alien to the hagiography of the High Middle Ages in general. Between the end of the fourteenth century and the beginning of the fifteenth, however, various reports are found on the miracle's diffusion, especially in the eastern regions of France. They continued until the prohibition of the synodal statutes of Langres in 1452 demonstrated that the phenomenon was already extensive enough to have provoked the fears of the ecclesiastical authorities.

Undoubtedly, toward the end of the Middle Ages, there was a profound change in the conception of baptism among the faithful, even if the precise facts and dates are difficult to pinpoint. The decree of the Council of Florence of February 4, 1442, has been indicated as a point of reference; there for the first time it was officially established that the ceremony of baptism ought not to be postponed but should take place "as soon as it is possible." In earlier centuries, this type of norm was lacking, and the tradition of administering the sacrament at fixed periods of the liturgical calendar was the norm, except when imminent death was feared. The "as soon as" of the Council of Florence seems to reflect a practice already followed in the West. The change had probably begun earlier, in the thirteenth century, following the repression of heretical movements that had denied baptism its tradi-tional efficacy (like the Cathars, who replaced it with the laying on of hands), or in 1274 when the Second Council of Lyons had felt it necessary to reassert the Augustinian doctrine that held that original sin was enough for the soul's eternal damnation (already adopted by the Synod of Carthage in 418) even if that damnation required different punishments than those for personal sins (as argued there for the first time). The point was reasserted by the Council of Florence on July 6, 1439, with language that repeated almost verbatim that of Lyons. This seemed to imply that there was still considerable disagreement about the issue at least among theologians.[59] Clearly, then, there was a rather slow evolution of theology, an evolution that makes sense in a Christian society in which debate was relatively free and official decisions had only limited and imperfect ways to reach the faithful. But the impact of a new mentality is easily recognizable in the second half of the fifteenth century. Already, in fact, in a region like Flanders one finds the almost frenetic preoccupation with baptizing newborns, day or night, and the equally minute care on the part of the adults to preserve the certificate of the ceremony, which became an essential instrument for life in society itself. In the countryside, especially, the very notion of not having been baptized became incomprehensible; it meant a genuine exclusion from the human community.[60]

Fear of witches certainly contributed to the growth in the anxiety to baptize babies as early as possible. The *Malleus Maleficarum*, the highly successful demonological encyclopedia of 1486, showed in ample detail that birth was one of the moments in life most susceptible to necromantic operations of all kinds. In this regard, Heinrich Kramer and Jacob Sprenger, the Dominican authors of this treatise, reported a series of frightening episodes, which were probably already a part of the popular discourse in several countries: in the region of Bern, witches had devoured thirteen infants in one year; in Basel one witch alone had killed more than forty infants, inserting pins into their heads as soon as they were born; in Strasbourg, a sorceress had confessed to so many crimes of this type that she could not even count them.[61] In popular belief, these malevolent interventions were the most common explanation for the very high rate of infant mortality; for the authors of the *Malleus*, they were primarily inspired by the devil, as part of a plan that aimed to postpone as long as possible the ultimate defeat of the infernal powers. Malign spirits, argued the two Dominicans, "know that these tiny children dying without baptism are sequestered and excluded from the Kingdom of Heaven because of the punishment of damnation and original sin: this will cause the last judgment to be put back and prolonged as long as possible. And the more men that are damned and delegated to eternal torments with them [these children], the longer it will be before the elect are chosen, which, when it occurs, will also mean the end of this world."[62]

Kramer and Sprenger especially warned against the role of midwives ("no one is more deadly to the Catholic faith than midwives") in such diabolical deeds that could take place even without murder, simply by pledging the newborn to the Evil One, before it was consecrated by baptism. The only viable remedy was to baptize the baby as quickly as possible.[63]

Because of these antecedents, one might say that the Counter Reformation largely perfected and extended to all of Catholic Europe an atmosphere of anxiety and fear which it found already formed and operating. From a doctrinal point of view, the Council of Trent did not add anything particularly new to previous attitudes toward baptism. In the *Catechismus ad parocos*, the necessity of administering the sacrament as soon as possible was again propounded with the same formula as the decree of 1442: "as soon as it is possible."[64] The difference came in the dissemination of the rule and in the care bishops took in their enforcement of it, even in the face of opposition from groups opposed to child baptism. In the synodal statutes that implemented the decrees of the council, the "as soon as" was generally understood as a limit of three days; in certain dioceses, to defer the ceremony for one week could bring grave spiritual sanctions, even excommunication. Particular attention was paid to midwives by the ecclesiastical authorities, so that they would be able to perform baptisms themselves, in case of the danger of the infant's death. Those [midwives] whom the *Malleus* had denounced for the most insidious complicity with the devil had become invaluable assistants to the clergy just one hundred years later. In fact the suspicion remained that many witches operated under the cover of being midwives; but to reassure the population, during episcopal visits midwives were examined carefully and required to swear an oath that they submitted to church authority and to kiss the Gospel. In fact, already in the sixteenth century in Belgium they were required to denounce to the authorities any Anabaptist parents who refused baptism to newborns. A similar requirement was made in France, aimed at Calvinist families, especially after the revocation of the Edict of Nantes.[65]

The midwife's role normally provided an element of security against the danger of death without baptism. In fact, midwives administered the sacrament even in circumstances in which the parents or relatives would never have dared to do so. At the beginning of the seventeenth century, the doctor Eustachio Rudio, for example, noted with approval that, in cases of abortion, some "pious and attentive midwives" immersed even the smallest embryos in hot water and if they gave the least sign of movement immediately pronounced the prescribed formula.[66] Many times, then, these women would have baptized already-dead newborns, creating the impression that they were still alive: thus it was no accident that an eighteenth-century writer admonished midwives not to deceive poor mothers, "pretending to baptize a fetus when it was born dead."[67] Even professional midwives, like doctors or priests, however, would have had little opportunity to reach the poorest classes, especially those who lived in the country or in mountainous regions; nonetheless, newborn children only rarely died without baptism, with the exception of abortions, which were numbered among the damned, even natural ones. It is easy to understand in this context the diffusion of the belief in temporary resurrections, which seemed to be the one means possible to escape from the painful situation that had befallen certain of the faithful, even with their good will. This was true especially in the seventeenth century, when religious culture had become more clearly defined even in rural areas and at the same time intransigent sermons on the theme of baptism were in vogue, often based on neo-Augustinian positions or on ones more or less plainly Jansenist in France. In Friuli, Dall'Occhio did not show much sympathy for the fate of infants who died without baptism, who were a damned group completely excluded from any consideration of Christian piety. But the same attitude can be found in the major theologians of the century; from Bellarmino to Enrico Noris to Bossuet, each was equally ready to denounce as

Pelagian any discourse that sought to reconcile church doctrine with the more human sentiments of parents and relatives.[68]

⅌ Belief in temporary resurrections can be seen, then, as the reaction of familial affections to an abstract and cruel theological doctrine, which required damnation without appeal. This was the position of those who invoked such a grace in the areas where the rite was practiced; but those who took a position against the supposed miracle also were reacting to Christian concepts, in labeling it abusive, superstitious, or even heretical. Nonetheless, there remained the suspicion that the phenomenon had deeper and older roots, of which the protagonists themselves, perhaps, were no longer aware or—better yet—were aware only to the degree necessary to keep things hidden from outside investigators. The sources consulted, hagiographic as well as inquisitorial, do not help very much in getting beyond official explanations, since they were all part of those explanations. To escape that seemingly closed circle of official voices requires relying on weak and marginal sources. But one thing is immediately clear moving beyond that closed circle. The parents who went to the sanctuary of Trava (or to other, similar places) asked not only for a miracle to save a soul; they claimed also that the tiny corpse should be buried in consecrated ground. It seems that they merely wanted to treat those dead souls like any other. In such cases the response of the ecclesiastical authorities did not leave much room for mercy. When the Dominicans of San Daniele surprised a father with his unhappy burden on the way to Trava, they sent him to the inquisitorial vicar and hurriedly buried the cadaver in the convent's garden; those who died without baptism, in fact, were excluded from burial along with other members of the community in holy ground.[69] Such a burial must have appeared customary at that time, at least for the clergy. For the families, however, exclusion from burial in consecrated land must have been a sad and sorrowful thing, especially in the country, where places such as a cemetery for non-Christians or other similar locales did not exist.

Infants' bodies rejected from the Christian community of the dead must have been buried secretly, wherever possible, without honor and decorum, much as the carcass of an animal. The church was probably reluctant to note that its norms were setting in motion a process that seemed to everyday people to involve a disturbing profanation of the dead. Honoring the dead, obviously, prefigured Christianity; and without a place where they could rest, without a series of rites which accompanied them to their last home, the dead could not achieve eternal peace and would continue to move among the living, as an unwelcome and feared presence. Perhaps behind the anxiety to baptize babies at all costs lay the fear that they would return after death to remind the family of their unhappy fate or to exact upon them dark vendettas.

In folklore, in fact, the motif of the unbaptized person unable to remain in the tomb is well known.[70] It was especially associated with young babies: throughout Italy one encounters the figure of a fairy [*folletto*] (called *massarol* in Veneto, *linchetto* in Romagna, *mazzamoriello* or *monaciello* in the south), almost always dressed in red with a little cap of the same color, disrespectful but not wicked, who represents the neonate who died without the sacrament, tenaciously attached to the people and places of its ephemeral existence.[71] French folklore also has apparitions of this type, although they are rather more sullen and sad. The souls of babies who died without baptism wander through fields and along riverbanks (perhaps the places where the bodies were most often abandoned) calling to wayfarers to be their protectors; or else they perform macabre dances in front of cemeteries, clamoring for admission. At other times they are transformed into birds with tortured songs, or into plants whose branches one must not cut.[72] These legends seem especially widespread in northeastern France, but they probably derive from a nucleus of much older traditions, originally to be found across a large stretch of territory. In fact, very similar beliefs are found in zones of Europe which are far apart and which have very different languages and customs. In Brittany, people a century ago told how the souls of infants who died without baptism were transformed into birds and were waiting for the end of the world, when John the Baptist would open the gates of Heaven to them, finally giving them the sacrament. Almost the same legend (especially in relation to John the Baptist's role) was recorded a few years ago in a valley of eastern Friuli, among the part of the population which still speaks Slavic dialects.[73]

The Slavic valleys of Friuli, a mountainous zone that constitutes the eastern border of Carnia and continues south into the high areas of the Natisone River basin, maintain—even amid their diversity of dialects—traditions that originally must have been common to the entire region. The figure of the *folletto* dressed in red is well known, but with more tragic and fearful connotations than appear in analogous legends from the rest of Italy, even from the nearby Bellunese Alps. The names of these characters are various: more often *fantìc* or *škrát* or terms derived from them; they have horns, and in aspect as well as in behavior they seem quite diabolical.[74] Gloomy and bloody stories are told about them: "The *škrát*," a woman of a village near Cividale reported, "is a man dressed in red: they are those who died without baptism. Around here one killed a priest. The priest was going home, accompanied by a nephew; the nephew was holding the lamp, he turned and did not see the priest anymore. He was down in a ravine, naked, tied to a tree. The *škrát* had killed him."[75] Rarely are those who died unbaptized described as so burdened with hate for the living. It is likely, however, that this was their original nature, which became popular again when all that was not Christian or Christianized became essentially a product or instrument of the devil. The penitential of Burchard of Worms records a grim custom that was evidently still in use at the beginning of the year 1000: if a baby died without baptism, the mothers would bring its body to a hidden place and transfix it with a stake, "saying that if they did not do so, the infant would rise again and harm many people."[76] Such behavior seemed to involve identifying the unbaptized infant with a being who not only remained without peace after death but who would cause harm to the living, a figure comparable to the more recent vampire, which not coincidentally could be rendered innocuous by the same macabre treatment.

The fear of dead babies must have been actually a foreign element in primitive religions. The dead were originally feared for what they were or had done when alive, because it was felt that they would remain obstinately attached to the honors, goods, and people dear to them during their life.[77] Newborns had not left anything behind, and thus when dead they did not elicit fear, nor did they have motives for returning among the living. If in the Christian world, at least in some parts of Europe, the situation was different, it means that the Augustinian conception of original sin, with all of its consequences, was deeply rooted in the souls of the population long before it would appear to have been from the resolutions of councils and the orientation of the official church in general. It must be remembered that in periods of aggressive and rapid evangelization the more terrifying and punitive aspects of pre-Christian beliefs were sometimes employed to reinforce the principles of the new faith, without concern for the theological issues involved. This impression is confirmed by examining other legends connected to baptism which have social control as their foundation or which simply express the condemnation of abnormal behavior. The maleficent *folletto* of Slavic Friuli is doubtless related to infanticide, and even to the abortions that were attributed especially to women of loose customs. "A *škrát*," reported a female informer from the valley of the Natisone in 1950, "is that type of baby who has been killed by an unmarried woman. I hope that now it no longer happens like that, perhaps it is no longer done, but at one time those kinds of girls made them die and then they were not baptized, they never had any happiness."[78] An analogous belief is the basis of a complicated Breton legend, still alive at the end of the last century. In this case the children, having been turned into squirrels, punished their "unnatural" mothers themselves by attacking them in the forest and tearing them apart.[79] These stories were evidently used to voice a complex of private remorse and fear, in situations that for the most part had probably escaped the control of the clergy or the authorities.

The morbid Breton legend, in any case, has a reassuring ending: the mother, before dying, manages to give her children a sort of baptism, and the cruel squirrels recover their former features, immediately dying once more and ascending like angels to heavenly glory. This tangled story is significant, because it clearly reveals the theme of the punishing presence of the dead juxtaposed with the belief in temporary resurrections; the fusion of the two motifs, however, is certainly much older. One can perceive its form in a miracle mentioned for the year 1393 by Jean Juvenal of the Ursins, the chronicler of Charles VI's reign in France, and from there it passed through various intermediaries to Bagatta. An "immodest woman" had suffocated her newly born son, burying him in a dunghill. A pious woman, "led by divine providence," found the body and placed it on the altar of a church dedicated to Saint Martin, praying fervently to the Lord to save its soul. The baby in fact came to life, was baptized, and three hours later died once more.[80] The background seems to be the same as that of the Breton legend and the Friulian tales; but it seems likely that behind the entire event there lies the same world of fear and remorse. Ecclesiastical sources, especially the relatively recent ones utilized here, did not leave much room for the theme of the survival of the dead; but the folkloric tradition offers a broader vision in which the various elements are embedded and form a more complete and convincing portrait.

❧ Temporary resurrections, then, sought to save a soul as well as liberate the living from the anguishing presence of the dead. This is the conclusion to be drawn, even if the initial conviction, the properly Christian one, still remains central and apparently seems capable by itself of explaining the entire practice. To separate the two motifs now, in any case, would seem unwarranted, for it is impossible to say to what degree one rather than the other has operated over the centuries the belief was widely held. To determine the precise origins of this notable convergence of folkloric themes and theological doctrines, each difficult to explain on its own, would be very difficult. It seems likely, however, that the pre-Christian fear of the dead was not associated with an Augustinian concept of original sin from the patristic era on, notwithstanding the existence of Augustine's sermon about the baby resurrected in Uzalis. One must look instead to the High Middle Ages and to populations less influenced by the Latin world.

One can find interesting suggestions, for example, in the Gaelic biography of Saint Patrick composed in Ireland around the eleventh century, but which surely includes earlier material. It is an obscure text, often indecipherable, which was not discussed earlier because it did not have much impact on the hagiography of continental Europe, at least until there were some late Latin reworkings of it shorn of its original characteristics. Among the miracles attributed to the Irish saint, there are at least four temporary resurrections of famous people, kings or warriors, who had died without baptism. It is certainly the oldest source that presents the phenomenon as a repeated fact, and the very structure of these episodes is reminiscent of more recent stories.[81] These miracles, however, were inserted into a particular atmosphere, not particularly Christian, in which a precise distinction between living and dead does not seem to have existed. Normally the dead, whether pagan or Christian, raised themselves up from their tombs to question the passersby, to respond to their questions, to describe their condition. In such a context the resurrections lose their supernatural character and become merely an expression of the thaumaturgic ability of Saint Patrick, infinitely superior to the Celtic magicians who vied with him. This is a world far distant from the world of theological rigor which is the foundation of Augustine's sermon on the miracle of Saint Stephen. The Irish story is an expression of a very different sensibility, glimpsed even today in the mythic world of the legends still diffused in Europe.[82]

Such ties to the most obscure elements of popular traditions, in sum, can help to explain the endurance of the belief in temporary resurrections long after papal condemnation—when the support the church had furnished in the earlier centuries, even if hesitantly and with controversy, was definitively removed. At Trava ex-votos demonstrate that the resurrections continued to manifest themselves until 1856. In France, the rite was common throughout the nineteenth century; even in 1912 the existence of such a practice was denounced, not without a scandal, in the countryside near Limoges, much farther west than the zone where it was found earlier.[83] In this regard, the famous tenaciousness of religious customs in agricultural or mountainous regions, where the *long durée* is an indisputable rule, was undoubtedly at work. But it seems equally legitimate to maintain that the ecclesiastical condemnations had only returned the belief in double death to the world of folklore, at the margins of, if not outside, the Christian tradition, where it had been formed originally.

Notes

1. Archivio della Curia Arcivescovile di Udine (hereafter ACAU), Sant'Uffizio, busta 80, fasc. "False resurrezzioni di bambini usciti morti da ventri materni," f. 2r in the modern pagination written in pencil. L. De Biasio was the first to utilize these documents, "Credenze ed atteggiamenti religiosi del mondo contadino friulano del Seicento: Un singolare rito battesimale amministrato nel santuario di Trava in Carnia," in the collective catalogue *Religiosità popolare in Friuli*, ed. L. Ciceri (Pordenone, 1980), pp. 39–53. [The quotations retain the spelling of the documents with considerable variations, especially in the notes of Dall'Occhio; only the accents and apostrophes have been corrected.]

2. ACAU, Sant'Uffizio, busta 80, fasc. "False resurrezzione," ff. 5 (the letter) and 6–9.

3. The minutes of the account by Dall'Occhio are in ACAU, Sant'Uffizio, busta 65, "Copia epistularum PP. Inquisitorum, ad S. Congregationem S. Officii," 4 vols., vol. 3, ff. 25v–26r, under the date of March 23, 1685. The original copy of the answer is in busta 63, "Epistolae S. Officii 1679–1766," at its date.

4. ACAU, Sant'Uffizio, busta 45, processo 2/542.

5. ACAU, Sant'Uffizio, buste 45 and 46, processi 543, 564, 571, 572, 574, 575, 578, 579, 582, all from the second series of the Acta Sancti Officii.

6. ACAU, Sant'Uffizio, busta 80, fasc. "False resurrezzioni," ff. 46r–49v, with an actual model of a trial to which the Dominicans of San Daniele had to conform; at ff. 54r–55r of the same fascicolo one can see the very rough copy of the first trial, sent to the vicar of Udine for examination, in which the name of the accused was changed to Fabio Britto, evidently for reasons of secrecy. A copy of the trial 2/543 is also saved in the fascicolo "False resurrezzioni," but here the true name of the accused is retained.

7. For these annotations, see ACAU, Sant'Uffizio, busta 80, fasc. "False resurrezzioni," f. 21v.

8. On the importance of the Beorchia family for Trava up to the fifteenth century, see G. Marinelli, *Guida della Carnia e del Canal del Ferro*, new ed., ed. M. Gortani (Tolmezzo, 1925), pp. 221–22 and 504; The family is still important in the region, as

attested by the fact that serving on the current Collegio di Carnia is Paolo Beorchia, a Christian Democrat.

9. A detailed reconstruction of events concerning the sanctuary may be found in the work of A. Roja, *Il piccolo Santuario della Madonna sopra Trava e suoi capellani: Memorie storiche* (Gemona, 1923), which reprints many original documents and uses the manuscript chronicals of Don Giovanni Paolo Beorchia, curate of the village at the beginning of the nineteenth century.

10. Roja, *Il piccolo Santuario*, pp. 8 and 12; the author, a priest from Carnia, describes the supposed resurrections as "an ignoble trick, which most of the people of the village probably never suspected."

11. ACAU, Chiese e paesi del Friuli, busta 111, fasc. "Trava," for the date December 31, 1663.

12. ACAU, Sant'Uffizio, busta 42, processo 2/396.

13. ACAU, Visite pastorali, busta F, fasc. 39, f. 229r.

14. ACAU, Acta Curiae, "Extraordinariorum 1686," f. 27r, at the date June 17, 1686; the document is reproduced in De Biasio, "Credenze," p. 43.

15. For similar testimony, see ACAU, Sant'Uffizio, busta 80, fasc. "False resurrezzioni," ff. 86r and 89r.

16. Ibid., f. 106r

17. ACAU, Sant'Uffizio, busta 45, processo 2/542, ff. 1r and 2r.

18. ACAU, Sant'Uffizio, busta 45, processo 2/543, f. 5r.

19. Ibid., ff. 2r–2v; the entire trial of Andrea Pinzan is published by De Biasio, "Credenze," pp. 47–50; but the quotations follow the original document.

20. ACAU, Sant'Uffizio, busta 45, processo 2/543, ff. 3v–4r.

21. ACAU, Sant'Uffizio, busta 46, processo 2/564, f. 2v.

22. All of these material considerations are in the long report, "Informationi di false resurrezzioni con abuso del sacramento," in ACAU, Sant'Uffizio, busta 80, fasc. "False resurrezzioni," ff. 42r–43v; this is a clean copy clearly put together at the moment as a summary: see ff. 93r–94r. It lacks a date, but it seems to be from the latest phase of the investigation, in the autumn of 1687.

23. ACAU, Sant'Uffizio, busta 80, fasc. "False resurrezzioni," f. 21r.

24. Ibid., f. 87r, the letter to the parish priest of Tarcento, March 22, 1687.

25. Ibid., f. 91r; for the deposition of the Third Council of Carthage, see J. De Mansi, *Sacrorum Conciliorum Nova et Amplissima Collectio* (Florence and Venice, 1759–98), vol. 3, col. 881; but on the argument, which is not all that clear, see E. Mangenot, "Baptême pour les morts," in *Dictionnaire de théologie catholique* (hereafter DThC; Paris, 1909 ff), vol. 2, cols. 360–64.

26. The "Memoria di false resurrezzioni," of March 3, 1687, in ACAU, Sant'Uffizio, busta 80, fasc. "False resurrezzioni," ff. 84r–84v, at the end; the document is edited by De Biasio, "Credenze," pp. 50–52.

27. ACAU, Sant'Uffizio, busta 80, fasc. "False resurrezzioni," f. 10r; for other information on Luggau, see ff. 66r, 68r, 88r, and Andrea Pinzan's deposition. On the Carinthian sanctuary, see: F. L. Hohenauer, *Kurze Kirchengeschichte von Kärnthen* (Klagenfurt, 1850), pp. 174–75 and 337.

28. On the diffusion of these temporary resurrections, especially in French-speaking countries, see J. Corblet, *Histoire dogmatique, liturgique et archéologique du sacrement de Baptême*, 2 vols. (Paris and Brussels, 1881–82), pp. 421–23; P. Saint-Yves [E. Nourry], "Les résurrections d'enfants morts-nés et les sanctuaires 'à répit'," in the *Revue d'ethnographie et de sociologie* 2 (1911): 65–74, later reprinted in the volume *En marge de la Legénde Dorée: Songes, miracles et survivances: Essai sur la formation de quelques thèmes agiographiques* (Paris, 1931), pp. 167–92, a very important source;

A. Van Gennep, *Manuel de folklore français contemporain*, vol. 1, pt. 1 (Paris, 1943), pp. 123–24. More specific works are discussed below: for Italy there is the rather disappointing work of C. Corrain and P. L. Zampini, *Documenti etnografici e folkloristici nei sinodi diocesani italiani* (Bologna, 1970), which does attempt to give a comprehensive treatment of the phenomenon on p. 389 and in table 12; the reference to Valle d'Aosta and the Piedmont Alps is accurate (there may have been an influence from the neighboring French regions), but the mention of Abano, the site of the noted baths near Padua, is totally misleading. The place was actually Alano, in the Piave Valley, where the presence of the rite is documented by the pastoral visit of San Gregorio Barbarigo in 1674; on this, see G. Rocco, *I luoghi di san Gregorio: Strade e paesi nell'itinerario pastorale del vescovo Barbarigo* (Padua, 1961), pp. 117–118. Moreover, in Corrain and Zampini there is no mention of Trava, about which V. Ostermann had already written in *La vita in Friuli: Usi, costumi, credenze popolari*, 2d ed. (Udine, 1940), vol. 2, p. 303 (1st ed., 1894). On the belief in some localities of the Trentino, see: C. Donati, *Ecclesiastici e laici nel Trentino del Settecento* (Rome, 1975), pp. 97–101.

29. Eleven testimonies of this type have been published by J. C. Didier in "Un sanctuaire à 'repit' du diocèse de Langres: L'église de Fayl-Billot, Haute-Marne, d'aprés des actes notariés du XVIIe siècle," *Melanges de science religieuse* 25 (1968): 3–22.

30. W. Gumppenberg, *Atlas Marianus quo sanctae Dei genitricis Mariae imaginum miraculosarum origines duodecim historiarum centuriis explicantur* (Munich, 1672); this is the third edition. The rich indices are of great help to research. Here are the numbers of the principal sanctuaries considered in this article: 14, 265 (Luggau), 290, 292, 312, 452, 559, 693, 704, 717, 995, 1031.

31. H. Platelle, *Les chrétiens face au miracle: Lille au XVIIe siècle*, (Paris, 1968), pp. 50–51.

32. A. Van Gennep, *Culte populaire des saints en Savoie: Recueil d'articles* (Paris, 1973), pp. 141–42.

33. For San Claudio and San Leonizio, see respectively *Acta Sanctorum, Iunii*, vol. 1 (pp. 665–66 in the reprinted anastatic edition of Brussels, *Culture et Civilisation, 1965–1970*), and the *Acta Sanctorum, Septembris*, vol. 5 (same edition, pp. 201–15 and 247); for San Modesto, see C. Donati, *Ecclesiastici e laici*, pp. 99–100.

34. P. Paravy, "Angoisse collective et miracles au seuil de la mort: resurrections et baptêmes d'enfants mort-nés en Dauphiné au XVème siècle," in the collective volume *La mort au Moyen-Age* (Strasbourg, 1977), pp. 87–102.

35. This had the goal of converting a Calvinist woman to Catholicism; on this, see Saint-Yves, *En marge de la Légende Dorée*, pp. 172–73.

36. Gumppenberg, *Atlas Marianus*, n. 717, pp. 769–71 (I have used the Italian translation of this work, 12 volumes in 16 parts, Verona, 1839–47).

37. Didier, "Un sanctuaire à 'repit' du diocèse de Langres," pp. 10–21.

38. At Fayl-Billot and at Aldeno, for example.

39. Gumppenberg, *Atlas Marianus*, n. 14, pp. 41–42.

40. Platelle, *Les chrétiens*, pp. 69–70.

41. Gumppenberg, *Atlas Marianus*, n. 292, p. 402.

42. Saint-Yves, *En marge de la Légende Dorée*, p. 193.

43. Donati, *Ecclesiastici e laici*, p. 100.

44. J. Lipsius, *Diva Virgo Hallensis: Beneficia eius et miracula fide atque ordine descripta* (Antwerp, 1605), esp. chapters 19 and 21.

45. E. Rudio, *Ars medica* (Venice, 1608), vol. 2, p. 293: "Sub Comitatu Hortenburgensi prope Tiroli Comitatus fines reperitur quaedam ecclesia Beatae Virgini Mariae dicata, quam incolae et vicini populi Sanctam Mariam de Licao nominant, ad quam si foetus mortui statim post partum deferantur et super aram Beatae Virgins ponantur,

reviviscunt et baptismate suscepto paulo post moriuntur. Cuius rei nedum nos, verum etiam innumeri alii clarum et indubitatum testimonium reddere possunt." Before moving to his post at Padua, Rudio had worked for a long time in Udine.

46. G. B. Bagatta, *Admiranda orbis Christiani quae ad Christi fidem firmandam, Christianam pietatem fovendam obstinatamque perfidiam destruendam Jo. Bonifacius Bagatta, Veronensis, clericus regularis Theatinus, collegit, selegit, in unumque redacta in lucem edidit,* 2 vols., 2d ed. (Augutae and Dilingae, 1695), vol. 2, pp. 93–94, 533–36, 542.

47. J. B. Thiers, *Traité des superstitions qui regardent les sacrements, selon l'Ecriture Sainte, les décrets des Conciles et les sentiments des Saints Pères et des théologiens,* 4 vols. (Paris, 1741), vol. 2, pp. 59–65.

48. N. Alexandre, *Theologia dogmatica et moralis secundum ordinem Cathechismi Tridentini,* liber 2, tract. 2, cap. 7, regula 3 (Venice, 1744), vol. 1, pp. 410–11. The text of the synodal statutes of Langres has been edited recently in J. C. Didier, *Le Baptême des enfants dans la Tradition de l'Église* (Tournai, 1959), pp. 191–92.

49. J. Mabillon, *Eusebii Romani ad Theophilum Gallum epistola de cultu sanctorum ignotorum,* (Paris, 1698), pp. 16 and 30–31.

50. Platelle, *Les chrétiens,* p. 51.

51. Donati, *Ecclesiastici e laici,* pp. 97–101. In 1674, instead, San Gregorio Barbarigo had suddenly prohibited a similar cult at Alano, where the miracles were attributed to an image of the Madonna; on this, see Rocco, *I luoghi di san Gregorio,* p. 118.

52. Benedictus XIV, *De synodo diocesana libri tredecim* (Rome, 1755), pp. 200–201, where the details of the various condemnations of the monks of Ursberg are also reported.

53. On the countryside around Paris, see: J. Fert, *La vie religieuse dans les campagnes parisiennes* (Paris, 1962), esp. pp. 294–98; on Marseilles and Provence in general, see the two articles by M. Bernos, "Réflexions sur un miracle a l'Annonciade d'Aix-en-Provence: Contribution a l'étude des sanctuaires à 'repit,' " in *Annales du Midi* 82 (1970): 5–20, and "Miracles chez les Servites en Provence à l'époque moderne," in *Revue d'histoire de la spiritualité* 49 (1973): 243–56.

54. From this phenomenon comes the French term *répit.*

55. According to Platelle, *Les chrétiens,* p. 51, Jean Huchon, author of a work in French on the seven sacraments, published in Lille in 1635, explicitly counseled a family to have recourse to the rite of temporary resurrections on the basis of the Augustinian text; for an analogous use, see Bagatta, *Admiranda orbis Christiani,* vol. 2, p. 533.

56. Augustine, *Sermo CCCXXIV* (P.L. 38, pp. 1446–47); for one interpretation of the sermon, see P. Brown, *Agostino d'Ippona,* tr. it. (Turin, 1971), pp. 390–91. (*Augustine of Hippo,* Berkeley and Los Angeles, 1967).

57. Jacopo da Varazze, *Leggenda aurea,* the Tuscan vernacular edition of the legend from the fourteenth century edited by Arrigo Levasti, 3 vols. (Florence, 1924–26), chap. 46 (12/3 of the Graesse edition), p. 387; after having adhered to the request to save Trajan, God gravely admonished Saint Gregory the Great: "Now that I have answered your prayer and I have forgiven the eternal punishment of Trajan, make very sure that from this point forward you make no plea for any other of the damned."

58. Varazze, *Leggenda aurea,* chap. 107 (12 Graesse), pp. 895–96. The reference here is to *De civitate Dei,* 22, p. 8, which, however, is not about resurrections; the writer probably had at hand the late compilation in two books *De miraculis Sancti Stephani protomartyris,* which in general constituted an appendix to the larger work; in this collection there are explicit references to temporary resurrections as a basis of the sermon 324 (see 1, p. 15).

59. The reference to the Council of Florence is in Paravy, "Angoisse collective et

miracles," pp. 87–89; for the texts of the various council decrees, see H. Denzinger and A. Schoenmetzer, *Enchiridion symbolorum, definitionum et declarationum de rebus fidei et morum* (Rome, 1967), nn. 780, 858, 1306, 1349.

60. J. Toussaert, *Le sentiment réligieux en Flandre à la fin du Moyen Age* (Paris, 1963), pp. 91–94 and 273–79, where there are numerous references to the belief in temporary resurrections.

61. *Malleus Maleficarum*, pars 2, quaestio 1, cap. 2 and cap. 13 (edition of Lyons, 1669, pp. 106–107 and 152).

62. G. Menghi, *Compendio dell'arte essorcistica et possibilità delle mirabili et stupende operationi delli demoni* (Bologna, 1590), p. 487, where he repeats faithfully what was written in the *Malleus*, pars 2, q. 1, cap. 13, p. 152.

63. *Malleus*, pars 1, q. 11, p. 68; pars 2, q. 1, cap. 2, pp. 105–7, and cap. 13, pp. 151–56.

64. *Catechismus ex decreto Concilii Tridentini ad parocos Pii Quinti Pont. Max. iussu editus* (Rome, 1566), p. 109.

65. On these topics, see Corblet, *Histoire*, esp. pp. 321–24. On the position of Calvin, who accepted the baptism of children but rejected as useless the administration of the sacrament to dying newborns, who were in any case Christians because of their parents' faith, see his *Institution de la religion chrétienne*, vol. 4, pp. 15 and 20–21, and J. D. Benoit, "Calvin et le baptême des enfants," in *Revue d'histoire et de philosophie religieuses* 17 (1937): 457–74. On the Christian duties of midwives in Italy, see the noted work of S. Mercurio, *La commare o raccoglitrice*, especially chapters 18 and 26 of the first book (Venice, 1676), pp. 73 and 98; the work is, however, from the end of the sixteenth century.

66. Rudio, *Ars medica*, vol. 2, p. 293; according to Corblet, *Histoire*, pp. 400–401, the practice of baptizing embryos began in the fourteenth century; but the church officially disapproved of it only in the eighteenth century.

67. G. Baruffaldi, *La mammana istruita* (Venice, 1774), pp. 53–54 (1st edition, 1732).

68. J. Bellamy, "Sort des enfants morts sans baptême," DThC, vol. 2, cols. 364–77, with extensive references to the texts.

69. Many of those who testified referred to this hurried burial of the tiny bodies by the Dominicans of San Daniele; see ACAU, Sant'Uffizio, busta 46, processi 2/574, 575, 578, 579, 582.

70. S. Thompson, *Motif Index of Folk Literature*, 6 vols. (Copenhagen, 1955–58), E 412.2 ("Unbaptized person cannot rest in grave"), and the related themes: E 501.2.7, E 501.5.4, E 613.02, F 251.3, F 360.1, V 81.2.

71. G. B. Bastanzi, *Le superstizioni delle Alpi venete* (Treviso, 1888), pp. 28–42; N. Borrelli, "L'origine e il fondamento storico di un'antica credenza popolare," *Il folklore italiano* 13 (1935): 77–82, and in the same volume G. Giannini, "Gli scongiuri contro il linchetto," pp. 224–28.

72. P. Sébillot, *Le folk-lore de France*, 4 vols. (Paris, 1904–7), vol. 1, pp. 148–49; 2:80; 3:210 and 526; 4:133–34 (for other references, see the ample thematic index).

73. A. Le Braz, *La légende de la mort chez les Bretons Armoricains*, 2 vols., 3rd ed. (Paris, 1912), vol. 2, pp. 34; for Friuli, see A. Ciceri, "Ancora sugli esseri mitici e sui personaggi della tradizione popolare in Friuli," *Studi di letteratura popolare friulana* 2 (1970): 114–27, esp. 118–19.

74. On these figures, see Ostermann, *La vita in Friuli*, p. 451; A. von Mailly, *Sagen aus Friaul und den Julischen Alpen* (Leipzig, 1922), p. 24; L. D'Orlandi and N. Cantarutti, "Credenze sopravviventi in Friuli intorno agli esseri mitici," *Ce fastu?* 40 (1964): 17–41; Ciceri, "Ancora sugli esseri mitici." In Friuli there is also found the *massarol* from the Veneto, who played jokes especially in barns, for example, pulling

the tails of the animals; the *folletto* of the Bellunese Alps was sometimes also blamed for evil deeds: see Bastanzi, "Le superstizioni delle Alpi venete," pp. 69–70 (where the *massarol* killed a girl who had offended him).

75. D'Orlandi and Cantarutti, "Credenze sopravviventi," p. 34. In Slovenian language *škrát* is the common term for gnome or *folletto*.

76. Burchard of Worms, *Decretorum libri viginti*, liber 19 ("De poenitentia"), P.L. 140, pp. 974–75.

77. On this, see the still useful essay of J. F. Frazer, *La Paura dei morti nelle religioni primitive*, tr. it. (Milan, 1978). (*The Fear of the Dead in Primitive Religion*, London, 1933.)

78. D'Orlandi and Cantarutti, "Credenze sopravviventi," p. 33; for an analogous definition of the *fantìć*, see Ciceri, "Ancora sugli esseri mitici," p. 118.

79. Le Braz, *La legende de la mort*, vol. 1, pp. 336–42; for this illustration, I have reduced the events of the legend to the essentials.

80. Bagatta, *Admiranda orbis Christiani*, vol. 2, p. 533; the immediate source of the Theatine was the Continuatio of Raynaldus to the *Annales ecclesiastici* of Baronius.

81. *The Tripartite Life of Patrick with Other Documents Relating to That Saint*, ed. W. Stokes, Rerum Britannicarum Medii Aevii Scriptores, n. 89 (London, 1887), pp. 123, 135, 179, 183; for an ancient Latin version of some of these episodes, see pp. 324–325. This biography of Saint Patrick is the only source for the themes of temporary resurrections recorded in the *Motif Index* (E. 176: "Resuscitation in order to baptize").

82. Given the regions in which the belief in temporary resurrections was widespread, one might hypothesize that a common Celtic origin is at the base of this, in populations later Latinized or Germanized; this is merely a hypothesis, however, perhaps only suggested by Le Braz's accounts, which seem most supportive of such theories.

83. For Trava, see P. Moro, *Gli ex-voto della Carnia* (Udine, 1970), especially the small picture reproduced on plate 34, from 1856; perhaps even more recent is the ex-voto of plate 40, which is, however, undated. For France, see Saint-Yves, *En marge de la Legénde Dorée*, pp. 180–81 and 190–91.

2 ⅋ Perpetuas: The Women Who Kept Priests, Siena 1600–1800

by Oscar Di Simplicio

The Housekeeper: When the parish priest is wealthy enough, he pays for a housekeeper, who plays a significant role in the life of the parish. Until recently, this pious woman, of canonical age, sometimes young and pretty and sometimes old and wrinkled, took upon herself a ministry that could have aided the pastor but was also an obstacle for him. Well known are those imperious housekeepers who once responded innocently: "Today there is no confession."[1]

This quote from G. Le Bras has even greater significance today, for in the context of recent social history, studies of domestics figure prominently and are a significant part of the new research on "women on their own." The priest's servant exemplifies both.[2] The "perpetua," as this type of domestic came to be called in Italy, was the priest's principal lay helper, and at his side she could play a truly multifaceted role: servant, lover, wife. To study the traces left by her activities across the seventeenth and eighteenth centuries requires an understanding of particular aspects of society both lay and religious (matrimonial forms, ecclesiastical celibacy, the forms of cohesion and disjuncture in the life of the village, and so on, and it requires understanding the evolution of these things over time. This study assays only some preliminary perspectives on three themes: (1) the nature of the relationship between the perpetua and parish priests in the countryside over these two

---

"Le perpetue (Stato senese, 1600–1800)," *Quaderni storici* 68 (1988): 381–412. Translated by Mary M. Gallucci.

centuries; (2) the comparison between such relationships and those found in urban settings; (3) a consideration of the factors that may have formed this particular personal and working relationship and how it changed over time.

ᢟ The Sources

Our information on perpetuas and parish priests comes from criminal cases in the episcopal archive of Siena: a group of seventy-one trials of concubinage which, even without any cases that could be labeled "normal," may be seen as representative.[3] Actually in these cases concubinage is often merely an "incident," an aside that had little to do with the reasons the priest chose a servant. And although the judicial nature of these records may have influenced the reconstruction of these cases, the historian may still be thankful that these domestics shared the beds of their employers as concubines, for otherwise we would know nothing about these perpetuas given the scantiness of the documentation for the history of servants.

At least this is the case in Siena—in the diocesan archive no other archival material has offered this type of information. No trace remains of any formal requests by priests to obtain permission to have a servant in their homes; and seventeenth- and eighteenth-century pastoral visitation records are silent on this matter. In fact, they make no references to the family or auxiliary personnel of the parish priest and lack any detailed descriptions of the priests themselves which might have allowed some speculation about a priest's ability to keep relatives or servants. And given this, as might be expected, they do not even hint at the existence of any irregular situations such as a priest's cohabitation with a known concubine. From this perspective the pastoral visitation should be regarded as an unreliable (or at least dubious) source. This observation is not new,[4] but in Siena the occasional coincidence of certain visitations and judicial investigations demonstrates the unreliability of the former.

In Ricenza, in 1653, the ecclesiastic carrying out the visitations recorded only a few "disagreements" between the parish priest and the brothers of the Società del Sanctissimo Uomo Gesù.[5] But in that very year, in the Curia, a trial was opened against the rector of the parish visited, the Reverend Carlo Saracini, denounced by the community for concubinage, with an alleged former prostitute who had already given him four children, along with usury and the squandering of church goods. In an even more explicit manner in Pari, in 1662, the normality of the situation was underlined: "And no parish is meanly controlled; great care is given to the health of souls."[6] Yet the parish priest there was Giovambattista Cioli, a powerful local tough whose past was strewn with various concubines and bastards and who at the time was facing serious problems because of a denunciation from a group of the community accusing him of concubinage, usury, and illegal trafficking (see Appendix A, n. 21).

?§ Rural Perpetuas

It is not possible to determine how many priests' housekeepers there were during any year of the period under consideration. In theory, each priest of the 107 communities of the Sienese state and the 14 suburban parishes would have been able to register one. But vacant posts existed (in 1640, for example, there were seven). And in the absence of a source that gives us a more complete picture at any given moment, there is nothing else to do but discuss the individuals in terms of the scarce data left by their trials and reassembled in Appendix A.

The Age of Perpetua in Manzoni's *The Betrothed*

"Perpetua, as everyone was aware, was the servant of Don Abbondio, an affectionate and faithful domestic, who knew how to obey and command, according to the occasion, to tolerate at times her boss's complaining and his bizarre deeds, and to make him at times tolerate her own, which became from day to day more frequent, since she had passed the synodal age of forty."[7] Manzoni, although he was a most adept creator of minor characters in *The Betrothed*, was indirectly responsible for an error about the synodal age which has been introduced virtually unnoticed into modern culture. This error gained authoritative status when S. Battaglia recorded the following definition in his *Grande dizionario della lingua italiana*: "Canonical age (or synodal): the minimum age of forty years established by the Council of Trent for the serving women of ecclesiastics."[8] This is an error regularly reproduced by the dictionaries in current use.[9] But at Trent, in the last session, the fathers of the council established nothing of the kind, affirming only: "[T]he Holy Synod forbids all clerics to keep in their home any woman whether concubine or not about whom there might be suspicions or with same to have any commerce." [10] In substance they were following the norms on cohabitation established by the council of Nicaea: "It is forbidden ... that any bishop, priest, deacon, or anyone else who is in clerical orders should seek to keep women, excepting perhaps their mother, sister, aunt or those who are free of suspicion."[11]

The underlying concept hinged on the avoidance of "suspicious women": a principle that for all its vagueness continued until the *Codex Juris Canonici* of 1917.[12] No general law of the church ever determined an age for the domestic servants of priests. Manzoni, in fact, by giving Perpetua the "synodal age of forty," seems merely to have committed the sin of anachronism, projecting an eighteenth-century practice on an earlier period. The Milanese synods of the years that provided the time frame for the novel, even if they frequently considered issues of priestly morality and cohabitation, never deviated from the Nicaean norm. It was only later that they interpreted it in a more restrictive manner.[13] Manzoni's source is later as well, going back to the period of his cultural formation. The peril of cohabitation with a "suspicious woman" could be avoided, according to the thinking of some eighteenth century canonists, if one respected two prerequisites when choosing a domestic: an honest life and an advanced age, generally forty years.[14]

In Sienese sources an "advanced age" never figured as a necessary prerequisite for becoming a priest's servant. There is an indication of the age of rural domestics in twenty cases: six were about twenty years old; six about thirty; five about forty; two under twenty; and one about fifty. The average age of housekeepers, thirty-one, and the range of ages underlines a noteworthy freedom of choice within an age span that began before twenty but of necessity ended before too advanced an age, when the strength and endurance needed to perform the functions of a servant became problematic. The questions of the investigators provide a further confirmation of the scant significance given to the age of the perpetua. In only two trials out of seventy-one (forty-one concerning the country, thirty concerning the city) did the investigator question the priest about the youthful age of his housekeeper. In Siena in 1623, the Reverend Giulio Tegliacci, a noble and the suffragan of the metropolitan church, was tried for having kept as a concubine Faustina, a young girl of about twenty: "He had been told that priests, particularly young ones like him, should not keep for a servant women as young as the one called Faustina, nor of such an appearance. And that because of this, it was clear why he was keeping her" (Appendix A, n. 5).

The charge, for all its details, is without any reference to an age limit. Moreover, it was perhaps not so much the age as the comeliness of the woman ("such an appearance") which generated suspicions. This seems to have been true in the case of the parish priest of Stigliano in 1653. The two perpetuas of Cosimo Vai in the opinion of one witness were not the motivation for a "scandal," but for another the suspicion and scandal were sustained because one of the servants "[was] young and a nice piece of woman" (Appendix A, n. 15a). Only in a late eighteenth-century trial do we find a reference to a rule, which was still, however, not specified. In 1792, the curate-chaplain of Pari, Giovanni Alberti, was denounced several times because "he scandalously kept a young servant, against the Synodal Constitutions . . . [a] certain Lucia Malocci of twenty-two years of age . . . and without others in the house" (Appendix A, n. 39).

Thus in these trials—with the exception of the last cited—there was never any concern about a local rule that restricted priests in their choice of a servant.[15] The market forces of the demand for and availability of perpetuas must have been regulated by ethical and behavioral rules that drastically limited the availability of women of marriageable age disposed to offer themselves for this service rather than the existence of any legal restrictions. These considerably reduced the options of parish priests and in turn raised the median age of the perpetuas.

The Civil Status of the Servant

The seventy-one trials provide information on the civil status of 70 perpetuas: forty-three from the country and twenty-seven from the city. Among rural perpetuas twenty-two widows (four were labeled as "gray") account for over 50 percent of the servants involved, a figure that invites reflection. Demographically in the *ancien régime*, widows constituted a significant minority of the population, oscillating perhaps between 10 and 14 percent. Regional and even local variations could be great. Moreover, it would be important for this study to know the number of widows who fell into the twenty- to forty-year-old age range, from which presumably most housekeepers were recruited. Without such data, it is impossible to talk about a meaningful majority of widow perpetuas over single and married perpetuas. Taking still a different tack, one might hypothesize that the existence of certain cultural attitudes and prejudices coincided to make widows the preferred female group for priests seeking a housekeeper.

Two opposing traditions colored contemporary perceptions of widows: on the one hand, the pious widow; on the other, the lustful one. The priest with a solid vocation, led by a "good bishop" active in promoting post-Tridentine pastoral responsibility, knew that there was a great Christian tradition supporting the choice of a widowed housekeeper. "The Maid-Servant of Martyrs, Disciple of Saints, Glory of her Sex, Ornament, Teacher of the fear of God, Guide to married women, Custodian and Sentry of the innocence of virgins, Mirror of Chastity and Trophy of Modesty":[16] this was a sample of the language that exalted the widow, at least those "who were true widows," as Saint Paul observed—who hoped in God, persevered in prayer, and did not waver about remaining in their status. Such a widow was the ideal choice for a priest/pastor; there were even practical benefits that grew out of the experience that a widow had gained managing a family.

But another image of the widow was just as viable for contemporaries: as a lascivious, lustful woman. Because she had been deprived prematurely of regular sexual relations, there lingered suspicions about her desire for renewed sexual intercourse. Such fears turned on widely diffused beliefs in early modern Europe aggressively reinforced locally by the salacious novellas of the Sienese Pietro Fortini (c. 1555).[17] The uninhibited sexual aggression that widows suffered could ironically be understood as the (perhaps) undesired consequence of the "liberating effect of widowhood in many historical contexts."[18] The advances a man could make to this type of "woman on her own" were of a more direct sort and were certainly a factor considered by a priest inclined to succumb to the temptations of sex. There is a significant lapsus in the language of the priest Rombolo Angelini, a schoolteacher in Pari in 1617, who had been denounced by the community and by his own parish priest for his extravagant behavior and for failure to perform his duty. It was reported widely in the village that he had said "that they all [the people of Pari] . . . were a pack of cuckolds and whores . . . and that if one had to remain for long in Pari, he would be likely to impregnate many women, actually widows of Pari" (Appendix A, n. 2).

If the demand for widows as perpetuas remained high because of these opposing views of the widow, a related issue helped to sustain it and discouraged single and married women from the profession as

Table 1.   *Rural Perpetuas*

Years	Widows	Single	Married	Total
1600	20	8	5	33
1700	2	7	1	10
Total	22	15	6	43

well. In Siena, clerics constituted a very unruly social group (see note 34), and as far as a woman's morality was concerned the most dangerous one. Their moral reputation in the city was so low that a simple meeting of a cleric with a woman was enough to arouse suspicions about sinful intentions.[19] In rural parishes the priest clearly could not act with as much freedom; nevertheless, their [low] standards were irreparably imprinted on people's consciousness. The availability of unmarried women was therefore limited and, not unexpectedly, was even lower for married ones. In the latter case supply was scant because need was low; but this was due especially to the extreme hostility of spouses to the idea (Appendix A, n. 15, 26, 35). Demand for married women was also low because the priest needed to have complete control of his servant's time. The figures in Table 1 show, however, that the relationship between widows and unmarried women was reversed in the eighteenth century, with unmarried women dominating in the later period. Perhaps this was due to demographic considerations, or perhaps it was because of a weakening of the factors discussed above in favor of the latter.

Toward Service

More often widowed than single, rarely married, how did a woman decide to serve a priest? The trials have not left much information, and this creates a serious problem for understanding the situation. This lack might be overcome by focusing on other sources in each village (marriage acts, wills, notarial documents, and so on). With such sources it might be possible to discover certain types of relationships between priests and their housekeepers (such as the claimed relationship of godparentage in the case cited in Appendix A, n. 14). We might also consider more closely how serving a priest would give importance to the perpetua's family. An ambivalent impression is given in these judicial records: although such service was sought after because it was a possible source of local prestige, to do so was a decision that had to be weighed carefully because of the possible risks from gossip and slander about one's reputation.

In two cases we learn that the woman assumed service in the tenth year of widowhood (Appendix A, n. 6, 30); in another, after only one year (Appendix A, n. 5). Perhaps such decisions stemmed from the acute need for a salary, for a house, for protection, and the like. This has a certain historical logic, but it is also so obvious that it explains little. In the absence of contracts to hire (probably never written out) and of information from other sources, a true case history remains impossible.[20] For the present, even if we cannot find out why a woman decided to serve a priest in a particular case, we do have information on how she found a post. In Siena, the presence of a female figure who worked as a "distribution center" for servants has been documented. A certain Christofana (Appendix A, n. 10) reported: "When I was in the Piazza [del Campo] selling a flask of vinegar and a bunch of thrushes . . . a peasant told me that she was a *mezzana* [procuress]. . . . [She said,] 'If you want to return to Marciano, I want to put you with a little woman [the mother of the priest] who is half a saint and with the priest of Marciano.'"[21]

Perhaps, then, female mediators worked to create such small living groups. This is suggested by the way the *mezzana* presented her offer: "I want to put you with a little woman." The cohabitation of the priest with relatives, especially women, seems to have been an important factor in convincing a woman to become the housekeeper of a priest. Likewise, moral concerns might press a priest to find a woman to live in his household. In Pari in 1662, a priest suddenly found himself without a servant; to safeguard the reputation of the young nieces he had in his home, he quickly hired a housekeeper, not without rousing suspicions.

The Place of Origin

The place of origin of the rural perpetuas, when it is indicated in the sources, always coincides with the parishes in which they took up service. This is an interesting coincidence; but as noted earlier, such data will only be adequately explained when additional documentation allows a better reconstruction of such situations. In at least one case, however, the provenance of the housekeeper was clearly different from that of the parish in which she served, and the path she followed before gaining the post—from the country to the city and back to the country—indicates perhaps another means of recruitment: from a pool of former servants who, as one might expect, kept up contacts with one another. Giovanna, from Monte San Savino, provides an example:

after having served for nine years at Siena for a noble family, she then became a dependent of the priest Alessandri in Montauto (Appendix A, n. 3b).

Characteristics of Service

The priest who cared for souls needed a helper who could dedicate all of her time to him; thus a perpetua normally had to live in the house annexed to the church. In fourteen apparently contradictory cases, however, the housekeeper did not live in there. Closer examination of ten of these nevertheless reconfirms the premise. In five instances the priest was chaplain acting as an assistant to the parish priest and did not have his own home but was living instead with a family where he was served by a housekeeper by the hour—often a member of that family (Appendix A, n. 17, 18, 34, 38, 40). In another four cases the servant was married and lived with her husband (Appendix A, n. 15d, 25, 26c, 35a). The last case is more complex (Appendix A, n. 5a, b, c): there no woman left her family; rather, the mother (a) and her two daughters (b, c) all lived together near the church.

In thirty-eight cases, however, the perpetua lived with the priest in the presbytery: she took care of it and kept track of him. Her other responsibilities beyond the usual "tending to" the curate—that is, preparing meals, "rearranging" the linen and the garments, cleaning the house—in the absence of written contracts (as noted earlier) one must generalize from the details scattered throughout the testimony of witnesses. In 1620, Anastasia, the young concubine of Mont'Antico, "always did the housework with his mother," taking her place, it seems, for the more difficult tasks—"when [it was time] to harvest, to shovel, to help make bread, to dig and to do whatever was needed" (Appendix A, n. 5b). The case of Olimpia at Casanuovole in 1753 was unusual. Like all the other housekeepers "she made bread, kept the house clean, cooked, bleached and tidied up the linens." But she did not get a salary because her husband worked on some of the property annexed to the church and, moreover, "he curried the horse ... kept the house in firewood, worked in a garden with the few vines, rang the bells whenever necessary, and the priest paid by giving him what he harvested and left him all the works and the salary of the wife" (Appendix A, n. 35a).

From such brief references, one gathers that the duties of a perpetua could include responsibility for a garden or the fields attached to the benefice of a priest and involve the intervention of others from the parish. A thorny question remains: did the perpetua have duties that were connected in some way to worship, such as ringing the bells or cleaning the church "furnishings"? That should have been out of the question. But the lack of (auxiliary) priests or of lay volunteers, in conjunction with an imperious housekeeper, could lead to just such a misuse of power: the source of notable disharmony in one documented case (Appendix A, n. 16).

Salary and the Length of Service

The salary of a perpetua is noted in the sources four times. In Montauto, in 1618, Giovanna was paid annually in grain—seventy-two *stiora*—and, in addition, had the right to glean the fields (Appendix A, n. 3b). In Mont'Antico, in 1620, Corintia earned instead a monthly salary of one *giulio* plus shoes, and her daughters "ate and drank" as well (Appendix A, n. 5). In Stigliano, in 1620, Margherita was paid annually twelve florins (Appendix A, n. 7); finally, Christofana in Marciano in 1637 received an annual salary of twelve florins plus a blouse (Appendix A, n. 10). The value of seventy-two *stiora* of grain would be hard to calculate. But even the other sums are unclear. Translating all the salaries into lire reveals that Corintia earned eight lire annually, while Margherita and Christofana earned eighty-four. Corintia's pay seems too low; at this same time a washerwoman in the hospital of Santa Maria della Scala of Siena earned twenty-four lire yearly plus "tips." The cost of feeding her two daughters must certainly have contributed to keeping her salary so low. In the end the exactly equivalent salaries of Margherita and Christofana provide evidence that appears solid enough. And it reveals a comparatively high remuneration. Margherita di Agostino, servant of Girolamo Turamini, a noble and the fiscal officer of the Hospital of Santa Maria della Scala, earned forty-eight lire annually plus her board in 1633, a little more than half of what the two perpetuas earned.[22] Such attractive salaries, if confirmed in other parishes of the diocese (Marciano was a suburban parish; Stigliano was in Val di Merse, not far from Rosia), seem to imply that the housekeeper to the priest enjoyed a prominent (but risky) social position in the village and, moreover, found in such service a desirable economic status.

As far as length of service, the norm was that most women had served more than five years (Appendix A, n. 1, 3b, 9b, 13, 14, 35a); and in six cases it was more than three years (Appendix A, n. 12, 20, 21b, 26a, 27b). But rapid turnover was also possible, always associated with priests well known for fornication. In Stigliano, for example, the priest between 1614 and 1624 admitted that he had had seven housekeepers (Appendix A, n. 6, 7); in Pari, in 1662, the records refer to many past servants in addition to the three investigated (Appendix A, n. 21); and finally, in Paganico, over the course of perhaps four years three perpetuas were employed (Appendix A, n. 26).[23]

The Servant-Concubine: Wife or Lover

The trial material studied provides rich evidence of another role of the perpetua—as concubine. The dominant theme of those records is that of a clergy given over to clandestine loves, but the distorting impact of the impressionistic voyeurism of the ecclesiastical courts must be kept in mind. Still, from the frequently repetitive stories it is possible to draw conclusions that allow a better understanding of the psychology of this group of perpetuas and certain characteristics of behavior which, though not peculiar to them, were particularly necessary for living without friction in their environment. The trials reveal an impressive range of human affairs. The account of the peasants of the Valle Pugna in 1651 provides a good example:

> In perpetual memory this is the good life of the priest Agostino Gabbrielli in Valle Pugna, who for twenty-four years continually has frequented and frequents an evil woman called Andrea, with whom he fathered two children when he was at San Giovanni that he sent to the Hospital. . . . His whore Andrea wanted to never see his mother . . . because she thought that then people would not notice her. . . . He called her his god-relative; and while his mother lived he went to visit her each holiday, and if he did not, he sent to say that his god-relative would go to where the poor thing lived in such pain and sorrow for she was aware that the whore was the boss and that she lived with what little they gave her and that is the truth.
>
> Item, it is true that he made his mother die miserably so that he could enjoy the whore who took her place and that is the truth known to all.
>
> Item, it is true that he chased out one of his nephews at the request of the whore in order to better become a notorious keeper of a concubinage, and this a fact.
>
> Item, it is true that on all holidays even if all of the people were assembled, until the concubine came, Mass was not said. All the people feel uncomfortable and this is the pure truth; and the concubine holds herself, all puffed up, and this is the truth.

Item, it is true that no one can say anything because at night he will come to find them at home, saying he wants to beat them up, and this is the truth.

Item, it is true that he lets poor people die without the sacraments, like a certain Francesco, a sharecropper . . . who four times sent for him, but he could not be found as he was enjoying himself with his concubine, which is true; whoever arrived there at night could no longer speak to him.

Item, it is true that on Saints [days] . . . he did not want to go to give people Holy oil . . . which likewise he did to the wife . . . of the sharecropper of Biringucci at San Pietro . . . which likewise he did to a boy of Mariano. . . .

Item, it is true that at Bulciano, last October 26 . . . a young girl had fled to the home of a tenant of Bulciano and they say that Agostino had taken her virginity and made a baby with her . . . this is public knowledge . . . and because she is a poor little thing and is without anyone, there is nothing to be done . . . and these things are discussed and known by all in these villages. He fears nothing though he has been warned by the Ordinary, condemned, summoned, and incarcerated, with his concubine restricted to Siena; nonetheless, he has kept her and keeps her. If God ordered him [to give her up], he says he would want to keep her anyway and this is true.

Item, it is true that the peasants have found a tale-singer who sings about his god-relative: "Agostino and the housekeeper / Pass the time happily / Through the lairs and the thickets / All day they enjoy themselves / Agostino and the housekeeper / Whoever is ill must wait / because few times do they find him."

His god-relative is none other than his concubine and boss because at his home she is everything, and he gives her meals, clothes, and he does nothing but what she wants and the people are suffering. They cannot say anything and she is hated by everyone, and this is public knowledge and report. . . .

Item, it is true that that young girl who publicly had his son this Agostino feeds and keeps at his expense, although she is in another house far from Valle Pugna near Bulciano. The son he keeps with his concubine, who brings the daily meals to him, organized and cooked by the said concubine, which is true. (Appendix A, n. 14)

The complaints of the community of Valle Pugna, whose aggrieved tone is interrupted only momentarily by the sarcasm of the tale-singer, combine the two extremes of concubinage between priest and perpetua: the marriagelike relationship and the prostitutionlike one. Andrea, a "whore" in the eyes of her contemporaries, appears to the historian also as the protagonist of a stable union, cemented for many years by a group of values (perhaps including "love" itself), which endured against the hostility of the social environment and the pressure of the law. The lives revealed by the trials very often fluctuated between these two contrasting realities.

The attitude of the ecclesiastical hierarchy brings to light the nature of another such relationship. The inquisitors were relatively relaxed about the occasional misbehavior of ecclesiastics surprised with a prostitute or woman of ill repute (at most they might fine him ten scudi, almost always less). But they were inflexible when they discovered a long-term union, strengthened by ties other than carnal ones associated with fornication: the widow Maddalena was reported to be the concubine of the curate of Vagliagli in 1666. She declared: "I am pregnant and close to giving birth. . . . I don't know by whom because I have had something to do with many men throughout the Cappanne . . . with people who have taken advantage of me and I don't know who else." This had occurred, she reported, while she worked in the fields. Maddalena also admitted to a relationship with the curate. "On my honor . . . he came to me in Coschini at my house where I had called him so that he would write down some things that I had collected; I told him about what happened to me [the rape], and he kidded me about it; the devil began then to tempt him and we fell into error [but I was] already pregnant."

Maddalena, in order to live more easily with the priest, moved to Coschini, where he had certain responsibilities. The couple took a house where they settled down. Their relationship resembled a very "typical" matrimonial bond, according to the customs of the time. Maddalena said, once again:

> [I went to him] because I had some credits [due], and I don't know how to read, and besides that there was no one there who understands me. . . . We began to be friendly; I did some services for him and I loaned him some grain and money . . . and I know that they are secure because he is faithful and I gave them to him without signing anything; and with them he bought the cattle, and an ox, and he has given the grain to the peasants.

As far as sex was concerned, they came to a mutual agreement. And as a result there were suspicions about a bastard, about affection, and the curate was subjected to intensive questioning:

> Question: The reason that you have taken those rooms [at Coschini] and put Maddalena there was so that you could have her and enjoy her as your woman, and this is the truth, admit it.
> Answer: This I will never say because it would not be fitting as a religious person.
> Question: It was not as a religious, nor as a curate that you got involved with Maddalena as you have, and it was worse because she was of your flock.
> Answer: This has been a simple failing . . ." (Appendix A, n. 22)

Inquisitors wanted to discover if behind carnal relationships there existed stable bonds.[24] Thus they examined closely the *amorevolezze*, that is, the attentions and the gifts, which were unusual for a relationship between an employer and a servant, or even for simple fornication. They asked if other gifts had been given (Appendix A, n. 37; Appendix B, n. 6); if the servant "[ate] at the small table of servitude" (Appendix A, n. 3b, 21c). In the case of Virginia (Appendix A, n. 21c), an additional reason for suspicion was the report that the priest had given her a ride "on horseback" while she was out walking with other women as they returned to the village.

In 1620 the priest of Mont'Antico nourished a suspicious and visible attachment for Anastasia. He pulled her near for "kisses in the street . . . with much scandal. . . . [He repeatedly said] to anyone who complain[ed] about him and this woman that he want[ed] to shoot him in the guts." Although proof of this young woman's alleged pregnancy and recent delivery was inconclusive, her movements created distrust: she always followed the priest to his various duties, even when her husband was working elsewhere (Appendix A, n. 5b). Such details suggest yet another reality, which will be investigated elsewhere: the marriage of convenience arranged by a priest. In eight cases, four from the country (Appendix A, n. 5b, 9b, 25, 35b) and four from the city (Appendix B, n. 5a, 9, 19, 26b), there is the strong suspicion that the perpetua's marriage was set up by the priest after he had enjoyed the woman, a method of recruitment not previously considered.

In the case of Mont'Orgiali, in 1632, it is evident that the local curate had the husband of Hortentia assassinated (Appendix A, n. 9b). Ottavio Baroni, the priest at Tonni in 1667, opted, however, for a more typical solution.

> Many years ago the curate of Tonni had been tried by his Tribunal because he was keeping a woman of about thirty-six years of age. At that time he was ordered by Your Most Illustrious Lordship that he leave her, as he did. A short time later, he rented a farm outside the gate of San Marco, and within weeks he married her to an old man of seventy; and they all lived together. . . . Within months the old man rendered his soul to God . . . and thus the priest continued to live with this woman . . . always as cohabitants. (Appendix A, n. 25)

In trial testimony the perpetua-concubine often appears as a marginal figure. The interest of the post-Tridentine church was directed toward the priest. Nonetheless, in some trials, serving women with strong personalities emerged. In the case of Andrea discussed above, his [the priest's] parishioners complained: "Mass was not said until the concubine arrived." (Appendix A, n. 14). Similar complaints were lodged about the treatment of Lorenza Ceccarelli at Murlo in 1790. The parishioners protested "about the openness of the wait to celebrate the Holy Mass and the feasts until that woman arrived at the church; so much so that among the people it was said that the shepherd does what pleases Ceccarelli" (Appendix A, n. 38). A high-profile personality gave the woman hegemony over the priest, with the servant's power and activities expanding beyond a conventional and accepted measure.

Laura from Ricenza "ha[d] been a woman of wicked ways, and [was] well known as such. She [was] kept as a servant by the reverend Carlo Saracini, priest . . . and by him she ha[d] had more than four children." Just before a pastoral visit, she was sent away, "but as he could not live without her . . . while she had gone to Valentano and remained there, [the priest] superstitiously made his tenant Donna Lucia go barefoot in devotion to the Hermitage . . . and he ordered the little girl Lisabetta to fast on bread and water on the next Sunday dressed in white and to take communion for him." Laura, strengthened by this fascination/bewitchment, took on untoward power. Thus the priest, "instead of with his breviary, was seen with a pistol, a small hand gun, and an harquebus . . . leaving the things of the church, its furnishings that is, and the care of the altar, and the ringing of bells for Mass in the hands of this servant Laura, to the disgust and scandal of the people" (Appendix A, n. 16).

An "imperious" servant could fall out with the community and transform the parsonage into an inferno. In 1620 Giovanna had been for seven years the perpetua of Alessandro Alessandri, priest of Montauto. She had even presented a son to the priest, but the union seems to have deteriorated. A witness reported: "I have heard many peasants who have been to his house say the priest and the servant are quarreling, they are always at war." Alessandri, taking advantage of an imminent pastoral visit, looked to use that as an excuse to get rid of the woman. "Persevering in the concubinage, but with the Archbishop's visit imminent . . . fearing that he would receive recriminations and castigations, he planned to have her leave. In order to escape her anger he gave her a formal injunction pretending falsely that it had been written by order of the Illustrious Vicar . . . in which it was stated that if she did not leave his house she would incur a certain punishment." In fact, it was the relationship with the woman that was in crisis, as Alessandri was moving through a phase of latent homosexuality. A young, seventeen-year-old clergyman had been sleeping for some time in his home, in bed with him. Giovanna reported: "When that boy began to come . . . my relationship ended with Alessandro. [I used to hear them] in the morning, playing together as they got up; and heard him kiss him while in bed." The mounting, biting jealousy in her account is evident. One day after dodging a pitchfork thrust from the young priest, Giovanna blurted out: "If this boy only knew how I have him by the horns, he would not come near me." Her pride had been injured, but she remained authoritarian with everyone. One witness complained, "She refused to touch my hand." Others complained about the role of moral censor which she had taken on, "having slandered an unmarried girl who had a baby." With this type of personality, it is not surprising that she took the initiative in a showdown, expressing doubts about the validity of the formal injunction. "If you send me away, I will ruin you," she threatened. And in the end she filed a denunciation. During the ensuing trial, she remained strong to the end, even under torture. In a scene that called up images of Dante, she maintained her charges while being tortured, "for the space of two Misereres," shouting toward the priest: "It's true, it's true . . . it is his son. . . . Traitor, without fear of God, blasphemer . . . Christ be buggered if you will make me break down" (Appendix A, n. 3b).

The perpetua was the most closely watched person in the village. Her principal attribute had to be discretion; exhibitionism was an unpardonable offense. Giovanna, Laura, Andrea, and Lorenza Ceccarelli were examples of servants who were overly visible and gave the impression (and proof) of having abused the position of privilege they occupied. The community (as is clear from the denunciations against priests who kept concubines) leaned toward toleration as long as no scandal occurred, if the personality of the servant was low profile. Discretion or exhibitionism: for contemporaries, the contrast was expressed in terms of "modesty" [*modestia*] and "showiness" [*vistosità*].

In 1610, the community of Cuna defended its priest by denying that the label "visible" [*vistosa*] fit his servant. While one might surmise much, accusations were not made: "We the undersigned have complete faith that as Parishioners we are satisfied with the charity and love toward us . . . given by our Parish Priest and Rector. . . . And although he has kept in his house a servant for the space of about nine years, nevertheless, because she is a woman of mature years, and not visible, nay very good, and fearful of God, to us it is not at all a scandal" (Appendix A, n. 1).

Hortentia, perpetua and lover of Marc'Antonio Niccolai, priest . . . in Mont'Orgiali in 1632, has left a perceptive definition of what was meant by "modesty" [*modestia*] in her village. Interrogated about illegal concubinage, she denied it and defended her behavior with an argument that was truly timeless: "I have not done such things, actually I would have made myself unseen and unheard if I had such sexual relations (with the priest). Just like the others, I would not go to his home to help him in those necessary chores. . . . I am talking about those women who are wise and leave with their eyes lowered, and then one hears them discussed by some man" (Appendix A, n. 9b).

For the perpetua, a lack of modesty was perhaps more serious than for other women. This attitude—it should be stressed—was understood as a reflection on the delicate role the servant occupied because of her association with the village priest. But the priest (and the church) were for the benefit of all, and nobody could pretend to be their boss. The term "boss" [*padrone*] occurs, however, four times in the trials, and each time its meaning is negative. In other cases the language of the witnesses, although limited, confirms that any perceived censorious actions by the perpetua were deemed unacceptable. This was seen in the case of Giovanna (Appendix A, n. 3b); others are equally explicit. During the Mass, the servant of the curate of Marciano assumed the function of a sentry, scrutinizing all the faithful "with little respect inside and outside the church; [because of her thousands of scowls] . . . the people of Marciano dislike[d] her intensely" (Appendix A, n. 10).

In 1662 Lisabetta, one of the servant-lovers of the priest Cioli of Pari, when compared with her sister who had preceded her in that role and was considered a prostitute, was described as "having a better name. . . . Of lovely aspect and a lady of good manners, she [knew] how to do everything. . . . She [was] a most modest woman." But, nonetheless, even her behavior came to be stigmatized. "She is the boss in the house. . . . She makes faces at everyone; she would like no one to visit the house; it is for this that [the people] don't like her." When Virginia, taking advantage of the absence of Lisabetta (because she was in Siena at the bedside of her dying sister), succeeded in ousting her from the curate's good graces, . . . the collision between the two women was immediate. Virginia said: "She reproached me saying that she wanted to remain with the priest; and that if he sent her out the door she would come back through the window" (Appendix A, n. 21a, b, c).

Jealousy and the desire for a much-envied higher social station (and a salary) fed the conflict between the two perpetuas.[25] Generally in the more developed trials, a sense of possession is evident, a metamorphosis of the perpetua into a custodian of the presbytery, with, at the same time, the moral role of the priest being transferred to her by osmosis.[26] Inevitably nicknames were coined. Among the most telling, the chaplain of Pari in 1617 called a servant a *pretaccia* ["evil female priest"], a perfect example of the slide in stature from servant to boss (Appendix A, n. 2).

In other trials, however, the perpetua was more like a prostitute who acted occasionally as a servant. For example, in Stigliano in 1620–24, the Reverend Bartolomeo Zoppi, who had earlier "gone bound to Siena and been imprisoned," continued to be unrepentant about his fornication, going through seven servants in ten years (Appendix A, n. 6, 7). Similarly in Mont'Antico the house of the cleric Buonsignori resembled more a brothel than the home of a churchman according to the men to the community (Appendix A, n. 27). Other examples reflect clearly the pure libertinage of the eighteenth century, as the language of the interrogators in several eighteenth-century trials reveals. A servant seduced by Lorenzo Pecciarini, chaplain of Pari in 1722, reported the priest's words of seduction: "Are you very scrupulous, are you afraid that I will make you pregnant? It requires some experience. But I have slept with other servants often and no one has known anything, nor have they seen anything" (Appendix A, n. 33).

In the case of the alleged concubinage of Olimpia, perpetua at Casanuovole, the testimonies of the female servants involved in the intrigues of the steward Franchi and the marquis Chigi, his rival, use expressions that evoke a different environment from that of the preceding century. Agnesa, a servant of Chigi, reported some of the verbal approaches of the priest: "Do you like your meat [flesh] raw or cooked? ... The marquis and I have done the reckoning of who between us should go to bed with you." Similar language was used with Lucia Bassi, a young and comely servant, for whose "charms" the priest and noble were contending. The priest said to her: "If you want to give it to me, give it to me; if not, I don't care because I have Olimpia, and the little brunette, and Teresa from Mont'Antico, and Agnesa from the Chigi house, who gives me as much as I want" (Appendix A, n. 35).

Merely a few phrases perhaps, but enough to show how language is a point of view on the world: "Words give the flavor of a profession ... of a generation, of an age."[27] And the actions of the priest Franchi truly provide a "taste" of the century. In the trial one of the main accusations against him was

> that with public scandal and against the laws of modesty, he held it licit to insinuate to the parishioners from the holy altar, with immoral terms, that those who had wives already pregnant when they married should satisfy themselves in their arms; just as those who were involved with single girls should ejaculate outside in order not to get them pregnant; and this he said repeatedly on several mornings, substituting similar most unseemly admonitions for the explanation of the Gospel. (Appendix A, n. 35)

The servants involved in this trial do not appear to have been true peasants. Rather, they seem to be domestics acculturated to the city, where they spent six months each year, and to the less restrictive noble environment that had accustomed them to such amorous ménages. But the real contrast does not appear to be as much between city and country as between the two centuries, even if evaluating the validity of such a generational explanation requires further research. Here I wish merely to suggest that the existence of similar cases involving perpetuas perhaps contributed to creating and diffusing a certain atmosphere, one that could provoke or diminish scruples or could propagate a general sense of malaise and, at the same time, a new attitude regarding domestic service for priests—new in the sense of more "normal," similar in part to the service performed as a domestic for a lay employer.

In the trials, sins of the flesh were condemned in both periods, but in the eighteenth-century records the atmosphere is less dark and bloody. The punishments that the hierarchy inflicted on such sinners were no longer those public expiations in which penitent and spectator were reciprocally purified. Punishment became discrete; it turned inward. Spiritual retreats into prayer replaced the public display in chains of concupiscent priests. Even for the laity, the old penitential practice was abandoned. In 1786, the ecclesiastical tribunal of Siena qualified as follows a verdict on a clandestine marriage:

> The change in circumstances and times constrains us to make a reasonable reply, since it has been well recognized that the punishments involving public penance in the form and manner in which they have been prescribed have brought with them not a good example, but rather pure pomp, and instead of protecting against scandal as they should have, they have lent themselves to spectacle ... with the sole object of displaying the guilty parties ... not lamenting them.[28]

Whenever one looks at the close of the eighteenth century, the cultural climate appears to have changed. And that means that it becomes less easy to discover the indiscretions that occurred within the walls of the presbytery.

⁓ The Urban Perpetua

In a comparison of the data on rural perpetuas with those of urban ones (Appendix B), a number of distinctions emerge:

Age. The median age is slightly lower for servants in the city: 28.7 as against 31.2.

Civil Status. There are differences also in the civil status. In the city, in contrast to the country, there is a slight predominance of single women over widows. The physiognomy of the priests' housekeepers is not as clearly delineated in the city as in the country. If the data are representative, in this context it may be true that traditional values still solid in the country may have been diluted in the complex social reality of the city.

The Provenance. This is a further element that distinguishes city

Table 2.   *Urban Perpetuas*

Years	Widows	Single	Married	Total
1600	8	9	6	23
1700	2	2	–	4
Total	10	11	6	27

from country. In twelve cases city servants were not native. Moreover, the scant number of cases in which provenance was specified does not allow the identification of a predominant area of origin. And when there is no mention, does it mean the servants were born in the city?

The Previous Occupation. Nineteen trials describe the activity of a woman before she became a perpetua. Five were former prostitutes; seven were servants; seven were domestics in the service of other employees who lent material aid to the priest under investigation. In four cases (Appendix B, n. 2, 6, 9, 26) the priest lived with or worked for a noble family.

The Characteristics of Service. The contrast here with the rural situation is revealing. There were twenty-one full-time domestics and thirteen part-time ones (in the country the figures are thirty-eight and fourteen, respectively). This difference could be explained logistically: the high concentration of priests in the city relegated many of them to precarious situations that did not allow them to maintain a regular servant. As one looks at each case, it becomes evident (as noted already for the country) that priests with a flock also tended to have a full-time servant. In three cases this is certain (Appendix B, n. 1, 22, 23); in six it is probable (Appendix B, n. 15, 16, 19, 24, 29, 30). When the source simply indicates a "prete" (a minor cleric?) instead of a sacerdote, the servant was always part-time (Appendix B, n. 2, 3, 6, 14, 21). The duties of an urban perpetua must have differed from those of her rural analogue, but there is little information in the sources to prove this. The numerous linen services used by the domestics investigated attest at least to the notable diffusion of part-time work. For their meals, the priests had frequent recourse to public inns [*osterie*].[29] Finally, in the urban trials there is no mention of the salary of servants.

The Servant as Lover or Wife

Licentiousness, depravity: these terms best typify the clergy as a whole in the urban environment (see note 34). Moreover, although clerics represented a high-risk category for the morality of women, that did not seem to have stopped a significant number of single women from serving them. Even the data on the servant-prostitutes (or at least the ones held to be such by their families) are not surprising. In the urban center, the sexual transgressions of clerics with suspicious women or with "registered" prostitutes were so numerous that inevitably there are examples of stable relationships: priests who lived with a prostitute "as if she were his wife" (Appendix B, n. 16). The result was most unlikely: women who moved from prostitute to perpetua. This reversed the path assumed to have been more normal, which led from domestic service to prostitution.[30]

In one case there is an overlap of the priest's place of origin and the prostitute's (Appendix B, n. 17), suggesting a possible earlier relationship. This is implied in other cases as well (Appendix B, n. 3, 6, 10). In some trials, the nature of the relations shows strong indications of the greater liberty of customs in a large city. The rape and prolonged abuse of a child carried out by Giovanni Vannetti, co-rector of the Church of San Salvatore, would probably not have occurred in the country. The priest deflowered Giovanna (Appendix B, n. 23b), the thirteen-year-old daughter of his perpetua who had died at home (Appendix B, n. 23a). He refused to give custody of Giovanna to her close relatives. Instead she remained in the house with the priest (as an unpaid servant) while he asserted that he was fond of her and wanted to take care of her future. Giovanna, occasionally helped by other domestics hired for brief periods (Appendix B, n. 23c, d), was, in effect, a prisoner. "The night when my mother died, he wanted me to sleep with him, and all night he mistreated me ... although I screamed when I felt hurt. And he forbade me to say anything ... because he told me he would kill me, and he did not let me leave the house, and when he went out, he locked me in."

Not quite so cruel, but typically urban, was the scam worked by Marta Griccioli (Appendix B, n. 24c) in 1692. The woman brought her two daughters with her (Appendix B, n. 24d) to help with the domestic chores. But she took advantage of her contacts and her mobility to prostitute them by the hour with priests and canons. One witness reported: "They came here almost every day and did this: the mother of that bride [speaking figuratively] came to the home of the [priest] Gallacini where the canon Fraticelli was also, and after talking a bit, they set the hour when her daughter, the bride, had to come, and at the fixed hour she appeared immediately, and the bride was locked in the room with the aforementioned canon."

The canon Fraticelli, who later became a notorious figure in the lay courts as well,[31] anticipated the licentious bravado of the eighteenth century—faced with the rebukes of a domestic reluctant to lend her services to a quasi brothel, he threatened dismissal and at the same time boasted of his amorous successes: "You think that I haven't had any but these [women]. I have had more than two hundred of them." And when the servant retorted, "You live that life even though every morning you celebrate [Mass]," he answered: "If my mother made me [a man of flesh], it is best that I accept it." The priest Antonio Boninsegni, canon of the collegiate church of Provenzano, was involved in comparable intrigues with similar language and situations (Appendix B, n. 30).

Even the social advancement of some domestics was well integrated within the complex social life of the city. Faustina, the twenty-year-old servant and lover of the canon Tegliacci, after two years of concubinage, was married by him to the mason Matteo. The canon subsequently had Matteo imprisoned for debts "so that he [the canon] could better enjoy his servant." It is evident that when a priest was well-to-do like the young Tegliacci, who was from a noble family, the original working and material conditions of the servant tended to disappear; the perpetua ceased to be a servant in order to become a kept woman. Other women were hired who provided temporary help: "Sometimes I cooked there in the house ... or we bought something from the *osteria* ... or I called in some woman who would help me."

The complicated case of the "possession" of Oriana, wife of Ippocrate Grazzini,[32] fits this same pattern. She was accused in 1625 of being the concubine of the aged canon Alberto Luti. The two were old acquaintances; the canon had met her in the house of the Elci family where Oriana was the personal maid of the Countess Laura. At her death, the noblewoman left Luti two hundred scudi to give to the servant, in recognition of her loyal service. The canon's attentions, however, continued. Eventually he found a husband for the well-off former servant, and, according to the accusations, he then tried to have him murdered, the better to enjoy the latter's new wife. Was this accusation true or false? To add the final touch to this already-complicated affair, a few months after the marriage, the unexpected occurred: the devil took possession of Oriana, giving rise to a case of possession which provoked a furor in Sienese ecclesiastical circles

(Appendix B, n. 9). Somewhat less uproar accompanied the social advancement of Caledonia, a servant in the Piccolomini house and eventual wife of Niccolo Castagnoli, a chemist. In 1712 the priest Selvi took up the duties of bookkeeper and agent in the Piccolomini household. This Selvi, who had already seduced a certain Rosa (Appendix B, n. 26a), the young orphaned servant entrusted to him by the hospital and dismissed when she "was found to be pregnant," now set out after bigger game. He became the lover of Caledonia, then married her off, and set up the new couple in his own house. Caledonia soon became the target of evil rumors spread by neighbors and by Selvi's old servant (Appendix B, n. 26b), because she took on "airs" and [went] about dressed with a luxury that exceed[ed] her condition and when she [went] out she [was] accompanied by Signor Selvi's manservant."[33]

In these urban cases, situations found in the country also recur— for example, the affectionate rapport between a priest and a servant which often was consolidated in a stable, marriagelike relationship. Bruno Valenti, priest of Angiano in 1636, had a bond with Donna Cassandra which lasted for twenty years (Appendix B, n. 11). The woman lived in Siena in the San Marco district, and twice a week she received regular visits from the priest under the pretext of "bleaching his collars and sewing them." In reality the "close friendship" had produced a "companionate marriage" reinforced by the birth of "seven or eight children." At the time of his investigation, his primary concern was the marriage of a daughter who had to be dowered. Despite the duration and force of the bond, the hostility of the priest's own family had not diminished. They continually reproved him, asserting: "[H]e never wants to leave her . . . Cassandra; and he would rather lose the benefice than leave her."

The young cleric Giobatta Tonci and Ersilia, servant in the Elci home, even shared a common birthplace, Radicondoli. In 1622 the palace where the girl worked served as a pied-à-terre for the cleric. The count's young sons, jealous because one evening Ersilia did not remain at their bedside to tell stories, discovered Giobatta in a room. The investigators suspected an emotional attachment behind what he asserted was merely a physical relationship, and Ersilia did not succeed in hiding her own feelings: "I love this boy, and I have had relations with him." The cleric, however, denied everything. And although he had only the "ministry of the Eucharist and a lectorship in the minor orders," which would not have imposed chastity upon him, he was tortured anyway. There was some proof of "affectionate deeds" and a letter that in fact belied the mere carnal side of the hidden love. The letter was addressed to Ersilia and dated April 6, 1622:

> Most affectionate and beloved aunt [*zia*], I have received your most enjoyable and long awaited letter. . . . Salvatore's arrival here has made me happy, hearing [the news] that you are well and happy which I cannot say for myself since I do nothing but think about you. It has made me think that [those thoughts] are like a continuous fever, indeed I hope to come to see you as soon as possible. You have shown yourself too loving toward me; I have received the sausage and earlier you sent me rice, yet I send nothing to you; however, I know that here there is nothing that is at all worthy of you. I will say nothing else except that I wish to remain in your good graces as I hold you in mine and that I keep you always engraved on my heart. . . . Your most affectionate nephew Giobatta Tonci. (Appendix B, n. 6)

⅋ The Causes of the Change

The progressive decline in the number of denunciations of concupiscent priests noted between 1600 and 1800 (from fifty-four in the seventeenth century to seventeen in the eighteenth) invites reflection, even if any conclusion can only be provisional. Such a phenomenon may be interpreted by placing the protagonists of the trials (the priest, the ecclesiastical hierarchy, the faithful, and the perpetua) within the context of the broad social change that accelerated in the concluding decades of the eighteenth century in Italy and the rest of Europe. In the brief space of this conclusion, hypotheses will be suggested that will be verified later in more focused studies.

The Causes of Ecclesiastical Concubinage. Before examining the reasons for a possible diminution in concubinage, it is wise to consider what factors may have favored its ubiquity in earlier centuries. Matrimonial models of the time, the benefice system, and ecclesiastical celibacy must be examined and questioned. In the Europe of the *ancien régime* at all social levels, rules to discipline matrimony existed. The clergy, however, could not marry. Moreover, evidently not all of those who became priests wanted to become one—such decisions were made within the family and were often an imposition on an individual. Concubinage arose also within the context of a traditional model of marriage, and surely many Sienese priests would have fit well the role of husband and father.

On the level of daily life, the results of the meeting of the Council of Trent on November 11, 1563, were decisive. The debate on the marriage of priests, reopened at the beginning of February, concluded with the ratification of twelve canons, the eleventh prohibiting marriage for the regular and secular clergy. With marriage denied and the prohibition against frequenting suspicious women by *quibusdam clericis* promulgated, chastity became a central issue in the decision to become a cleric. If that decision had been limited to accepting a vow of poverty, chastity, and obedience, perhaps then the phenomenon of sinful cohabitation would appear today as a marginal human weakness. But a shadow of suspicion was projected over the quality of faith of the entire ecclesiastical order of the *ancien régime* by the "system of benefices," which had the potential to make clerical life a career decision that was both socially and economically advantageous. In such a scenario, while it was possible to accept the marginal "frailty" of a few, it was better to require the adaptation of the many to a general custom. Selective matrimonial models, ecclesiastical celibacy, the clerical status as "profession": these three closely related factors give meaning to a phenomenon such as the inobservance of chastity, which given its widespread practice (see note 34), cannot be explained merely by individual caprice.

The Decline in Ecclesiastical Concubinage. The apparent decline of such activity, if real, was evidently accelerated by the weakening of the matrimonial model discussed earlier. But perhaps other changes also had an impact on the ecclesiastical world from both within and without. A "civilizing process" seems to have played a central role. This transformation of individual behavior in the *ancien régime* appears to have been to a large degree a result of the consolidation of the modern state: the improvement of its power to control and repress; the domestication of elites and their transformation into a ruling class responsible for order and promoters of a disciplined morality; the growth in juridical culture; the development of the civility of good manners, of civilized behavior in public and the affirmation of the sense of the "private." These are some factors that contributed to a notable transformation of collective behavior—a metamorphosis intended to control drives, to discipline gestures, to promote the evolution of a sense of shame. Churchmen were involved in this no less than lay. A more civilized clergy was created as a consequence, who abandoned their former way of life insofar as it was no longer suited to the times. On the specific matter of ecclesiastical concubinage, the change in the church's strategy in the modern era began its decline. If in the thirteenth through fifteenth centuries the concubine was persecuted first, with the sixteenth century the priest became the focus of the inquisitors.[34] After Trent, then, the church reorganized and reinforced its powers in order to purify the ministers of the faith. The diffusion of models of civilized behavior was accompanied by a process of the moralization of clerics and priests which came from within the church.

Unfortunately, the limited nature of local research on any qualitative improvement in the religious sense of eighteenth-century priests in Siena renders problematic for the present the acceptance of this hypothesis. But the history of the relations between parish priests and their housekeepers can perhaps act as a litmus test of the development of the pastoral sense in the diocese. In addition, the hypothesis is supported by the fact that a smaller number of concubines would govern the nineteenth-century presbyteries.

And the perpetuas? There would continue to be housekeepers in the nineteenth century and beyond because priests were still in need of their material assistance. But the documentary evidence ends at the end of the eighteenth century, and in the absence of trials silence falls anew upon the servants of priests. In 1832 a special note of the archbishop of Siena suggests that obedience was still far from absolute:

> From the beginning of our Spiritual Governance we admonished
> Priests . . . about the selection of serving women. . . . But since
> these provisions have not had the desired effect and since it would
> be wise to establish a system to insure that the Canonical Constitu-
> tions be observed . . . we decide as follows: no parish priest or sim-
> ple priest will be able, in the future, to keep in his service any
> woman younger than forty, and about whom we have not had au-
> thentic proofs as to her spotless morality and wisdom. If someone,
> constrained by necessity, wishes to take as a servant some woman
> of proven honesty and of good reputation but younger by a bit
> than forty years, let them petition us on this matter.[35]

Other documentation is lacking to decide whether or not these perpetuas were similar to earlier ones. Surely they lent their help at the time to a person [the cleric] who was partly an outsider in the village. Perhaps the priest, always less integrated with his parishioners in terms of culture and manners, finding himself at the margins of the sociability of the village, ended up seeking to overcome his solitude through closer relations with other clerics. This change accentuated the distinction between lay society and ecclesiastical society and even transformed the nature of the relationship between priests and perpetuas in the eyes of the faithful. The differentiation between priest and the village relegated the priest more and more to his presbytery, whose walls increasingly marked out a private world. What happened within those walls remained a matter of debate, but nurtured now with increasing insistence by "opinions" rather than by a "mentality." And in whatever direction the priest transformed the companionship given him by the perpetua (leaving aside her material aid), it became simply a matter of an individual decision, not an acceptance of a diffused practice. The twentieth-century anticlericalism of the Third Republic offered a similar picture: "Mon bon Ponosse, puisque nous ne pouvons entièrement nous détacher de la matière, faveur qui fut accordée seulement à quelques saints, il est heureux que nous ayons à domicile les moyens de lui accorder secrétement l'indispensable, sans occasioner la scandale ni troubler la paix des âmes. Réjouissons-nous que nos misères ne portent pas préjudice au bon nome de l'Eglise."[36]

Appendix A: Rural Perpetuas

Number	File/Year	Woman	Age	Status	Full-time?	Years	Children, Pregnancies, Abortions	Reputation
1	5522/1610	a			yes	9		good
2	5523/1617	a		widow	yes			
3	5523/1618	a						prostitute
		b		older widow	yes	7	1c	
4	5524/1620	a	40	widow	yes	various		scandalous
5	5524/1620	a		widow	no	9		
		b	26	widow	no	1		controversial
		c	16	widow	no			
6	5524/1620	a		widow	yes	2	1	controversial
7	5529/1624	a			yes			scandalous
8	5531/1627	a			yes			
9	5534/1632	a		widow	yes			
		b		older widow	yes	7/8	3c	scandalous
10	5539/1637	a		older widow	yes	3	1c	controversial
11	5539/1638	a		widow	yes		1?	
12	5539/1639	a		single	yes	3	1	scandalous
13	5540/1641	a	22	single	yes	11	1	
14	5545/1651	a			yes	9		scandalous
15	5548/1653	a	24	single	yes			scandalous
		b			yes		1	
		c					1	

Number	File/Year	Woman	Age	Status	Full-time?	Years	Children, Pregnancies, Abortions	Reputation
		d		married	no			
16	5547/1653	a		single	no			
17	5551/1654	a	30	married	no			
18	5551/1656	a		widow	no			
		b	17	single	no		1	
19	5551/1658	a	30/40	widow	yes		1p	
20	5552/1659	a			yes	3	1c	scandalous
21	5558/1662	a	40	widow	yes			
		b	40	older widow	yes	3	1c	scandalous
		c	30/40	widow	yes			
22	5560/1666	a	35/40	widow	yes	2	1p	
23	5561/1668	a		widow	yes			scandalous
		b		single	yes		2a	
24	5565/1674	a						
25	5565/1677	a	35	all	yes		1c	scandalous
26	5568/1680	a				3		
		b						
		c	40	married	no	1		controversial
27	5572/1686	a						
		b	50?	married	yes	3		scandalous
		c		widow	yes		1p	scandalous
		d		single	yes		1p	scandalous
28	5580/1697	a					2c	
29	5580/1697	a			yes			
30	5582/1722	a	44	widow	yes	1	1p	controversial
31	5590/1725	a			yes			scandalous
		b		widow	yes		1p	
32	5591/1725	a		single	yes		1p	
33	5591/1729	a						
34	5593/1740	a			no			scandalous
35	5595/1753	a	30	married	no	7		scandalous
		b	20	single		1		scandalous
36	5604/1775	a			yes			
37	5606/1790	a		single	no		various	
38	5606/1790	a		single	no			scandalous
39	5608/1792	a	22	single				scandalous
40	5608/1793	a	20	single	no			
41	5608/1794	a		single	yes			scandalous

Appendix B: Urban Perpetuas

Number	File/Year	Woman	Age	Status	Full-time?	Children, Pregnancies, Abortions	Origin
1	5520/1605	a		widow	yes		Florence
2	5521/1608	a	20	single	no		Pienza
3	5523/1617	a	40	widow	no		Colle
4	5525/1620	a			no		
		b					
5	5525/1620	a	20	married			Casta del Piano
		b					
		c					
6	5527/1622	a	25	widow	no		Radicondoli
7	5526/1626	a		single	yes		
		b		widow	yes		
8	5526/1628	a					
9	5530/1629	a	35	married			
10	5532/1629	a	17	single			Monte S. Sovino

11	5538/1636	a		widow	no	7/8c	
12	5538/1639	a					
13	5544/1641	a		single	no		
14	5544/1642	a			yes		
15	5544/1648	a			yes		
16	5544/1648	a			yes		
17	5544/1648	a			yes		
18	5549/1654	a		married	no		Sarteano
19	5561/1667	a		married	yes		
20	5563/1667	a			yes		
21	5564/1678	a		single	no		
22	5565/1675	a			yes	1p	
23	5570/1682	a	39	widow	yes		Sinalunga
		b	12	single	yes		
		c			yes		Pisa
		d			yes		Pisa
24	5578/1692	a	48	widow	yes		Montevarchi
		b	25	single	no		
		c		married	no		
		d		single	no		
		e		married	no		
25	5578/1693	a		single	yes		
26	5585/1712	a	50		no		
		b		single		1p	
27	5589/1720	a	30	single	yes	1p	
28	5602/1768	a	18	single	yes		countryside
29	5606/1790	a		widow	yes		
30	5606/1794	a			yes		

Notes

1. G. Le Bras, *La chiesa e il villaggio* (Turin, 1979), p. 113. This article anticipates in part a chapter from a forthcoming book on the behavior of the popular classes in the city and the country: *Amori nascosti: Sentimenti e sessualità in antico regime (1600–1800)*. I would like to thank Claudio Donati and Adriano Prosperi for their comments.

2. Various periodicals have dedicated entire issues to the theme of "women on their own." See *Annales de demographie historique* (1981); *Journal of Family History* 7 (Winter 1982); *Memoria: Rivista di Storia delle Donne* 18 (1986).

3. Archivio Arcivescovile di Siena (hereafter AAS), Cause criminali, nn. 5519–5610 (1604–1800). These files are not foliated.

4. R. Sauzet, "Considérations methodologiques sur les visites pastorales dans la diocèse de Chartres pendant la première moitié du XXVIIè siècle," *Ricerche di storia sociale e religiosa* 1 (1972): 95–137.

5. AAS, Sante Visite, 43 (1653–61), ff. 9r–10r.

6. AAS, Sante Visite, 48 (1668), f. 22r.

7. A. Manzoni, *I promessi sposi* (Milan, 1906), chap. 1.

8. S. Battaglia, *Grande dizionario della lingua italiana*, vol. 2 (Turin, 1962).

9. See, for example, the *Dizionario Garzanti della lingua italiana* (Milan, 1965) under: *canonico, sinodale*; or Devoto-Oli, *Vocabolario della lingua italiana* (Florence, 1979). Similarly, the error has penetrated even the commentaries of certain editions of Manzoni's novel—for example, the edition edited by L. Caretti (Bari, 1972). The phrase *età sinodale* (later also *età canonica*) does not appear in the *Vocabolario degli Accademici della Crusca*, or in any of the great dictionaries of the early decades of the nineteenth century, such as Manuzzi's or Costa-Cardinali's. It appears in dictionaries only after

the novel, and for the first time, obviously, in the great Tommaseo-Bellini under *sinodale*. The error of attribution to the Council of Trent seems to appear for the first time in Zingarelli (1992).

10. *Concilium Tridentinum*, sess. 25, cap. 14. An eighteenth-century edition of the *Acta* reports an interesting commentary: "In ultimo autem decreto agitur de clericis concubinariis, eorumque punitione. Nimium autem rara, ac hodie forte nulla est citra montes huius decreti quaestio in foro, cum etiam in laicis in Italia non de facili permittatur usus concubinatus, multo minus in clericis. Quandoque autem in Rota audiri consueverunt istae quaestiones in clericis ultra montes." *Sacrosantum, Oecumenicum Concilium Tridentinum Additis Declarationibus Cardinalium Concilii Interpretum, ex ultima recognitione, Joannis Gallemart, . . . cum decisionibus variis Rotae Romanae eodem spectantibus* (Trent, 1752), p. 534.

11. *Concilio de Nicea*, dist. 32, can. 16.

12. "Caveat clerici ne mulieres, de quibus suspicio esse possit, apud se retineant aut quo modo frequentent. 2). Eisdem licet cum illis tantum mulieribus cohabitare in quibus naturale foedus nihil mai possit suspicari, quales sunt mater, soror, amita et huismodi, aut a quibus spectata morum honestas, cum provectiore aetate coniuncta, omnem suspicionem amoveat." *Codex Juris Canonici Pii X . . .* , can. 133.

13. For the period when the novel took place, roughly from the synods of Carlo and Federigo Borromeo until 1650, see volume 4 of the *Acta Ecclesiae Mediolanensis*, ed. Angelo Ratti.

14. Pope Benedict XIV (1675–1758) stated on this: "ipsarum quoque [famularum] aetas cognita sit, ita ut parochi famulae, qui consanguineis caret, quadraginta iam annos iam absolverint. Aliter tamen decernendum eat, si cum parocho etiam mulieres consanguineae etiam versentur . . . magnum sane discrimen interest cum plures simul mulieres . . . eadem domo continentur; diverso tamen modo res se habet cum sola mulier, nulla sanguinis propinquitate sed famulae tantum conditione accita, cum parocho versatur, qui forte per hiemem longissimae noctis spatium . . . cum ipsa famula prope ignem vanis colloquiis insumit." I have taken the quotation from Benedict XIV (Inst. eccl. 82–2) from the entry "cohabitation" in the *Dictionnaire du droit canonique*, vol. 3 (Paris, 1942), pp. 970–82.

15. AAS, Libri edictorum, 6481–85 (1594–1795). Naturally the age of the perpetua at the moment that she was hired was younger than that noted when a judicial investigation began. For this see the following trials: Appendix A, n. 13; 21b; 22; 26c; 27b; 30; 35.

16. C. M. Moroni, *Dizionario di erudizione storico ecclesiastica* vol. 88 (Venice, 1852), pp. 250–85.

17. See, for example, the fourth and fifth *novelle* in P. Fortini, *Novelle, Le giornate delle Novelle dei Novizi*, vol. 1 (Florence, 1967). On a more general level, see Lawrence Stone, *The Family, Sex, and Marriage in England, 1500–1800* (London, 1977), p. 281. For a local example, see G. R. Quaife, *Wanton Wenches and Wayward Wives* (London, 1979), pp. 143–64.

18. N. L. Roelker, "Introduction," *Journal of Family History* 7 (Winter 1982): 376.

19. In the criminal records of the AAS, numerous petitions remain from clerics who felt that they had been persecuted by families.

20. Constructing case histories of some of the perpetuas would be possible in the case of Pari. Giovambattista Cioli, a native of the area, became the parish priest in 1631 at the age of twenty-seven and remained there until 1673. Gifted with a strong personality, he left a rather detailed parochial register (AAS, n. 1686). Traces of his rectorate are dispersed in other local archival holdings (for example, Archivio di Stato di Siena, Quattro Conservatori, nn. 951–81; ASS, Vicariati, 329–30).

21. The Piazza del Campo apparently continued without interruption to be the appointed place for finding housekeepers. After the Second World War, the function

of the *mezzana* [procuress] was performed by an old *bananaia*, today dead, who kept a list of women willing to serve in one of her notebooks.

22. ASS, Ospedale di Santa Maria della Scala, 3118, f. 3r.

23. In the voluminous trial against the priest Niccolai (Appendix A, n. 9), a very old servant turned up in the presbytery (9a), half deaf but not unaware; she was kept perhaps as a cover for concubinage with Hortentia (9b).

24. In the case of "young Angela" (Appendix A, n. 28), taken to Siena to give birth at his home by the priest Gerfalco under the pretense that she was his sister, the diligent questioning of the inquisitors brought to light the priest's deep paternal feelings. The nurse to whom a previous son of Angela's had been entrusted at the hospital reported: "He received money, too. [Once the priest] took up the baby, kissing him . . . and he always said to me that he would look after him. And when he came with those women [Angela and others], they all held him and played with him as if he were his child."

25. In one of Virginia's comments there is a possible reference to the economic advantage of working as a perpetua: "She [Lisabetta] used to say that she did not want to lose the house but that she could be certain that I want to stay in my poverty."

26. P. Boutry refers to a probable growth in power of the priest's housekeeper: "Il arrive bien souvent . . . que les curés se laissent dominer par elles. . . . Elles font des rapports à leurs maîtres et ensuite disent indiscrètement dehors ce qui se passe au presbytère. . . . La première année . . . elles disent: 'Les poules de Monsieur le curé'; peu de temps après, elles disent: 'Nos poules'; elles finissent par dire: 'Mes poules . . .' " cited in Boutry, *Prêtres et paroisses au pays du Curé d'Ars* (Paris, 1986), p. 223.

27. M. Bakhtin, *Estetica e romanzo* (Turin, 1979), p. 101. I owe this quote to my wife, Dasa Silhankova.

28. AAS, 5607.

29. The sources make frequent references to the arrest of priests surprised during their revelries in taverns.

30. This conventional itinerary, from servant to prostitute, is rashly taken as a given in many works. For another opinion, see E. M. Benabou, *La prostitution et la police des moeurs au XVIII siecle* (Paris, 1985), pp. 300–306; K. Walser, *Frauenarbeit und Weiblichkeitsbilder um 1900* (Frankfurt, 1986), pp. 59–73. I owe this reference to Angiolina Arru.

31. Archivio di Stato di Siena (hereafter ASS), Capitano di Giustizia, 682 (1700), ff. 71–72. This involved a case of pandering. Angela Fantini was investigated for having prostituted her twelve-year-old daughter Angela. Caterina Useppi, widow and servant of the canon Fraticelli, was also implicated. The latter "took Angela's virginity this past August . . . and this past September, when she refused to submit again to canon Fraticelli, he took her and having violently placed her on the bed, he evilly sodomized her from behind."

32. On Oriana's possession, see my forthcoming book.

33. In the documentation, this is the only reference to a male servant.

34. See R. Saez, "La trasgression de l'interdit amoureux: Le prêtre, la femme, et l'enfant dans l'archevêché de Tolède (1565–1620)," in *Amours légitimes, amours illégitimes in Espagne (XVI-XVII siècles)*, under the direction of A. Redondo (Paris, 1985), pp. 93–100. The following figures for clerical crime are drawn from the Cause Criminali: 1604–28, assaults 144, homicides 5, bad conduct 122, sexual transgressions with prostitutes 100, sexual transgressions with suspect women 55, robberies 33, carrying arms 23, minor crimes 27; 1629–53, assaults 75, homicides 3, bad conduct 40, sexual transgressions with prostitutes 58, sexual transgressions with suspect women 9, robberies 10, carrying arms 16, minor crimes 24; 1654–78, assaults 181, homicides 7, bad conduct 67, sexual transgressions with prostitutes 91, sexual transgressions with suspect women

34, robberies 21, carrying arms 32, minor crimes 35; 1679–1704, assualts 129, homicides 6, bad conduct 37, sexual transgressions with prostitutes 37, sexual transgressions with suspect women 1, robberies 4, carrying arms 17, minor crimes 18; 1705–29, assaults 64, homicides 2, bad conduct 16, sexual transgressions with prostitutes 16, sexual transgressions with suspect women 2, robberies 15, carrying arms 2, minor crimes 4; 1730–54, assaults 32, homicides 3, bad conduct 9, sexual transgressions with prostitutes 2, sexual transgressions with suspect women 4, robberies 9, carrying arms 0, minor crimes 5; 1755–79, assaults 19, homicides 0, bad conduct 9, sexual transgressions with prostitutes 0, sexual transgressions with with suspect women 6, robberies 8, carrying arms 0, minor crimes 5; 1780–1800, assaults 13, homicides 0, bad conduct 10, sexual transgressions with prostitutes 0, sexual transgressions with suspect women 8, robberies 5, carrying arms 0, minor crimes 23.

35. AAS, 6486, f. 135.

36. G. Chevallier, *Clochemerle* (Paris, 1934), chap. 3.

3 🐜 The Old Vinegar Lady, or the Judicial Modernization of the Crime of Witchcraft

by Giovanna Fiume

One night in October 1788, Giovanna Bonanno, a seventy-five-year-old widow and beggar, who was widely believed to be a witch, was arrested in Palermo. She possessed all the classic characteristics of a witch: she was at once an old woman, a widow, and a beggar.[1] Undoubtedly, Giovanna practiced magic, as it was said of her that she went out at night with "the women from beyond" [*donna di fora*].[2] These were supernatural beings whose unpredictable decisions and fickle desires people believed were responsible for their good or evil fortunes.[3] We do not know how much of their notion of "going out" is conserved in the contemporary belief that witches "flew."

In any case, people went to Giovanna Bonanno for spells and magic potions. Agata Demma, a widow of forty-two from Palermo who sold bread, asked Bonanno for some magic to use against her son-in-law, Francesco Mistretta, a "special courier"[4] for the prince of Trabia. Widowed six years before, he had recently fallen in love with a domestic servant who worked in the same noble household. As a result, he had stopped supporting his four young children, whose maintenance now fell to Demma. For her the question was how could she transform this "illicit friendship" into "disgust," or better yet, how could she kill his mistress, in order to redirect her son-in-law definitively back to his paternal duties. The old woman advised her to throw "unsalted water from the tannery" along the stairs and corridors where the servant usually passed, and told her that she could get this

"La vecchia dell'aceto, o la modernizzazione giudiziaria del reato di maleficio nella Palermo del tardo Settecento," *Quaderni storici* 66 (1987): 855–77. Translated by Margaret A. Gallucci.

water from an authentic "tanner," Rosa Billotta, called the "Night Singer." Unfortunately for Demma, the potion did not have the desired effect, not because of the lack of efficacy of the magic but because of the malice and spite of Billotta, who inopportunely added salt. Demma later lamented to the judges that she had been tricked out of eight *tarì*.[5]

Despite Bonanno's protests of incompetence each time someone asked her for magic or witchcraft, they were the only reason women went to her. Moreover, the magic sought was lethal and had to kill its victim through occult powers—thus leaving whoever understood or mediated those powers morally and legally without blame. In short, those who went to Bonanno went with the intent to murder. Even when her mixtures and spells did not attain their desired effect, the intent to kill remained.

Yet Giovanna Bonanno made a casual discovery that changed her life: she heard that a child who had ingested a "lotion to kill lice"— devised and concocted by an herbalist, Saverio La Monica, who lived in Via Gioia Mia al Papireto[6]—was cured *in extremis* by being given abundant doses of common olive oil. The old woman intuited immediately that she could use this mixture in another way and earn money selling it. Thus a lotion used to kill lice became, in her eager and unbiased hands, a "mysterious vinegar liquor," a miraculous resolver a familial conflicts, as efficacious as it was untraceable as a cause of death. This secret mixture, which Bonanno always guarded jealously, guaranteed her from that moment on her daily bread: "Not having a formal means of subsistence, the aforementioned woman . . . was determined to earn a living through the sale of the said vinegar, killing anyone so that she could earn four *tarì*."[7]

But before using the vinegar, Bonanno had to test it in order to ascertain its effects. Without delay, she lured a stray dog found outside the Porta d'Ossuna, tied it to the bulwark of the wall with a rope, and gave it a piece of bread soaked in the vinegar to eat. Returning later that night to verify the effects, she discovered that the dog was already dead. She then tried to skin it, since skinning was the most basic proof of poisoning, but could not. Satisfied with her discovery that she believed would resolve the more pressing problems of her subsistence, she spread the news among her customers that she possessed a "mystery" that, when ingested with food, caused a certain, quick, and inexplicable death. From this moment on, she recommended it to everyone who came to her for spells or magic charms.

The vinegar really was a "mystery," a mysterious liquid that had a natural smell and tasted like water. It could be mixed undetected in food or drink or in the more common remedies that doctors administered to the sick: water and lemon rind, "seasonal water,"[8] and "simple broth."[9] As a result, the women who came to Bonanno for magic accepted it with equal naturalness. If anything, they showed some disbelief when the old woman boasted about the vinegar's marvels, and reconsidered for a moment only when faced with the atrocious sufferings of their husbands after they administered the first doses. Moreover, the vinegar required from eight to fifteen days to reach its full effect: just enough time for the sick husbands to go to confession and receive communion, so that not even the danger of eternal damnation of their spouses' souls weighed upon the consciences of the wives. The vinegar was a secure and economical remedy. People bought it because they preferred to spend money on magic that worked rather than waste money on spells of dubious success. The vinegar—Margherita Serio said, supporting the old vinegar lady's claim—"[was] better than [most] magic that only wasted money."[10]

Angela La Fata used this vinegar concoction against her husband, Giuseppe, as did Rosalia Caracciola against hers, Don Agostino; Rosa Costanzo against her spouse, Francesco; Maniela Lo Piccolo against hers, Ferdinando; Marianna Ballo against her husband, Cesare; and finally Giuseppe D'Ancona against his wife, Rosa. Rather than a marital crisis, the internal dynamic of each case turned on a precarious social position whereby a lover represented either the possibility of moving up the social ladder, through a new marriage, or, at the very least, the possibility of attaining a more satisfactory social position.

Such stories may appear very common, but the court records provide so many details that one can reconstruct several years in the lives of these people—their actions, conversations, thoughts, movements, feelings, future plans, and so on—reconstructing not only networks of complex social relations but also many aspects of the mentality of the time which allow us to measure its distance from the contemporary world. Rather than tell the personal stories of the six wives who murdered their husbands, tales of passion, power, and poison, this essay will focus instead upon the old vinegar lady, Giovanna Bonanno, the poisoner, whose contacts with many of the other characters were brief and uncommon. Moreover, the six poisoners in question cannot be linked solely to her, for it appears that in two cases the poison was dispensed by Maria Pitarra, in another by Margherita Serio, and in a different case by Rosa Billotta.

Who really was the "old vinegar lady" then? Were the judges in Palermo putting a witch, a sorceress, or a diviner on trial, as the Holy Office had been doing for centuries? In studying the approximately fifteen hundred pages of court proceedings, it appears clear that in this trial a double agenda was being pursued: first, the judiciary in the period of Viceroy Caramanico (1786–95) appears to have been following a strategy of acculturation to lay and Enlightenment justice by Caramanico's predecessor Viceroy Caracciolo (1781–84). This in turn meant a drastic break with the retrograde practices of the Inquisition. None of this seems surprising when one considers the political context in which this case developed.

Caracciolo will be remembered for one notable gesture: the abolition of the tribunal of the Inquisition in 1782. And if it is true that at that moment "taking a stand against the Inquisition was not an act of heroism,"[11] it was not an ordinary act of administration either. Like French Enlightenment figures, Caracciolo believed that the tribunal of the Inquisition was a "tribunal that [should] be abolished in all political regimes [and that] in a monarchy it could only make men into hypocrites, informers, and traitors."[12] He did indeed abolish it, at the same time informing his friend D'Alembert of his deed in a letter that was published in the *Mercure de France*.[13] "Following this act"—the viceroy wrote to the marquis of Sambuca—"I will free three poor women from the horror of the prisons [of the Holy Office], since they are the only ones there. One whose sentence had already been served did not want to be freed because she had no means of subsistence, adding that she relied on charity; the two other women found themselves locked up, accused of witchcraft and magic spells, without having been [formally] sentenced."[14]

For Caracciolo, what witchcraft and magic must have signified with their cabalas, sorcery, charms, divination, healing of illnesses with mysterious practices, and the gifts of prophecy and finding lost treasures can be deduced from the definition of magic in the *Enciclo-pedia:* "The human spirit is not capable of such bizarre acts! It has surrendered to all these strange fantasies ... but today finally, in countries where people think, reflect, and doubt, the devil plays a very small role, and diabolical magic enjoys neither praise nor belief."[15]

Here, then, is the fundamental shift in the trial against the "old vinegar lady": a series of witchcraft practices became poisonings, as demonstrated by the questions of the judges. From the very first questions on, they imposed their interpretation by focusing the entire investigation on the chemical composition of the poisonous vinegar, which was scientifically examined. Their initial inquiries centered on the alchemical formulas of the herbalist Saverio La Monica, who was asked to duplicate his compound before a panel of noted experts.[16] The compound was then observed, smelled, and compared with the one confiscated in Bonanno's house; both were then experimented with on two stray dogs, who were tied up in a locked room and fed bread soaked in the vinegar. The two poor animals died on the fourth and fifth days of the judicial experiment, respectively, with symptoms similar to those observed in the victims.[17]

Here too, then, were people who knew how to "think, reflect and doubt" and who did not believe in witchcraft. The judges' questions—which can only be surmised, as the examinations were recorded in the form of long depositions—forced the accused to feign contempt for magical practices, a position that seems far from their own beliefs. Bonanno first claimed that she had a "mysterious liquor" for the foolish women who asked her for it, but then went to the herbalist for a supply of the lotion to kill lice. This inconsistency was too apparent to be casual. When Angela La Fata went to Bonanno and asked her "if she knew anyone who had a magic potion to kill her husband Giuseppe," Bonanno answered, "I told her I knew no one who practiced magic."[18] When Margherita Serio, later drawn into the sale of the poison, said to her: "One of my friends asked me to look for a magic potion capable of killing my friend's husband," the old woman replied: "Really there are none."[19] Billotta, who entered into this group for selling the vinegar, said in her first deposition that "she [Bonanno] never led [her] to believe it was magic."[20] The same was true for each confession.

In Inquisition trials women had also denied practicing witchcraft (except in cases in which they confessed fantastical events under torture), and without confessions it was difficult to burn them at the stake. The old vinegar lady in this trial replicated the traditional denial, without realizing that it was precisely her denial that would cause her downfall and that, if she had confessed to practicing magic, she would have been treated with the same condescension as the women found by Caracciolo in the hidden dungeons of Palazzo Steri.

The trial became, in a way, a type of Rorschach test, whereby the judges could read out their own expectations onto it.[21] From this perspective one can explain, for example, the great similarities in the depositions which otherwise are difficult to attribute to a prearranged agreement, even a hidden one, between those questioned. Even if the witnesses insisted on witchcraft more than the accused, the judges' questions rejected any element that might turn the discourse to that subject. And with their decision to pursue only those elements that pertained to poisoning, the judges had already attained their first goal of intimidating the accused.

Concerning first the old vinegar lady, Giovanna, she was tortured even though she had already made an ample confession when she was cross-examined by the judges on October 9. "Brought to the torture chamber," the records note, "she was tied to a rope, then hung from the high cord with a suitable weight on her feet . . . so that she touched and did not touch [the floor]."[22] Since torture could not last more than thirty minutes, the ropes were loosened while her earlier long deposition was read.

In the economy of this trial, her torture seems to have been a pure formality, done as quickly as possible without the nihilistic logic of "harsh torture" more typical of the Inquisition.[23] Surely a woman nearing her eighties had to have been very tempted to confess when the rope was yanked violently;[24] yet she did not provide the dramatic "confessions" typical of those tortured by the Inquisition for witchcraft and other crimes.[25]

On May 7, 1555, Pellegrina Vitello, a woman of about thirty from Genoa, the wife of a silk weaver who lived in Messina, for example, was tortured even though she had already confessed that she had falsely claimed to work spells together with an accomplice in order to trick gullible people.[26] But the inquisitors were not satisfied with this version of the facts and wanted to hear her recount tales of pacts with demons and other such diabolical machinations. So they tortured her on the cord, prudently adding in the transcript that, if she "died or broke bones" while she was being tortured, "it was her fault and not theirs."[27] After hearing their decision, Pellegrina replied "that she did not know what else to say." Hung once again on the cord, she said: "If I knew what to say, I would say it." When she was given a *strattone* [the rope was allowed to drop a person, stopping them just before the ground], she exclaimed: "Oh my, Oh my, Oh Holy Spirit, help me for I have done nothing wrong." "And as she swung there above the ground sweating and moaning, crying 'Help me, Christian souls,' she turned to the inquisitors and said, 'You have tortured me unjustly.' And when the weight was put on her feet, she cried out: 'What do you want me to say? Oh Saint Catherine, Oh Holy Spirit!'

The cord was pulled up and she was left hanging and silent."[28] She was dropped in the same manner [*strattonata*] numerous times in a half-hour, continuing to lament and deny the charges under oath. At one point she turned to the inquisitors and said, with a tone that may have been sardonic: "I do not know what to say; I must not seem dead yet to your Holynesses."[29] Her firm denial that she made a pact with the devil, even under torture, permitted her to escape being burned at the stake. Instead she was paraded through the streets of the city and whipped as a "witchly diviner" holding a candle in one hand and crowned with a miter.[30]

Harsh torture combined with ecclesiastical mercy in Pellegrina Vitello's case in contrast to mild torture and the severity of capital punishment in Giovanna Bonanno's case highlights the question, why was the disparity so great? To answer that, it is necessary to look more closely at several aspects of this case which led up to the final surprising verdict. First and foremost, what were the cultural values of the judges, how did they relate to the reconstruction of the facts, and were they the dominant ones? Trials offer occasions for a cultural confrontation between accusers and accused; but have the criminals actually broken the rules of society, and are the judges the true guarantors of those rules? To what degree was their normative system shared, and to what degree did it clash with general and more traditional values?

"In shifting from the perspective of one social level to another, the action of a play is not at all that different from that of a trial, where the plaintiff and the defendant construct different versions of the same situation, with one being judged real and the other illusory in the end."[31] Reading the records of this trial repeatedly suggested this ambivalence, both the possibility of the reversal of the real and the illusory and the believability of both versions: the judges' and the accused's (even if for the latter that was only a hypothetical possibility).

That ambivalence turns on the pivotal distinction between witchcraft and poisoning. Did the deaths of Giuseppe La Fata, Don Agostino Caracciolo, Rosa Caschera, Cesare Ballo, Francesco Costanzo, and Ferdinando Lo Piccolo result from a poisonous potion sold by an old woman and administered by their respective spouses, or were they caused by "putrid fevers" accompanied by a burning sensation and vomiting, symptoms typical of cholera, which killed them in ten days despite medical treatment? In short, did these six people die because of illness or because of foul play?

Even in the progressive eighteenth century, medicine was in the dark when it came to distinguishing the symptoms of arsenic poisoning from the symptoms of cholera, and ironically pharmacological remedies cured cholera with arsenic. The confusion made sense, since the effects produced by ingesting arsenic were similar to the symptoms of cholera.[32] In fact, arsenic destroyed internal organs, causing an acute inflammation of the esophagus and intestine as well as liver deterioration. Grave cases of dysentery, often bloodied, caused by the rapid elimination of liquids, through vomit and diarrhea, lead quickly to delirium, cardiocirculatory collapse, and death. Such symptoms, including both a fever and a cadaverous odor on the breath, caused by the necrosis of internal tissues, were normally diagnosed as "putrid fevers." Even in the mid-eighteenth century the etiology of cholera was unknown, and doctors at the time wrote about an illness whose contagion was uncertain, tied instead "to the changing seasons, poor nutrition, [and] continuous contact among men on muddy riverbanks."[33] Paradoxically, arsenic was prescribed to cure cholera, since arsenic "relieves and cures the patient through an excessive burning in the stomach, through intense thirst, through diarrhea . . . through cyanosis, an intense coldness, and suppression of urinary fluids."[34] Moreover, arsenic was prescribed for "typhoid fevers accompanied by symptoms of putridity, inflammatory fevers . . . gastric fevers, [and] headaches." And, in addition to curing "extreme melancholy accompanied by suicidal tendencies,"[35] arsenic was prescribed, not least of all, as a tonic, since after a few doses it caused weight gain.

Arsenic's use was so widespread among surgeons, chemists, and doctors and so highly regarded by homeopathic medicine that its abuses were virtually uncorrectable. At the end of the eighteenth century, what doctor would have been able to distinguish a person who was ill with cholera from a person who was suffering from arsenic poisoning? Legal medicine and toxicology both advanced rapidly, and yet the former was able to single out the poison with certainty only when an autopsy revealed the presence of arsenic crystals and its residues; otherwise, there could be no certainty, especially if the crystals were ingested in another solution. Thus toxicology focused its energies on finding an antidote and a plausible remedy. Most schools proposed taking massive doses of emetic medicines, differing only about the type. The use of olive oil and flax oil, and milk and hot sugared water, advised by some doctors[36] was condemned by those who proposed taking massive doses of lye or soaped water,[37] or solutions of iron sulfate, found in ink.[38]

There was also no consensus on the corrosive nature of this poison. Nor was there any relevant difference that distinguished the cures of learned medicine from the so-called popular cures, which used olive oil, flax oil, and lye as emetic medicines, garlic for its diuretic effect and as an intestinal disinfectant,[39] and enemas made from tobacco as stimulants.[40] In this period of feverish research and experimentation, medical knowledge, even as it ruled out many cures, was characterized by an empirical willingness to use others from popular medicine which had sometimes themselves been taken from a learned tradition: never more than at this moment was the exchange of knowledge so reciprocal.

This in part explains the uncertainty of medical opinion about these cases even though it attempted, nonetheless, to offer an explanation of the causes of death. But natural causes did not exclude all the other possible questions that could be asked about why it was that particular person, on that specific day, and so on, who died. Magic "could become the true 'cause' [of death] because it explained the goal, the motive, or the intent of those who hid behind a death."[41] Such deaths were subject to a double level of causality where natural and magical explanations were not mutually exclusive. Considering that Catholicism explained pain and human tragedy within the context of several possible types of intervention, then more than one explanation was possible given the nature and diffusion of popular religious beliefs in the late eighteenth century.

Let us suppose that Giovanna Bonanno, like the three old witches locked in the secret dungeons of Palazzo Steri, was a witch. Witchcraft often used poisonous potions that sometimes caused death. Then why free the other three witches and hang her? The old vinegar lady was the last in a long line of followers of the great "School of Palermo" which produced the most famous poisoner of the early modern period, Teofania di Adamo, whose name gave us "acqua tofana," a potion with arsenic as its base, found in manuals of toxicology.[42] "Acqua tofana" and "water from Palermo" are cited in pontifical court sources in the seventeenth century[43] as well as in German court sources in the nineteenth.[44] From Teofania di Adamo, to her daughter Giulia Tofana,[45] to her stepdaughter Girolama Spana, and on to the women executed in the area in the last three centuries,[46] poison appears to be the feminine weapon par excellence. The domestic world, with its hearth in particular, the place set aside for food preparation and manipulation, was also an archaic laboratory where women not only exercised a basic form of alchemy which presupposed knowledge of substances' secrets and properties; there they also experimented first-hand on the real or imagined qualities of animal, vegetable, and mineral materials. Their knowledge crossed the boundary between the natural world and the magical realm; it contained elements of a naturalistic type of religious belief as well as elements of sympathetic magic. The ritual elements of folk healing provide an example: they included an oration (prayer, exorcism), a natural cure (animal, vegetable, mineral), and symbolic gestures. But the question remains, first, why up through the modern period did poison liquids remain the feminine method of resolving conflicts, and second, why was poison part of a ritual medicine cabinet used by women?

These six stories of murdering wives can be narrated either as a series of interrelated steps that led in the end to murder, or as tales of magic believed in and used to satisfy the desire to get rid of a spouse. Giuseppe D'Ancona's story seems most suited to being told from the first perspective. The thirty-five-year-old baker from Magione was married to Rosa Caschera for fourteen years. Marriage in no way prevented him, helped by the seamstress Rosa Billotta, from having affairs even if his trysts were the cause of continuous "domestic disputes." He confided to his friend Giuseppe Lo Cicero, who earlier had helped him beat up his wife: "Did you hear about the fight I had with my wife the other day? She's always making a big fuss, saying that I am taking advantage of her. I'm afraid that one of these days my wife is going to poison me."[47] D'Ancona seemed to want to claim the status of a potential victim, as unlikely as that may seem, while he himself contacted Billotta and Bonanno and bought some poison vinegar for his wife. Rosa's father later testified with bitterness that his son-in-law had subjected his daughter to physical and verbal violence. In particular, he threatened her daily: "One day you will learn from my fists, because you deserve to be treated not like my wife but like a whore."[48]

In reality even Billotta had had some reservations about selling her vinegar to D'Ancona, whom she considered a "bad Christian," a violent womanizer with a hot temper and a bad reputation. From the beginning relations were strained. When she told him about the vinegar's effects, he replied sarcastically: "You are full of it!"[49] He did not pay the *carrabella* in advance ("I'm broke," he told Billotta), nor would he carry the poison to his house himself ("Surely I can't bring three small flasks with me—they'll break. And anyway, I'm not even taking one!"[50]). Eventually, he only paid a part of the ten gold coins he promised freely as payment. After the women hounded him, he threatened physical violence if they spoke to anyone about his affairs ("If even one word comes out of your mouths about what's been going on, I'll grind you up like grain and break your bones like Saint Sebastian"[51]). Despite these threats Bonanno had no intention of losing her earnings, especially on such a good deal.

At first it might appear that D'Ancona killed his wife because he was in love with Maria Anna Zuccaro, a girl of barely fourteen, whom Billotta introduced to D'Ancona (falsely) as her niece. After long discussions between D'Ancona and the girl's mother, Dorotea Zuccaro, the two parties reached a satisfactory agreement: the well-off baker would pay the mother ten gold coins and four *tarì* per day for Maria Anna's maintenance. She in turn would reject the marriage proposal of a cook at the Palazzo Reale for this more satisfactory arrangement. In the end, however, after killing his wife, D'Ancona reneged on his promise to Dorotea and Maria Anna, because—according to Billotta— "he wanted to get back in God's graces,"[52] and soon after married a certain Emanuela Porcello.

Public opinion immediately branded the case a poisoning: numerous people testified to this effect including, besides the aforementioned Giuseppe Lo Cicero, Aloisio and Isabella Sergio, who owned a tavern in the Magione;[53] Nicola Schiavo, a butcher in the same piazza;[54] Andrea Bassani, a rope vendor;[55] Salvatore di Genova, a shopkeeper;[56] and finally, Caterina Messina, who washed the clothes for the D'Ancona's. Messina suspected poisoning either because Rosa and Giuseppe argued constantly or perhaps because she thought it odd that they ate from separate plates.[57] Giuseppe's assistants, Jacopo Balatti from Milan and Antonio Plantera, testified that Giuseppe was the only one who prepared the medicine for the ill Rosa, in the hearth near the oven, and that he could easily have mixed in poison without anyone's knowledge.[58] Neither his neighbors nor his employees sided with Giuseppe, universally held to be violent, unscrupulous, and overbearing in his confidence about the crime and about his several earlier attempts against his wife. Everyone detested and disapproved of his continuous wife beatings and his sexual exploits. His sexual affairs were far from the normal ménage that often escaped moral strictures, especially for men who had the wealth to support two families.

Only the well-off baker had the means to pay a lawyer, who counseled a successful line of defense, and the firmness necessary to deny every charge to the last. Accused by his in-laws, D'Ancona responded to the judges' questions with doubts about the doctors who treated Rosa. The latter still had not ruled on the cause of the death that they had witnessed, either for fear of admitting their own error or perhaps because of professional scruples. Concentrating on the complete lack of proof surrounding the purported uxoricide and the lack of credibility of the witnesses, D'Ancona argued that two of those who testified, Maria Anna Zuccaro and her mother Dorotea, acted out of resentment, while two others, Giovanna Bonanno and Rosa Billotta, were untrustworthy, "guilty and infamous." And in that context he petitioned that the investigation be terminated.[59]

In other cases a witchcraft interpretation rather than poisoning seemed to provide a better explanatory model, as the power of such explanations should not be underestimated for the period. Maria Anna, a twenty-two-year-old woman from Palermo, was Cesare Ballo's wife and Nunzio Tabita's lover. Tabita, a peasant of twenty-three, had free access to the couple's house and was slated to become godfather to one of their sons. One night Cesare returned home unexpectedly and discovered the two lovers. Confused and surprised, he could not find the courage to confront them in the bedroom; thus, from behind the door he reassured his wife: "OK, OK, I know what you're up to, I'm leaving."[60] The neighbors calmed him down and made him make peace with his wife. Returning home, he began to believe an alibi about a brawl in the street: when the police intervened, Nunzio had fled and hid in Cesare's bedroom. Cesare truly wanted to believe his wife's lies, and for his neighbors he demonstrated a severity toward her which was far from real as he shifted her punishment to a generic time in the future ("Next time I'll cut your head off and hang it in the window sill"[61]). Still he became worried because his wife was not eating, and he went out to buy bread and cheese, which they ate frugally together.

Cesare was "a good young man," Maria Pitarra said, not without a bit of irony about a goodness that bordered on stupidity given his toleration of his betrayal and dishonor. Yet his wife did not seem to appreciate these qualities and complained about the meager existence she had to lead because Cesare spent everything he earned at the tavern and how often she had to ask Nunzio for money for her and her two sons' sustenance. Oh, if a potion could only free her from him! "So many good Christians who go in search of something find it," she said to her neighbor, Maria Pitarra; "if only there were someone who had a potion to make my husband Cesare die!"[62] Maria Anna believed, then, that magic could resolve people's problems. Moreover, experience proved it, since she had heard many stories that demonstrated that magic actually did work. At this point Pitarra suggested Bonanno's "mystery liquid," which would make Cesare "die slowly,"[63] and advised her to ask Nunzio if he would be willing to marry her at some future time. Nunzio kept his distance from the plot, perhaps because he saw such magic as women's work. Nonetheless, after hearing her out, he gave her the first installment of money needed, saying: "I did my part—I gave you the money. The rest is up to you,"[64] in this way trying to distance himself from the moral responsibility of complicity with his lover. Actually, apparently troubled by Cesare's suffering, he also gave her the money needed to buy the medicine the doctors prescribed to cure the sick Cesare.[65] It is evident that both Maria Anna and Nunzio believed they were dealing with a "magic potion that induced death,"[66] not a poison; and later they suggested it to Emanuele Cascino, who used it to solve his own tangled amorous affairs.

One night in October 1788, the old vinegar lady was visited by an acquaintance, Giovanna Lombardo, who came to ask her if the rumor she had heard about a "certain water that caused death" was true. When she told her that it was, Lombardo wanted to know if someone could have used this "water" to kill Maria Costanzo's son Francesco. Bonanno then slapped Lombardo's face, for it was true that she had sold it to various people; however, if she thought for even an instant that someone would use it to kill Francesco Costanzo, she would have gone in person herself to warn his mother of the imminent danger. "And his mother would have thanked me and then saved my reputation,"[67] she added. The old vinegar lady, regretting the unanticipated results of her endeavor, was also surprised by the reaction of the mother of the dead man. In fact, Francesco Costanzo's mother went to the police, who, to expedite the matter, sent four would-be buyers of poison to the old woman's house in an attempt to catch her red-handed.

The trap was successful, and "Don Matteo Fodale, Commissioner of the Illustrious Captain of Justice of this city, together with various agents went to the house of the said suspect, captured her, and led her, imprisoned in a cage, to the house of the said Illustrious Captain."[68] A diarist of the period, however, wrote that the old vinegar lady's crime was "denounced to the High Court of Justice by a group of women who lived in her neighborhood after a dispute."[69] Whatever the true explanation, it is clear that something shifted the delicate balance that up to that moment had permitted the "silent slaughter of husbands."

At this point one might wonder how such a massacre (six cases of wives who killed their husbands in these proceedings alone) could continue for a good two years (from 1786 to 1788) without authorities having at least a suspicion or without the herbalist Saverio La Monica, to whom Bonanno went "often,"[70] suspecting an improper use for his "vinegar that killed lice." Moreover, how was it that the doctors who were called to the bedsides of the sick were so convinced that they were dealing with gastric-enteric infections and typhoid fevers that they were not even curious enough to go and observe the rapid decomposition of the cadavers, notoriously quicker in cases of poisonings?

Actually the talk and rumors that circulated about the poison were encouraged by the quickness with which the widows remarried, and of course, the risk that the crime would be proven was also implicit in the poison's widespread use. The old vinegar lady had to advertise her vinegar, with the result that the qualities of this "miraculous water" were widely discussed, provoking the same reactions of belief and disbelief as any efficacious magic would have. In addition, Bonanno was reputed to be a witch. Linares would call her a witch some fifty years later, a witch crouched before a fire in her shadowy and filthy coven.[71] The old woman's secrets were judged boastings without any foundations by disbelievers; the husbands' deaths were deemed accidental rather than the result of her arts. Those arts were merely a ruse to scrape together some money in order to live. In her conversation with Maria Pitarra about attempting to poison Giuseppe D'Ancona's wife, Pitarra cried out: "Christ, what kind of yarns are you spinning?"[72] Many also believed that the old woman's vinegar was one of those evil concoctions or magic potions that only wasted money. Yet disbelief is often transformed into belief: and in this case public opinion proclaimed the deaths were caused by magic.

How, then, did the whole affair come out into the open? Maria Costanzo was a wine seller in the district of Olivuzza. One night in August her son Francesco came to her house and asked if he could stay with her. He told her that a few days earlier he returned home from the countryside and caught his wife together with Emanuele Cascino. Several days later, after a few important neighbors intervened, the couple made peace, but Francesco insisted they move to the countryside near Olivuzza so that his mother could keep an eye on his wife while he was away. When Francesco fell ill, he himself moved to his mother's house, where he died several days later despite the efforts of local doctors. Maria, therefore, knew of her daughter-in-law's amorous affair; in addition, some elements of her son's sickness made her suspect witchcraft. She confided her thoughts to Francesco's godmother, Giovanna Lombardo, who took the initiative and went to the old vinegar lady's house, where her suspicions were confirmed.[73]

In other cases a similar outcome could have been reached without ever going to the authorities to confirm the suspicions and verify the rumors. Maria Costanzo, "inconsolable" about her son's death, however, confided in her confessor, and it was he who suggested she go to the authorities so that other innocent victims would not suffer the same fate. The priest was, then, the mediator between the crime and the law, because he did not believe in witchcraft, and where Costanzo suspected the intervention of occult powers, he saw murder. If this formal denunciation represented an example of the acculturation of justice, then it was the result of an external intervention on the part of those who, like the priest, only partially shared the culture of the people in this story and who broke the code of silence about the vinegar. The small group of women involved to various degrees in Francesco's death must also not be forgotten; the disagreements within this group provoked the public fight that Villabianca believed led to the discovery of the entire affair. There followed the formal denunciation to the authorities; the trap that caught the old vinegar lady red-handed; and the arrest of each person involved in this tale of passions, one after the other.

It is surprising how quickly this trial went given how often in this period there were long waiting periods before trials began. Such delays often ruined the families of the accused economically and threatened their own health and thus also provoked a large number of appeals and escape attempts. In sharp contrast, this trial was begun in October 1788 and concluded after only nine months with a verdict that called for the execution of Giovanna Bonanno. That sentence was carried out on July 30, 1789. Yet for all its speed, a large number of witnesses were brought in to testify, including blood relatives, in-laws, and minors, thanks to a "dispensation" that ruled: "[G]iven that the crime is serious and difficult to prove, [it is permitted that] other witnesses deemed not competent or unreliable be interrogated, even those suspected of complicity, because they will provide us with more information; these include blood relatives, in-laws, all male relatives, brothers-in-law, minors, unreliable and noncompetent witnesses, and all others who would otherwise by law not be able to testify or be excused from doing so."[74]

In this as in other exemptions allowed in the trial, there was an overruling of ordinary procedure which allowed the bringing together of different material relative to several crimes. The trial then was simultaneously against Bonanno, Pitarra, Serio, and all those who murdered their spouses. The judges met even during holidays and prevented any delay in the legal process by not observing "any communal or municipal law, statute, custom of the monarch or viceroy, act or constitution of the Kingdom . . . lest crimes remain unpunished for lack of evidence [with the scope of] maintaining public order by exercising the public vendetta."[75] It is true that the "criminal laws of the viceroy period constitute[d] a confused series of acts and customs designed to curb the most atrocious and common crimes, to correct or to tolerate preexisting laws,"[76] but that actually gave the judges more freedom and discretion.

Entire family groups and everyone who lived on a particular street or square were brought in to testify; anyone who supplied any piece of information or who had any knowledge of a couple's quarrels, about public opinion on the deaths and why they were believed to be caused by witchcraft, or about slander or gossip was called in. For example, for the uxoricide case against Giuseppe D'Ancona, the following people testified: the victim's father, mother, and brother, two doctors who treated her during her supposed illness, her sister-in-law who prepared her meals, D'Ancona's young lover and her mother, the laundry woman, his two assistants at the bakery, the two owners of the tavern next to the bakery in Piazza Magione, the butcher, the proprietor of the rope shop, the pork butcher, the merchant, and finally the neighbors. And this was, of course, in addition to Bonanno and Billotta, who sold the poison. Similarly, in the trial against Rosa Costanzo those who testified were the victim's mother, the wife's adopted mother and aunt, the "representative" of the square and the powerful neighbor who made the couple make peace after their fight, the stable master and tavern owner in the district of Zisa in whose tavern Francesco fell ill, those who were at the tavern who witnessed this, the baker in Olivuzza and the neighborhood woman who sold bread, two other female neighbors and two male co-workers, and finally Francesco's godmother, Giovanna Lombardo. Once again this was in addition to Bonanno and Pitarra, who sold the poison. The same was true for each of the other murders as well.

This seemed to create virtually a modern maxi-trial ["*un maxi-processo*" refers to the currently popular Italian large show trials used primarily against people accused of Mafia activities or terrorism which have become as much media events as trials—EDS.] in which the number of defendants and witnesses made up for the lack of modern means of mass communication to provide the maximum publicity. This maxi-trial was essentially a large cultural workshop in which, given the social distance that separated judges from witnesses, it was possible for the former to mold the latter to their dominant cultural vision. Their tactics were authoritarian and designed to terrorize: the terror of the Inquisition's justice based on the secret nature of both the charges and the accusers' identity was replaced by the terror of secular justice based on the evidence of the charges and the notoriety of the accusers. Certainly it was not yet the age of "mild punishments" involving jail sentences if the roughly contemporary Tommaso Natale, a self-proclaimed forerunner of Beccaria, who supported reforming penal codes and criminal procedures, could suggest punishments proportional to crimes, such as amputating one or both arms, branding various visible parts of the criminal's body, lopping off a nose or an ear, or gouging out the culprit's eyes.[77] In using a theater of grand punitive exemplum, the goal was to "modernize" the habitus of the governed, who would be pressed toward skepticism regarding magic and a greater individualism.

But was medicine or natural causes in general able to explain life and death matters adequately? At one level an initial victory for medical explanations was won when Maria Costanzo was persuaded by her confessor that a concrete individual was "humanly" responsible for her son's death and she went to the authorities to denounce Bonanno. The defendant's denial brought with it, often unintentionally, the charge that relatives, friends, and neighbors were complicit. As a result the disintegration of tightly woven webs of relations helped to formulate a new individualistic spirit; and thus, from social units such as families, classes, and guilds the modern "citizen" who sought not privileges but rights developed.

Such ideas were easily imposed on the *popolo minuto*[78]—everyone in this story belongs to that social group—and yet they encountered one obstacle that sheds light on the whole modernizing process of the judges. Rosalia Caracciolo and Gastone [her lover] with her mother's consent poisoned her husband, who had squandered her dowry. This warrants closer examination, as it seems rather anomalous. The motive for the murder involved, as in other cases, a lover: no woman was foolish enough to murder her husband without having a lover aspiring to take his place. In fact, lovers, for the most part, were the ones who gave these women the money they needed to buy the poison and sustained their morale when their legitimate spouses slowly died in agony. Rosalia told the women who sold her the poison that the reason she wanted it was because her husband was against her desire to prostitute herself. The first odd thing about this case is that the trial proceedings contain neither Rosalia's deposition nor her mother's. Their testimony can only be surmised through Bonanno's and Billotta's confessions. The latter's curiosity about Rosalia's motive for buying the poison evidently was satisfied by her confession about intending to become a prostitute. But there were other possible scenarios:

a. Early nineteenth-century literature had made explicit reference to this episode, interpreting it in two ways: first, as an allegory about aristocratic arrogance that would stop at nothing short of murder,[79] or, later, representing Rosalia as the illegitimate daughter of Donna Maria di Altofonte and Gastone del Carretto, who, by killing Rosalia's husband, vindicated the adulterous affair between his son-in-law and his wife.[80]

b. Rosalia Caracciolo and her mother, Michela Belviso, were acquitted of murder, while the other wives who murdered their husbands were punished and sentenced to twenty years in prison despite the fact that numerous witnesses testified in their defense. It is easy to imagine that Rosalia's lover was a noble, who remained mysteriously anonymous thanks both to the two women's prudence and to the judges' questions, which carefully avoided this area. Only a nobleman's protection, and one who was high up in the hierarchy of power in Palermo, could have changed the outcome so drastically. Moreover, the marquis of Villabianca, the unreliable diarist of eighteenth-century Palermo, who wrote scathingly about the entire affair, cited neither Rosalia's nor her mother's name in his *Diario* even though he did recount the details of the verdict. His silence seems most significant.

Little or nothing is known about these judges—a topic to be investigated—nor will we ever really understand the incongruities in their final verdict which called for Agata Demma's and the herbalist Saverio La Monica's release from prison and Rosalia Caracciolo's and her mother Michela Belviso's silent acquittal without their even being named. Giovanna Bonanno was sentenced to be hanged in the center of Piazza Vigliena. Maria Pitarra followed the procession that led the old vinegar lady, with a noose tightly around her neck, to her execution. She was required to help, even kissing the gallows, and then was imprisoned for life in the Quinta Casa.[81] Rosa Billotta was sentenced to ten years in prison, Margherita Serio to five. These women were the "dispensers" of the poison. Those who administered it included Emanuela Molinari, widow of Lo Piccolo, who was sentenced to twenty years, as were Maria Anna Tabita, widow of Cesare Ballo, and Rosa Mangano, widow of Francesco Costanzo. Angela La Fata was sentenced to three years in prison, while Giuseppe D'Ancona was exiled to an island for eighteen years. As for the accomplices: Anna Campo, Lo Piccolo's laundry woman, was sentenced to three years in the galleys, and Emanuele Cascino and Nunzio Tabita were sentenced to fifteen years rowing on the royal galleys.

How disproportionate the punishments were to the crimes in this verdict! First of all, not sentencing Caracciolo or Belviso is an absolute mystery; then giving the same sentence to the laundry woman, an accomplice, which was given to Angela La Fata, a wife who murdered her husband, makes little sense. Did the judges think this particular crime was not a poisoning? And why was she sentenced to three years in prison? And why was the herbalist not guilty at all? He was required by law to sell products with an arsenic base only to people who could show a "doctor's permission in writing signed by the doctor" under penalty of a monetary fine.[82] And why were there such drastic differences in the sentences given to the women who "dispensed" the poison? Bonanno was hanged; Pitarra got life in prison; Billotta got ten years; Serio got five. In fact, the old vinegar lady only personally gave the vinegar to two women, Angela La Fata and Rosalia Caracciolo, whose true roles were the most uncertain of all. Or again, why was punishment so harsh for Bonanno when, although she was the one who thought up the vinegar's improper use, Billotta, Pitarra, and Serio were the ones who decided to use it? Is the person who instigates a murder more guilty than the one who executes it? Was the old vinegar lady really more culpable than the women murderers themselves?

Apparently yes, given that she was the only one who paid with her life. The Compagnia dei Bianchi assisted her during the three days she spent in the Cappella del Conforto, received her confession, and escorted her to the place of execution.[83] On July 30, 1789, Giovanna

Bonanno was hanged, atop a very high gallows, a metaphor for her horrendous crime. Her head[84] was buried in Saint Anthony's cemetery, known as "Lo Sicco," beyond the Porta di Vicari. A large crowd gathered for this spectacle of justice: "When the time for the execution arrived, the spaces that earlier that morning contained empty carriages were replaced by their owners. The throng of people who gathered for this spectacle was incredible."[85]

Everything about this spectacle seemed to respond to an opportune moment politically to offer a grand punitive exemplum and show the efficacy of public vengeance when, driven by the light of reason, such powers resided solidly in the hands of a centralized authority. The solemnity of this ceremony may only be compared to the ceremony of the last burning of a witch, celebrated in the distant year 1724. And yet a disquieting suspicion remains: that the judges, despite their intentions, had actually unwittingly burned one last witch.

Notes

1. Alan Macfarlane's well-known thesis argues that witchcraft accusations were produced by feelings of guilt when, as ancient communal values broke down, people refused to give charity to old women, for the most part widows, who were forced to beg. See A. Macfarlane, *Witchcraft in Tudor and Stuart England* (London, 1970).

2. Maria Pitarra's confession, October 20, 1788, in Archivio di Stato di Palermo (hereafter ASP), Miscellanea Archivistica 2 (hereafter Misc. Arch.), vol. 32, f. 186v.

3. "Unpredictable and fickle spirits, but not by nature evil, these women live almost perennially in the house where they had chosen to live ... making nocturnal flights in the form of toads or reptiles." See G. Pitré, *Usi e costumi, credenze e pregiudizi del popolo siciliano* (Bologna, 1969), vol. 4, pp. 153–77.

4. A valet employed by patriciate families who delivered urgent messages.

5. Agata Demma's testimony, October 28, 1788, ASP, Misc. Arch., ff. 329v–333r.

6. Less dangerous than the French ointment made in the same period described by P. Orfila, *Trattato dei veleni* (Rome, 1817), vol. 1, pt. 1, pp. 154–56.

7. Giovanna Bonanno's confession, October 9, 1788, ASP, Misc. Arch., f. 84v.

8. In other words, water "at the temperature of the season, not cooled or heated"; see V. Mortillaro, *Nuovo dizionario siciliano-italiano* (Palermo, 1876).

9. "A thin, unsalted broth, given to the sick"; ibid.

10. Giovanna Bonanno's confession, f. 92v.

11. See C. Trasselli, *Da Ferdinando il Cattolico a Carlo V* (Soveria Mannelli [CZ], 1982), p. 149.

12. *Enciclopedia (1751–1772)* (Milan, 1966), vol. 2, p. 413, under Inquisizione.

13. Published June 1, 1782.

14. Letter from Viceroy Caracciolo to Sambuca, dated March 28, 1782, cited by V. La Mantia, *Origini e vicende dell'Inquisizione in Sicilia* (Palermo, 1977), p. 145.

15. *Enciclopedia*, p. 436.

16. Composed of Francesco Moleti, physician for the Royal Court; Stefano Di

Pasquale, chief doctor at the Ospedale Grande; Giuseppe Catanese; the priests Giuseppe Serra and Andrea Vitale, also doctors; and Don Giuseppe Chiarelli, Antonio Valenti, Francesco Chiarelli, and Salvatore Cangemi, all herbalists/alchemists.

17. See the minutes about the experiment conducted by the panel of experts, ASP, Misc. Arch., ff. 534v–543r.

18. Giovanna Bonanno's confession, f. 95r.

19. Ibid., f. 98v.

20. Ibid., f. 98r.

21. I am paraphrasing P. Boyer and S. Nissenbaum, *La città indemoniata: Salem e le origini sociali di una caccia alle streghe* (Turin, 1986), p. 34. (*Salem Possessed*, Cambridge, Mass., 1974.)

22. In the margins of the first page of the minutes of Giovanna Bonanno's cross-examination, f. 83v, is written: "The mildest torture was called a *tocca e non tocca*, where the accused was suspended high up in the air: a mercy conceded to those who, according to the doctors, could not be given harsher forms of torture." See G. Pitré, *Del Sant'Uffizio a Palermo e di un carcere di esso* (Rome, 1940), p. 119.

23. Part of the principle of "torqueatur tamquam cadaver in capite alieno, ad vocandos complices."

24. The condemned were bound with their hands behind their backs and suspended. The rope was then jerked violently. This is the *garrucha* of the Spanish Inquisition, described by B. Bennassar, *Storia dell'Inquisizione spagnola* (Milan, 1980), p. 101.

25. M. Yourcenar does not analyze as text Campanella's cross-examination by the Inquisition. See his *Il tempo grande scultore* (Turin, 1985), pp. 42–47.

26. See Pellegrina Vitello's cross-examination under torture on April 17, 1555, cited by C. A. Garufi, *Fatti e personaggi dell'Inquisizione in Sicilia* (Palermo, 1978), p. 69.

27. Ibid., p. 76.

28. Ibid.

29. Said without malice in L. Sciascia, *Morte dell'Inquisitore* (Bari, 1971), p. 205.

30. Sententia, in Garufi, *Fatti e personaggi*, pp. 77–78.

31. N. Frye, *Anatomica della critica* (Turin, 1969), p. 220.

32. See J. Mezger, *Geschichte Homöopatische Arzneimittellehre* (Heidelberg, 1977), vol. 1, pp. 238ff.

33. C. Cavallaro, *Nuovo corso teorico-pratico alfabetico di medicina omiopatica* (Palermo, 1844), vol. 1, p. 235.

34. G. Schultz, "Preservativi e metodo curativo del colera secondo le vedute omiopatiche," read to the Accademia Omiopatica di Palermo on August 8, 1854, Palermo.

35. B. Tripi, *Manuale della materia medica omiopatica* (Palermo, 1846), p. 63.

36. G. Belluomini and L. Giobbe, *Biblioteca medico browniana germanica* (Naples, 1802), vol. 5.

37. P. Orfila, *Soccorsi da dare alle persone avvelenate* (Palermo, 1812), as well as C. Cavallaro and J. Berzelius, *Traité de chimie* (Brussels, 1838).

38. G. Frank, *Manuale di tossicologia, ossia di dottrina di veleni e contravveleni* (Parma, 1804).

39. Learned medicine considered garlic effective in curing cholera. See G. Ingianni, "Azione bactericida ed antisettica del succo d'aglio e del solfuro di allile (essenza d'aglio) sui bacilli del colera," *Archivio italiano di clinica medica* 4 (1874).

40. G. Pitré, *Medicina popolare siciliana* (Bologna, 1969), pp. 381–82.

41. A. Macfarlane, "Stregoneria in Inghilterra tra il '500 e il '600," in *La stregoneria in Europa*, ed. M. Romanello (Bologna, 1981), p. 249.

42. F. Gmelin, *Allgemeine Geschichterder mineralischen Gifte* (Nuremberg, 1777), and Frank, *Manuale di tossicologia.*

43. A. Ademollo, *I misteri dell'acqua tofana* (Rome, 1881).

44. F. L. Voget, *Lebensgeschichte der Giftmörderin Gesch Margarethe Gottfried* (Bremen, 1831).

45. "In Sicily there is an ancient custom that is still practiced today: if a parent has a baptismal name that is uncommon or unusual, the people give it as a surname to all his or her children"; see S. Salomone Marino, "L'acqua tofana," *Nuove effemeridi siciliane* 9 (1881): 293.

46. Angela Sileci and Gattino, executed May 20, 1665, in Palermo; Giovanna di Bernardo and Chiavello di Monreale, executed May 21, 1712; Giovanna Greco di Montaperto, executed July 23, 1764; Caterina Lo Sardo di Canicatti, sentenced April 11, 1771; and Giovanna Bonanno, sentenced July 30, 1789. See A. Cutrera, *Cronologia dei giustiziati di Palermo (1541–1819)* (Palermo, 1917).

47. Giuseppe Lo Cicero's testimony, ASP, Misc. Arch., ff. 582v–588r.

48. Giuseppe Caschera's testimony, ASP, Misc. Arch., ff. 573r–575r.

49. Rosa Billotta's cross-examination, ASP, Misc. Arch., October 17, 1788, f. 114r.

50. Ibid., ff. 117v–118r.

51. Ibid., ff. 128r–129v.

52. Ibid., f. 182r.

53. Testimony, ASP, Misc. Arch., 631r–633v.

54. Ibid., ff. 633v–634v.

55. Ibid., ff. 634v–635r.

56. Ibid., ff. 635r–636r.

57. Ibid., ff. 613r–618v.

58. Ibid., ff. 622r–627r and 627r–630r.

59. Exceptiones defentionis, ASP, Misc. Arch., unnumbered pages at the beginning of the trial proceedings.

60. Maria Anna Tabita's (widow of Ballo) cross-examination, ASP, Misc. Arch., November 19, 1788, f. 294v.

61. Ibid., f. 295r.

62. Maria Anna Tabita's testimony, ASP, Misc. Arch., f. 296r.

63. Maria Pitarra's testimony, ASP, Misc. Arch., f. 189r.

64. Ibid., f. 301v.

65. Ibid., f. 303r.

66. "A lethal potion" from the testimony of Nunzio Tabita, October 19, 1788, ASP, Misc. Arch., f. 318v.

67. Giovanna Bonanno's testimony, Misc. Arch., f. 143r.

68. Ibid., f. 146v.

69. Villabianca, *Diari*, vol. 16 (1789–90), ms. in the Biblioteca Comunale di Palermo (hereafter BCP), Qq D 108.

70. Saverio La Monica's deposition, November 25, 1788, ASP, Misc. Arch., f. 72v.

71. V. Linares, "L'avvelenatrice," in *Racconti popolari* (Palermo, 1840).

72. Giovanna Bonanno's testimony, ASP, Misc. Arch., f. 122v.

73. Maria Costanzo's deposition, ASP, Misc. Arch., 1788, ff. 342r–350v.

74. I am utilizing N. Ratti's Italian version, "Il processo di Giovanna Bonanno, la 'vecchia di l'acitu,' " *Archivio storico siciliano* 38 (1913): 384.

75. Ibid.

76. V. La Mantia, *Storia della legislazione civile e criminale di Sicilia* (Palermo, 1874), vol. 2, p. 167.

77. T. Natale, *Riflessioni politiche intorno all'efficacia e necessità delle pene* (Palermo, 1772), pp. 90–91.

78. See G. Fiume, "Il sordo macello dei mariti: Un processo per veneficio nella Palermo di fine Settecento," in *Ragnatele di rapporti: Patronage e reti di relazioni nella storia delle donne* (Turin, 1988).

79. Linares, "L'avvelenatrice," pp. 61–125.

80. L. Natoli (W. Galt), *La vecchia dell'aceto* (Palermo, 1927).

81. The Quinta Casa was one of the Jesuit houses used as a women's prison after the Jesuits were expelled from Sicily.

82. "Bando del Protomedico," Palermo, 1767, quoted in V. Parisi, ed., *Capitoli ed ordinazioni della felice e fedelissima città di Palermo sino al corrente anno 1768* (Palermo, 1768), p. 440.

83. Cutrera, *Cronologia dei giustiziati*, p. 291.

84. According to Villabianca, Bartolomeo Pollini made an etching of her head for the Milanese Carlo Gatti. See "Delle vendette piu clamorose di giustizia che dai tempi andati fino ai presenti si son prese sopra i malfattori con laccio, ferro e fuoco in atti di pubblici spettacoli ai popoli palermitani per legge di buon governo," in *Opuscoli*, 19, BCP, Qq E 95, p. 371.

85. Villabianca, *Diari*, f. 212.

4 ‮ၔ‬ A Secret to Kill the King: Magic and Protection in Piedmont in the Eighteenth Century

by Sabina Loriga

The State Archives in Turin contain a set of witchcraft cases heard by secular courts in the first decades of the eighteenth century. Nine of these cases, which involve more than seventy defendants, are complete, while ten contain either only the judicial investigation or the arrest of a suspect without reaching the trial stage.[1] All, however, revolve around the untimely death of the young prince Vittorio in March 1715 and for the most part involve small dolls made in the image of a member of the royal family. Each case was compiled not by judges of lower courts—who investigated peripheral and local matters—but by the Senate, the highest body of the Piedmontese government. This body often saw the intervention of individuals from the highest echelons of Savoyard politics and frequently sentenced people to death or to life in the galleys. Thus these cases were not minor later flareups, insignificant aftermaths of earlier prosecutions, or events marginal to the sociocultural realities of Piedmont under the rule of Vittorio Amedeo II; rather, the number of people involved, the limited and compact span of time in which the trials took place,[2] and the importance attributed to them are but the first and most evident signs of their major significance. This was truly a wave of persecution which had its own peculiar physiognomy, which expressed and illuminates some of the contradictions that prevaded society in Piedmont in the first decades of the eighteenth century.

The documentation is rich and raises many important issues for

---

"Un secreto per far morire la persona del re: Magia e protezione nel Piemonte del '700," *Quaderni storici* 53 (1983): 529–52. Translated by Margaret A. Gallucci and Corrada Biazzo Curry.

both comparative history and the history of witchcraft persecutions. First, these trials, focusing on small figurines of the king or other members of the House of Savoy, pose the issue of the nature of the popular perceptions of the royal image—its meanings and the impact of the king's presence on the daily lives [of the people]—particularly in a monarchy of relatively small geographic proportions, and reveal the strong link between the crime of witchcraft and the crime of lese majesty. Moreover, these trials demonstrate a ferocious drive to persecute witches by both the highest levels of government and the king, thus raising significant questions about the current historical truism that holds that the end of the legal persecution of witchcraft was due to rising skepticism among the ruling classes and which sees later trials (from the late seventeenth and early eighteenth centuries) as merely the casual residues of a phenomenon already in decline, the result of the social pressure of the people on provincial judges.[3]

But rather than begin with these topics, first I wish to utilize these trials to examine an apparently unrelated topic: the issue of confinement, and more precisely, the culture of confining individuals in charitable institutions or of locking them up in prisons. This documentation offers many possibilities for studying the relationship between the individual and such institutions. More traditional studies of poverty and total institutions have focused on the political programs of the church, state, or wealthy social groups adopted in regard to the poor and "marginals," but here I wish to use these trial proceedings to study popular attitudes toward these institutions.[4]

"I heard there was a man in prison who made a doll of the king, and that he put on it a piece of blessed palm leaf, and that the king had the said man quartered, and then rewarded and compensated the man who revealed who made the doll." It was June 2, 1717, and Clara Ribolletta was trying to explain to the judges who were cross-examining her why the previous December she had accused her father, sister, husband, in-laws, and many other important people of witchcraft, sex with the devil, going to the sabbat, and above all making three small dolls. One of the dolls had caused the premature death of the young prince Vittorio in the spring of 1715; the other two, still in the basement, were directed against the reigning prince and king. Realizing that she was trapped in her own accusations, she was trying in vain to play down her previous testimony and free herself from the witchcraft accusation that had been brought against her. Thus she recalled that she was not the first to formulate similar accusations and explained that she "said all this in good faith, believing that she would be rewarded."[5]

Seven years earlier in the senatorial prisons of Turin the prisoner Antonio Barbero claimed that he had important revelations to make and recounted how "in these cells a prisoner plotted to make a wax figure of His Royal Highness and then to melt it with the intent to kill the said king." He accused his cellmate Antonio Boccalaro, sentenced to twenty years in prison for the murder of prosecutor Franco Vercellino, of making a magical doll of Vittorio Amedeo II. In exchange for his testimony, Barbero asked that "His Royal Highness decide to set him free."[6] His accusation was corroborated by two other prisoners, and when the judges searched the cell, they found the evidence: a cloth doll, sewn with white thread, the size of the palm of a hand, its head the size of a nut, eyebrows drawn on, black eyes, a nose that stuck out, with arms, a penis, and legs. The doll's discovery was fatal: after maintaining his innocence through three interrogations, Boccalaro was sentenced to death as an example to others. The execution took place in the Piazza delle Erbe on January 30, 1710. Barbero was given a reduced sentence, as Clara Ribolletta had remembered.

Two elements of the Boccalaro-Barbero affair recur regularly in these trials: first, the magic/witchcraft was directed against a member of the royal family, and second, they regularly occurred in charitable or punitive institutions, "places and spaces governed by authority."[7] In most cases (seven out of nine) the accuser was confined in a poorhouse, a shelter, or even a prison: Cattarina Cuore, who denounced various people for causing the death of the young prince Vittorio by means of witchcraft in 1716, was confined in the Deposito dell'Opera Pia San Paolo in Turin; Clara Ribbolletta, who, as already noted, accused several people of witchcraft in 1716, had a long and troubled history of confinement (in the Deposito dell'Opera Pia Buon Pastore in Asti, the Ospizio dei Poveri in Aosta, and the Deposito dell'Opera Pia San Paolo in Turin); Onorato Daniele, who accused the priest Albanelli along with Giuseppe Peiron of making "a secret doll to kill the king our Royal Sovereign and the Royal Prince of Piedmont his son" in 1712, was imprisoned in the senatorial prisons of Nice; Joseph Laurencet, who accused Count Depleoz of bewitching his wife in 1723, was imprisoned in the Cittadella in Turin; Martin Barro di Vico, also imprisoned in the Cittadella, accused his cellmates in 1725 of casting an evil spell on the prince in the castle of Ivrea; Onorato Arnaudo, who accused Carlo Faro of casting an evil spell on the late princess and reigning prince of Piedmont as well as of wanting to cast an evil spell on the queen in 1726, had a long history of imprisonment in the senatorial prisons in Pinerolo; and finally, Biaggio Forno, for whom the trial proceedings are missing and who in 1718 accused many people of practicing "sorcery,"[8] was locked up in the senatorial prisons in Turin.

The number of accusers who were already confined in institutions is striking, even considering that many people were confined or imprisoned in this period[9] and that charitable institutions and prisons were fertile fields for witchcraft accusations, places where denunciations more readily found legal and formal expression. This fact originally led to the hypothesis that there was a causal link between a concentration of witchcraft accusations originating within institutions and the closed nature of these institutions. Such a connection is not entirely new: both historical and anthropological scholarship on witchcraft have touched on it in slightly different contexts with various interpretations, two of which warrant closer examination.

Robert Mandrou and other historians who have studied "institutional epidemics," that is, collective episodes or chain reactions of cases of possession or witchcraft accusations within religious institutions, believe that both the religious and communal nature of these institutions created an atmosphere that encouraged the persistence of archaic and superstitious beliefs and, above all, forms of cultural and psychological regression. This theory, however, does not seem helpful for explaining the sociocultural causes of these particular witchcraft trials in Piedmont in the first decades of the eighteenth century for two reasons: first, because in the cases the accusations were made by individuals who were from different institutions and acted at different times, with no sign, therefore, of a craze or epidemic; second, Mandrou's analysis limits the theoretical and historical importance of later witchcraft accusations and reduces them to a problem of cultural backwardness and psychological pathology, thus tautologically viewing them as peripheral or atypical with respect to the rest of society.[10]

In contrast, several anthropologists—in particular Mary Douglas and Godfrey Lienhardt—have theorized that communal, total social settings in which relations are intense, personalized, and limited prevented the direct and explicit expression of tension and aggression. In such situations individuals may resort to witchcraft accusations as a way of expressing these hostilities. This theory seems much more useful, since it focuses on the concrete and relational meaning of belief.

Witchcraft accusations in this context become positive strategies in relationships between individuals or groups. The strength of Douglas and Lienhardt's hypothesis lies in attempting to analyze the possibilities for expression and communication available to individuals in contexts that can be defined as total.[11]

Still, this theory cannot answer all the questions raised by these cases. Perhaps this is due to their particular historical nature, which reveals a plethora of information about society and culture in Piedmont in the early eighteenth century. Surely witchcraft accusations can be ways of expressing and "resolving" aggressive impulses,[12] especially as relationships among the confined/imprisoned were often highly charged emotionally and inmates normally were unable to choose or change cellmates. Undoubtedly, for example, in these terms Barbero and other prisoners could express their hostile feelings toward Boccalaro, who throughout his imprisonment showed disdain for his cellmates, refused to talk to them, treated them as "scoundrels," and chose as his only interlocutor and confidant the prison warden.[13] Nevertheless, there were other motives for Barbero's accusation, which makes it seem likely that such hostilities were merely a part of a more general context of relationships which an accusation often was not very successful in expressing.

Actually, in most of these cases, only the accuser was imprisoned or confined, while the accused live outside the institution and generally was a person the accuser knew in a period preceding internment. Moreover, even when—as in the Boccalaro case—the accusation involved and reflected relationships that were internal to institutions, they did not represent an explosive, aggressive situation. Significantly in this context, the emotional detachment of the accusation was not even broken by an expression of compassion for the victims of the witchcraft—almost always a member of the royal family—and it showed few signs of tension or anxiety. A similar detachment was evident in the depositions of other persons confined or interned as well, who often reacted with extreme indifference to the entire investigation. The responses of witnesses in the 1726 trial are only one possible example. Early that year Onorato Arnaudo, pardoned by His Majesty, was released from the senatorial prisons in Pinerolo and went to Count Michele Antonio Borda both to thank the Senate for its act of clemency and to provide some important information concerning "His Royal Highness and the whole Royal House in order to relieve his conscience." He then denounced his former cellmate Carlo Faro for making a small figurine that would have killed "the late Royal Princess of Piedmont, during childbirth, along with the Royal Prince" and for wanting "to kill Her Majesty the Queen and the entire Royal House of Savoy." To corroborate his story, he said that he had publicly accused Faro in front of the other cellmates. These latter, when they were interrogated as to why they had not come forward with what they had heard from Arnaudo, gave evasive answers: "But, sir, I neither thought about it nor reflected upon it"; "I thought these things were improbable and probably made up by him"; "It seemed talk without merit."[14] It seems that the accusation neither involved nor affected very much the relationship between accused and accuser, nor even the relationships among those interned or imprisoned. The discourse focused instead on the relationship between accuser and institution, and the real protagonist of the judicial episode was the accuser, with the accused merely playing the part of the unwilling stooge.

In this context it is interesting to note how beliefs in witchcraft were modified in an institutional setting. In other social contexts, revealed primarily in the testimony of witnesses,[15] such beliefs functioned to explain misfortunes and to interpret relationships.[16] The setting that was created around Clara Ribolletta, when she reached Ivrea after she had run away from her husband for the third time and had spent many months as a vagabond, serves as an example. To obtain aid and protection from both the parish of San Maurizio and the parish of Sant'Uldarico, Clara not only accused her kin of witchcraft but sustained also—perpetuating the tradition of the sixteenth-century Cerretani[17]—that she never received a Catholic baptism and that her father had sacrificed her to Beelzebub. She herself played the part of a woman possessed. This episode immediately gained for her the sympathy of the two parish priests and did not go unnoticed in the city. It created fissures and provoked conflicts between the curates and their congregations and forced many to judge Ribolletta and to ask themselves if "she was making it all up, possessed, or mad."[18] What is interesting in this affair is the incredible diversity of opinions expressed. Although everyone believed in witchcraft, those who followed and participated in this affair chose to interpret the case in different ways. Belief, therefore, was not homogeneous and undifferentiated: far from having a prescriptive value, belief was a cultural matrix where possible positions and conflicting attitudes existed simultaneously. Reading an event within the "ideology" of witchcraft was only one of the possible interpretive choices. What determined the decision, in this case whether or not Clara was a witch, possessed, or a charlatan, was the relationship of each person to Ribolletta herself. Their judgement reflected tensions and feelings, both personal and social, which they felt and lived out in their relations with the new arrival. What was at stake was the meaning of their interrelatedness, "the total relationship."[19]

The internal debate of the cleric Gamacio, about whether to see the sudden deaths of his two sisters, which occurred during Ribolletta's stay in the Canavese, as witchcraft and thus to consider her a witch, is particularly revealing:

> Actually I spoke [with others] about the death of my two sisters, and they told me that perhaps it was Clara who killed them. But I replied no, because I could not know for sure ... it could be that I said to someone that my sisters were strong and robust and that I could not understand why as soon as Clara left our house, my little sister aged four had an accident and that in spite of medical attention she did not recover. ... I do not understand what you are telling me because it is bad to suspect people, even if I have heard it said that the said Clara was "marked" ... like witches are, but I did not see it. As to my other sister who also died in a short span of time, she was also strong and robust and died in five days. ... I do not know what I should think, but when that Clara was in our house she was always with my sisters and I do not know if she picked them up or hugged them.[20]

In noninstitutional contexts witchcraft beliefs, then, allowed individuals to defend themselves "from the risks of an existential crisis when they confronted the abyss" and to express and define the tensions and ambiguities that arose in their relationships.[21] It is significant that these accusations rarely found legal expression and instead were controlled and resolved through various mechanisms of psychological protection—for example, magic—which E. De Martino believes allowed a "protected life style" to be established, or else were resolved on a metacommunicative level, within the relationship between the accuser and the accused. The ritual nature of the peace made between Matteo Rostagno's wife (one of the people accused by Cuore) and a certain Cattarina, following a dispute over money which involved insults and curses, illustrates the point:

> Finding myself near [the Church of] San Francesco, I wanted to buy a black beret. Cattarina ... who was passing by at the same time said to me. "Oh, you pimping whore, it would be better if

you paid for the socks your husband bought than buy berets and pretend to be somebody." Since she said these words in public and had insulted and dishonored me in front of other people, I told her that she would never again be able to say the truth about me and that even if she went to confession, she would never go to Paradise. So the said Cattarina went home and told her mother and husband that I told her that the child in her womb would not live, and so they came over ... to my house and reproved me ... and I calmed them down and said that was not true and after my husband paid ... Cattarina's mother said to me, "[My] daughter said things to you and you said things to her, you two should forget about it, make up, and be good friends again."[22]

In an institutional context this aspect of witchcraft belief—its relational and explanatory nature—was less significant. Rather, accusations functioned as a mean of negotiation: through which the accuser addressed the institution and established a relationship based on threats and demands. In part these accusations were a threat because they normally involved the making of a small doll in the form of a member of the House of Savoy. This accentuated the fears and sense of conspiracy which accompanied political life in Savoy at the time, in particular after the unexpected and untimely death of Vittorio Amedeo II's first son followed rapidly by the death of the young prince Tommaso, son of Emanuele Filiberto of Carignano. Such accusations were also a threat because they showed how vulnerable the royal image really was, creating doubts about the king's charisma and about what Marc Bloch has called the "echo of regality."[23] Significantly, the accusers' words hit home and seriously worried both the ministers and magistrates. These anxieties were expressed explicitly in the declarations of the prime minister, Pietro Mellarede, who in 1719 said that "these types of dolls" were "the talk of many people," and he argued that little information should be made public about "certain types of dolls which everyone was talking about ... since curiosity led the human spirit to try evil." Thus the magistrates were forced to conduct minute interrogations about "secrets that jeopardized the health" of the princes and of the king himself[24] and to alternate show executions—like Boccalaro's—with limited and controlled displays of justice where "the spectacle element [was] neutralized,"[25] or to imprison the accused without a trial in one of those "dungeons, where the King Vittorio put all those whom he wanted to die and whom he did not dare execute publicly."[26]

In short, accusers stirred up and played upon fears that turned upon the royal image. This was the reason why they could then ask for a reward. Barbero was not alone in asking for something in exchange for making his denunciation. All the other accusers shared the hope that they, too, would benefit. Onorato Daniele, Biaggio Forno, Joseph Laurencet, and Martin Barro all asked, as did Barbero, that their sentences be reduced, a typical request for a judicial order that sought and rewarded public accusations. But in other cases the reward sought was different: Francesco Freylino, a twenty-five-year-old who had worked in a notary's office and then became a beggar, confessed on his deathbed that the witchcraft accusations he had made against Antonio Borda and Giuseppe Cernua were "inventions in order to obtain work." Onorato Arnaudo, after serving a year in prison for illegally carrying weapons, denounced Carlo Faro in the hope of "obtaining a reward and a job from His Majesty in order to make a living." Clara Ribolletta's motivations were quite different; she made several denunciations with various goals: first, to avoid returning to her husband, whom she had fled; second, to be placed and accepted in the community where as a beggar she had ended up; third, to be admitted to the Deposito dell'Opera San Paolo of Turin; and finally to get out of the Deposito. Cattarina Cuore hoped that, "[once she] said these things, His Majesty would see to it that [she] would always have enough to eat for [her] whole life . . . and that His Majesty would be moved to have pity on [her]."[27]

The reward sought through these accusations was not always release from prison or immediate economic benefits. In many cases the accuser hoped to obtain a job, to receive special treatment, to be admitted to a charitable institution, or even to cut through the red tape of institutional hierarchies altogether in order, for example, to be admitted to San Paolo instead of being locked up in the home for the poor.[28] Accusations were not simply motivated by economic or material gain. Information on the wealth of those who made accusations indicates that most did not belong to the lowest or poorest social class; rather, they fell among the poor who lived in conditions of extreme instability and precariousness not only economically but also socially.[29] In the interrogations of the accused and accusers, socioeconomic conditions were continually discussed, as demonstrated by Cattarina Rama, who, denounced by Cuore, commented: "I do not get along with that Cuore, as she is an ignorant animal because she stays now eight days in one place, now eight in another . . . even Anna wanted to throw her out . . . and even her brothers do not want her at home . . . *nonethe-less she has a big trunk full of her stuff.*"[30]

Here it seems that what was hidden within the charges turned not so much on charitable institutions or prisons as totalizing spaces (self-contained and separated from society) but rather on institutions as dispensers of assistance which also provided opportunities for social placement.[31] The issue, then, was not simply the conditions imposed by confinement but crucially how to live without "protection" or belonging to a disciplining body.[32] This sheds new light on several characteristics of the mechanisms of assistance in Piedmont at the beginning of the eighteenth century. The motivation for several accusa-tions—the hope of finding a job, of obtaining economic assistance, of being accepted into charitable institutions, and so on—and the use of charges of witchcraft as a tool for affirming individual needs were rooted in a situation characterized by a demand for social protection, or better, for social recognition that was not satisfied by such institutions. Moreover, this call for help became more and more pressing as the streets and piazzas of Turin were invaded by aggressive mendicants and beggars.[33] Such a phenomenon promoted new assistance programs[34] and clashed with a system of charity-based social programs which allocated funds in a limited and arbitrary manner.

The moral goal of charitable politics, rehabilitating the poor, was in fact accompanied on a daily level by a management of funds which privileged certain groups. In other words, the criterion for choosing how funds were distributed was based not so much on helping strata of the population who lived in particularly precarious and difficult conditions but rather on protecting and defending the anxieties about status and honor of "old noble families and the nouveaux riches—functionaries of various degrees, notaries, lawyers, doctors, [and] mod-est court dignitaries" who experienced sudden periods of economic difficulty or who had fallen into conditions they deemed inadequate to their social position.[35]

Alongside preoccupations about the integrity of social groups, there were also concerns about kinship and patronage. This tendency, reflected in the documentation produced by the institutions responsi-ble for assistance,[36] is confirmed by the biographies of a number of the protagonists in the trials. Whether they were seeking a job, eco-nomic aid, or admission to a charitable institution, the issue of who mediated between the poor and the authorities was clearly evident, often violently so. Lucia Giordano explained how, after running away from her paternal home and then surviving a trying existence as a vagabond and beggar, she was able to gain admittance to the Institute of the Buon Pastore of Asti thanks to the intervention of Madama Orsetta. Cuore sustained that she was admitted to the Deposito San Paolo of Turin following the intervention of the head of the Carmelite order in that province. Finally, Marianna Muratore recounted that she had been brought to Asti "to the tavern of San Giorgio run at that time by Signora Testa." [Muratore explained,] "I told her that . . . my husband had abandoned me and that she could help me by telling me how I could be admitted to the Convertite [a charitable home], and she told me that I must speak to the man who ran things, Signor Conte di Revigliasco."[37]

Thus the charge of witchcraft fits in the context of an unsatisfied request. In a society based entirely on groups and communities, the accusers, individuals who did not belong to any social unit, used the accusation of witchcraft to make up for their lack of legitimation and protection and to jump over the patronage networks that distributed economic assistance.

Clara Ribolletta's case is significant in this regard. Her reasons for accusing family members and friends of witchcraft, which at first glance seem contorted and forced, begin to make sense when one takes into account how she gained admittance to the Deposito dell'Opera Pia San Paolo of Turin, one of the principle charitable institutions at the beginning of the eighteenth century funded through private donations.[38] In fact, Ribolletta tried unsuccessfully several times to be admitted to San Paolo: Lucia Giordano, who was confined in San Paolo, described her as "at the entrance of San Paolo to see if the signora [the director] would accept her, but . . . the Lords of the Congregation of San Paolo did not want to accept her." Ribolletta herself said she went to Princess Francavilla for support "[because] she could get [her] in, since she had many powerful friends."[39] Thus Ribolletta early on had come face to face with the criteria of selection which regulated access to San Paolo, criteria that were predicated on corporate interests and patronage networks, which influenced the whole range of activities of the Compagnia San Paolo.[40] It was only because of, or to be more exact on the merit of, her witchcraft charges that she was able to overcome these criteria by interesting influential and important people in her case. Thanks to their influence the earlier decision to deny her admittance because she was "poor" and a "foreigner" was revoked:

Father Fea [an official of the inquisition and parish priest of the Church of San Maurizio in Ivrea] told me he would write about it to Father Alfieri, vicar of the Holy Office of Turin, who would speak to the lord president Pallavicino. Father Fea replied that I could not be admitted because I was a foreigner, and since I was poor, I was not even able to pay the pension as was customary for foreigners. Once I heard that, I went to beg President Gabutto so that he would work to get me a place in the Deposito, and Father Fea went too and begged Signor Pinchia to help me. This Signor Pinchia replied from Turin that there was a chance I would be admitted to the Deposito and that His Majesty had become involved in getting me accepted. Then I asked Father Fea who would provide me with clothes and all the other things I needed. The said Father Fea told me not to worry, that they would tell His Majesty all about the nature of my husband, father-in-law, and father [all accused by Ribolletta of making dolls of the king and his sons], and thus returning home to such people would not be allowed and everything would be taken care of.[41]

And, in effect, the intervention of powerful people, obtained through the charges of witchcraft, opened the doors of San Paolo to her. Ribolletta—like Freylino, Arnaudo, and all the other accusers—was correct when she saw that an accusation was an effective tool for affirming her needs and when she declared explicitly the link between the threat and the request for social protection which such an accusation expressed: "So I said all these things about the dolls because I told myself that . . . I would be taken care of by His Majesty for what I had disclosed, and that His Majesty would reward me with some allowance, so that I could support myself without having to return to my husband, who I detested and still detest."

Cattarina Cuore recalled sorrowfully that she hoped that the witchcraft charge would move "His Majesty to compassion for me *even though he did not want to.*"[42] The other protagonists of these trials, the accused and the witnesses, also realized that witchcraft charges hid similar hopes. Many people emphasized the instrumental motive for the charge, sustaining that it was "nonsense invented by them to gain their Lords' favor," to "gain His Royal Highness's graces," to "earn a reward," or to "gain a position." But, above all, as several of those accused explained explicitly, the motivation for the charge turned on the arbitrary criteria that dominated the distribution of economic assistance and the ease with which one could be excluded. Many witnesses in the 1716 trial sustained that the poor in Ivrea complained that Ribolletta, following her charges, "took the charity that was rightly theirs" and that "if it was a matter of some miserable beggar from their city, they would let him die and [that] that sponger [Ribolletta] would get it all."[43]

In addition to indicating the deficiencies of the institutions and the limits of charity-based politics, profoundly imbued with corporate group interests and patronage networks, witchcraft charges shed light on the social needs that stood behind and invested such institutions. The continued need, even if only implicit, for legitimation and social protection characterized these institutions not only as a repressive and punitive space (and institutes as places where individuals were separated from society and subjected) but also as mediators for unprotected individuals.

This can be seen in biographies of several of protagonists of these trials, chiefly in their interrelationships with charitable institutions. These reveal the complex ties that bound the individual to the institution, going well beyond mere resistance or subjection. Ribolletta's relationship was one fraught with ambiguities and tensions. Her economic and especially her social insecurity, which forced her to play all the cards at her disposal to gain admittance to the Deposito dell'Opera San Paolo of Turin, went hand in hand with problems that she had in accepting the life of confinement there. Thus, after she won the difficult battle of being accepted, at the moment of crossing the threshold at San Paolo, she could "only cry," already regretting that she "resolved to withdraw into that House."[44] Her stay was punctuated by fear of being thrown out, and by continual attempts to escape or change the rules imposed on her by the administrators, and by trying to obtain special treatment—being allowed to meet with her friends or extorting a special diet. Far from being a behavior characteristic of only Ribolletta, this ambivalent reaction to institutionalization was an experience common to many, who alternated between intolerance, escape attempts, disobedience, and attempts to gain admittance to other charitable institutions. Lucia Giordano, who was thrown out of the Buon Pastore of Asti for "being disobedient to the director of that House," after only two months applied to be admitted to the Deposito in Turin. After being accepted and staying for a short time, she was expelled again "for her bad behavior and disobedience to the director." Marianna Muratore, who like Giordano spent time in the Buon Pastore and the Deposito, behaved in a similar manner: during her third stay in the institution in Asti she was put under strict discipline and fled in April 1716. Seven months later she reappeared at the house of treasurer Berlenda requesting that she be readmitted to the Deposito in Turin.[45]

It seems clear that institutions were not simply perceived in a negative way; popular attitudes toward them were characterized by profound ambivalence.[46] This ambivalence in turn was linked to an ambiguity intrinsic to the history and social implications of the institutions themselves: being both punitive spaces and places where the poor and vagabonds were separated from society, they were also "the ruling class's solution to a problem posed by the lower classes."[47]

Witchcraft accusations, then, when they were used as a tool for correcting the mechanisms of exclusion of these institutions and to obtain social legitimation, reveal both an awareness of and an ability to manipulate the culture of institutions. Here one is not encountering the stereotypical passive subject before judges. The accusers knew not only, as noted above, how the institutions functioned and how they distributed assistance but also the states of mind and the cultural values of institutional representatives and agents (administrators, king, judges, priests, members of confraternities).

For example, they knew that the death of Vittorio Amedeo II's firstborn son in 1715 created a moment of concern about magical death, just as they understood the importance of the symbolic and political meanings of the royal image. Through their charges of witchcraft they tried to aggravate the doubts that surrounded the death of the young prince as well as the anxieties that someone was plotting to overthrow the House of Savoy. In fact, when they made their denunciations, they emphasized their deference to the authorities and stressed how these acts were threats, underscoring "the horror of such a loathsome deed" and reminding the authorities that a similar fate could await other members of the royal family. In addition, they stressed the symbolic gravity of such an act against the king, especially because it revealed his vulnerability.

Thus many accusers insisted on stating that they were not just making a "normal" denunciation but that it was "an affair of the utmost importance concerning the Royal Family." Several emphasized this element of their charge in their description of the magical figurine, which they described as "a bust ... with a band in the shape of a crown which was separate and removable." Others preferred to emphasize literally the "deadline": Martin Barro stated that Vittorio

Amedeo's second son, the future Carlo Emmanuele III, "would die within five years," while Cuore maintained "that the statue [of Carlo Emmanuele] was already well underway, and that if they put it in the fire, it [would] be too late to save him." Ribolletta, in turn, spoke of a genuine conspiracy against the House of Savoy. Among the army of "more than three million people who were professional witches," she claimed that there were many influential members of Piedmont society who "wanted to become king." They had been responsible for the death of the young prince Vittorio and were now plotting against Prince Carlo and the king himself, "knowing that the dolls [were] already being made in their images and that if [they began] to put them in the fire, it [would] be too late to save them." Among the conspirators she included the president Pallavicino, who "complained that he was not made president earlier," and Count Massetto, who wanted to use the figurine to see "if His Majesty was more powerful than them [the conspirators]," and others who "had a longer reach" like the governor of Turin, Vittorio Amedeo II's personal confessor Father Dormiglia, and the prince of Carignano.[48] Moreover, the witchcraft charge was often accompanied by statements designed to underline the seriousness of the threat to the royal family, not only physically but also in terms of the symbolic and representational images of their power. Thus the sacrilegious theft of the lamp and silver candelabra in September 1716 from the Chapel of the Santissimo Sudario, the royal family's favorite chapel, was often referred to by the accusers.

Several protagonists in the trials demonstrated that they knew the different attitudes of their interrogators about witchcraft. In fact in this period, the position of the secular court and that of the Holy Office were vastly different. The former still prosecuted witchcraft stubbornly and vigorously, [49] while the latter exercised its repressive apparatus wearily, meting out milder penalties[50] and stressing demonic possession over witchcraft. Possession permitted the inquisitors to stress the centrality of dogma about the devil, protect the innocence of the possessed person (an unwilling victim of the devil), and at the same time exercise an effective cultural control (acting, through exorcisms, on the intimate levels of an individual's conscience), without having to use juridical sanctions. Significantly some of the accusers were aware of these differences and changed their behavior accordingly. When Ribolletta, Freylino, and Cuore, who had begun their testimony accusing others of witchcraft, realized that they had become trapped in their own charges and were incriminating themselves of witchcraft, they began to insist "that these matters concerned the Holy Office more than His Majesty." Cuore explained the reasons that led her to choose the Dominican convent, despised by Radicati di Passerano,[51] over secular justice:

> The differences between these prisons are many. It is easy to get out of ecclesiastical prisons: all that is necessary is that one go there and say certain words in Latin, that is, spontaneously admitting their guilt, and they obtain absolution and are set free. As to worldly prisons, that is, secular prisons, when people go there of their own volition to accuse themselves, they are punished. I have seen many people who were hanged or torn by pincers. Ecclesiastical justice does not kill anyone, least of all those who go there of their own volition.[52]

Ribolletta—who in Ivrea played the part of a woman possessed when she appeared before the inquisitors— made sure she did not play that part when she appeared before the secular magistrates. Instead, she chose to hide her previous behavior and concentrated on her accusations against powerful people, an argument never mentioned when she was before the Holy Office.

It is clear that the capacity of magistrates, inquisitors, and institutional administrators to distinguish between the statements made before them was neither linear nor obvious. What is significant is that the politics of institutions was limited both in its distribution of funds by corporate group and patronage network interests and in the control it could hope to exercise on a cultural level—limited precisely by those individuals who should have been the principal victims of their mechanisms of exclusion and subjection. A study of the behavior of the accusers changes, at least in part, the recent scholarly stereotype of individuals imprisoned, confined, or receiving charity within institutions as inert and domesticated victims. In that vision they were nonexistent as individuals—unless discussed in terms of what institutions did to them[53]—and were only considered on the social or collective level, to confirm their impotence and inferior culture.

I believe that these witchcraft trials give us a very different image of institutional life in Piedmont at the beginning of the eighteenth century. The accusers— for the most part, people who were imprisoned, confined, or receiving charity—neither seem to be people who were culturally deprived, nor do they seem, in their attempts to manipulate institutions, to have been clinging to archaic or traditional cultural beliefs. Instead, they show that they were well informed, that they had mastered knowledge of events that were culturally significant (how quickly they utilized events such as the young prince's death or the robbery at the Chapel of the Santissimo Sudario), and that they understood the anxieties and cultural values of institutional administrators and mediators.

Another explanation for the high concentration of witchcraft accusations involving institutions is that the accusers were knowledgeable about the discourses of their interlocutors and that they used these adeptly, *precisely because* they were imprisoned, confined, or receiving charity. Charitable and disciplinary institutions, intended as cultural spaces where individuals and social groups were controlled and subjected, were characterized in their daily workings rather as spaces where information circulated (whether internally, among those confined, or externally, with those on the outside)[54] and where individuals had many opportunities to come into contact with the models and cultural values of their superiors, learning both to appropriate and to manipulate them.

Witchcraft accusations brought before the secular tribunal tell us about individuals' hopes, attempts to utilize and to gain access to institutions, the strategies they employed to survive, and not merely materially, and the records that those hopes and attempts engendered. All the accusers were able to obtain their desired reward; they were all able, if only for that day, to be important to that institution and at the same time through it to find a moment of legitimation and social protection. The final verdicts, however, varied greatly. Several accusers—Barbero, Onorato Daniele, and Biaggio Forno—obtained a reduction in their sentences, while the people they accused were found guilty. Boccalaro was hanged and quartered. It should be remembered, however, that his case was taken up again a month later by three magistrates very loyal to the king (the general counselor Riccardi, the chancellor de Bellegarde, and the minister de Gubernatis), who expressed disapproval of his sentence. These men espoused a hierarchical conception of punishment based on matching the level of suffering in the penalty with the crime. They believed Boccalaro's execution was faulty and the punishment unjust and inadequate because "it was used for many, diverse crimes that [were] inferior":

> We have come to feel that in the case of such an egregious case of Lese Majesty, aggravated by heretical sorcery, it should merit . . . a

more rigorous and exemplary punishment like being hanged and quartered by horses, letting the piety and clemency of the king modify with an act of grace, or similar act, the form or mode of death for the good of his soul ... although the death penalty is in itself the best punishment ... and therefore chosen by the laws and legislators with the terms and superlatives of the ultimate punishment ... still punishment by death has its gradations, if not in its substance that is death, in its form and modes of causing death.[55]

Count Depleoz, Father Albanelli, Guid, Chichiastro, Father Duret, and many others accused were also condemned to death or to life in the galleys. But in other cases it was the accusers who followed Boccalaro's fate. Ribolletta, thanks to her accusations, did not go back to her husband; supported by the curates in Ivrea and admitted to the Deposito in Turin, she ended up incriminating herself as a witch and was condemned to be hanged. For Cuore and Freylino, the verdicts were similar: they too were victims of their own words, and both were judged guilty of witchcraft. Freylino was condemned to the stake, while Cuore, sentenced to life in jail, was locked up in the Fortress of Miolans, where she died several years later following an escape attempt.[56]

Notes

1. This latter group of cases where the accused was imprisoned without trial includes those detained awaiting trial, those imprisoned by royal decree, and so on. In general, these were controversial cases that the authorities wanted to give as little publicity as possible and where there was a discrepancy over whether they fell under civil or ecclesiastical jurisdiction. Archivio di Stato di Torino (hereafter AST), sez. 1, Materie Criminali. Information on persons imprisoned for witchcraft without trials is contained in Visite dei Carcerati, a section of the Materie Criminali, as well as in the registers of the Segreteria Interna.

2. There were only two trials for "sorcery and magical spells" tried by the secular court in the years prior to our cases (one from 1417, the other from 1618). I have not found any investigations of such cases after 1727, excepting several arrests for witchcraft between 1730 and 1740. AST, sez. 1, Materie Criminali, mazzo 1, fasc. 3, and mazzo 4, fasc. 3, as well as Materie Criminali, Pareri e Memorie, mazzo 1, not inventoried.

3. Such theories argue that the decline in witchcraft prosecution either was due to the diffusion of a new jurisprudence from center to periphery or was a result of a decision passed from "high" to "low" and thus was the result of a [new] awareness on the part of the High Magistry and the king. Such theory is grounded in the dichotomy center/periphery and on the conception enlightened/superstitious which runs throughout Mandrou's *Magistrati e streghe nella Francia del '600*. While Mandrou is the primary exponent of this thesis, it is shared by many scholars. Hugh Trevor-Roper and Keith Thomas, for example, explain the decline of witchcraft persecution with the concept of distance, or inequality between the High Magistry, minor judges,

and the people. On this, see Mandrou, *Magistrati e streghe nella Francia del '600* (Bari, 1971, Ital. trans. of *Magistrats et sorciers en France au XVII siècle* (Paris, 1968), pp. 198, 214, 299, 428, 544, 627; Trevor-Roper, *Religion, the Reformation, and Social Change* (London, 1967), Ital. trans. (Bari, 1975), p. 213, n. 140; and K. Thomas, *Religion and the Decline of Magic* (London, 1971), pp. 546–48, 694–96, 798–99.

4. G. Ricci, "Da poveri vergognosi ad ex-nobili poveri: Un episodio sulla Toscana del primo Ottocento," paper presented at the conference "Pauperismo e assistenza negli antichi stati italiani, sec. XV–XIX," Cremona, March 1980 (hereafter "Pauperismo").

5. AST, sez. 1, Materie Criminali, mazzo 13, Testimony of Clara Ribolletta, June 2, 1717, d. 19.

6. AST, sez. 1, Materie Criminali, mazzo 12, fasc. 3, Atti criminali contro GioAntonio Boccalaro, Antonio Barbero's testimony, December 18, 1709.

7. E. Grendi, "Ideologia della carità e della società indisciplinata," paper presented at the conference "Pauperismo."

8. AST, sez. 1, Materie Criminali, mazzo 13 and 14, Processo criminale contro Clara Ribolletta, Cattarina Cuore e Marianna Muratore; mazzo 15, fasc. 10. Processo criminale contro il prete Albanelli accusato di diversi sortilegi; mazzo 23 and 24, Informazioni, lettere, ecc. sulla causa del conte Depleoz della Valle d'Aosta e suoi complici inquisiti di sortilegio; mazzo 25, fasc. 4, Atti criminali contro Martin Barro; mazzo 28, fasc. 4, Copia d'informazioni prese contro Carlo Farò. AST, sez. 1, Segreteria Interna, Serie 4 Giuridico-Ecclesiastico-Economico, Registro 7.

9. B. Pullan, "Poveri, mendicanti, e vagabondi," in *Storia d'Italia, Annali* vol. 1. (Turin, 1976), p. 994; Grendi, "Ideologia"; G. Levi, "Mobilità della populazione e immigrazione a Torino nella prima metà del Settecento," *Quaderni storici* 6 (1979): 546–54. See also D. Carutti, *Storia di Torino* (Turin, 1846; reprint, Turin, 1979), pp. 533–34.

10. Mandrou, *Magistrats.* Also M. Craveri, *Sante e streghe* (Milan, 1980).

11. Mary Douglas, "Thirty Years after Witchcraft, Oracles and Magic," and G. Lienhardt, "The Situation of Death," in *Witchcraft: Confessions and Accusations,* ed. M. Douglas (London, 1970), pp. XIII–XXXVI, 279–89. Also Thomas, *Religion,* pp. 796–97. A. Macfarlane, *Witchcraft in Tudor and Stuart England* (London, 1970), pp. 168, 200–201. P. Boyer and S. Nissenbaum, *Salem Possessed* Cambridge, Mass., 1974, pp. 69, 143–46.

12. On witchcraft accusations as expressions of aggressive impulses, see in particular J. Demos, "Underlying Themes in the Witchcraft of Seventeenth-Century New England," *American Historical Review* 75 (1970): 113–26. J. Middleton and E. H. Winter, eds., *Witchcraft and Sorcery in East Africa* (London, 1963). C. Kluckhohn, "Navaho Witchcraft," in *Witchcraft and Sorcery,* ed. M. Marwick (London, 1970), pp. 220–27

13. AST, Materie Criminali, mazzo 12, fasc. 4, Atti criminali contro Gio Antonio Boccalaro, Boccalaro's cross-examination, December 19, 1709.

14. AST, sez. 1, Materie Criminali, mazzo 28, fasc. 4, Copia di informazioni prese contro Carlo Faro, Gio. Domenico's testimony, January 11, 1726; Cesare Berarda's testimony, January 11, 1726; Marco Lorenzo Brun's testimony, January 12, 1726.

15. On witnesses' testimony as "superior records" and thus as documents that are of particular relevance to the concept of witchcraft and their use as sources of popular beliefs, see R. Kieckhefer, *European Witch Trials* (London, 1976), pp. 29, 45; also Thomas, *Religion* p. 531

16. Macfarlane, *Witchcraft,* p. 176; E. Evans-Pritchard, *Oracles and Magic,* ital. trans. (Milan, 1976), p. 146; P. Mayer, "*Witches,*" in Marwick, *Witchcraft,* p. 56.

17. Pullan, "Poveri," pp. 1013–14; P. Camporesi, *Il libro dei vagabondi* (Turin, 1973).

18. AST, sez. 1, Materie Criminali, mazzo 13, Processo contro Clara Ribolletta, trial proceedings at Ivrea n. 16, Marco Antonio Pitolio's testimony, July 22, 1717.

19. Macfarlane, *Witchcraft* p. 176.

20. AST, sez. 1, Materie Criminali, mazzo 13, Processo contro Clara Ribolletta, trial proceedings at Ivrea n. 35, Domenico Gamachio's testimony, July 26, 1717.

21. E. De Martino, *Sud e magia* (Milan, 1959), pp. 2, 27, 96–97, 112–13, 181. On the concept of reassurance, see G. Levi, "Regioni e cultura delle classi popolari," *Quaderni storici* 41 (1979): 720–31.

22. AST, sez. 1, Materie Criminali, mazzo 13, Testimony of Giovanna Cattarina Rama, April 2, 1717, d. 42.

23. M. Bloch, *The Royal Touch: Sacred Monarchy and Scrofula in England and France*, trans. J. E. Anderson (London, 1973).

24. AST, sez. 1, Materie Criminali, mazzo 16, fasc. 20, Copie di biglietti del conte Mellarede al cavaliere Leblanc, August 23, 1719. Segreteria Interna, Serie 3-Economica, Registro 87, letters from Count Mellarede to Marquis Foschieri, to chief prosecutor Giusiana and to [cavaliere] Leblanc, September-October 1721. Segreteria Interna, Serie 1-Giuridico, Registro 1, letter from His Majesty to President Gand, February 1716. Lettere Particolari, lettera P, letter from Count Mellarede to [intendente] Palme, October 1716. AST, Materie Criminali, mazzo 13, request of magistrate Deville to Cattarina Cuore, January 10, 1717.

25. M. Foucault, *Discipline and Punish: The Birth of the Prison* (New York, 1977).

26. A. Radicati di Passerano, *Histoire de l'abdication de Victor-Amédée*, cited in F. Venturi, *Saggi sull'Europa illuminista, Alberto Radicati di Passerano* (Turin, 1954), p. 166. The concerns over not giving the trials too much publicity were in part determined by serious jurisdictional conflicts with the papacy, and in particular with the Inquisition, which were typical of the reign of Vittorio Amedeo II and inhibited the magistrates: for example, in 1717 Ludovico Guid, accused of witchcraft and of making a pact with the devil by Cuore, was sentenced to be imprisoned in the Fortezza di Miolans rather than to death for fear that "the death sentence would give rise to disputes with Ecclesiastics." The same fate befell Father Albanelli and Giuseppe Peiron. AST, sez. 1, Materie Criminali, mazzo 12, fasc. 16, letter from Count Mellarede to the Cavaliere Leblanc, November 1717; mazzo 14, letter from Senator Bally, September 20, 1717; AST, sez. 1, Segreteria Interna, Serie 3-Economico, Registro dei prigionieri, n. 87, letter from Count Mellarede to Count Foschieri, October 31, 1721. On the jurisdictional politics of the Savoyard government, see Venturi, *Saggi* pp. 63–100. G. Quazza, *Le riforme in Piemonte nella prima metà del Settecento* (Modena, 1957), pp. 29, 358–63, 399–403. G. Ricuperati, *L'esperienza civile e religiosa di Pietro Giannone* (Milan and Naples, 1970), pp. 305–6, 493.

27. AST, sez. 1, Materie Criminali, mazzo 16, fasc. 10, Atti criminali contro Francesco Gerolamo Freylino; mazzo 28, fasc. 4, Copia d'informazioni prese contro Carlo Farò; mazzo 13 and 14, Processo criminale contro Clara Ribolletta, Cattarina Cuore, e Marianna Muratore.

28. For data about the confinement of beggars in Piedmont, see Levi, "Mobilità, " pp. 546–54.

29. J. P. Gutton, *La société et les pauvres en Europe (XVI–XVIII siècles)*, ital. trans. (Milan, 1977), pp. 8–10. Pullan, "Poveri," p. 1039. S. Woolf, "Problemi della storia del pauperismo in Italia, 1800–1815," paper presented at the conference "Pauperismo"; G. Ricci, "Povertà, vergogna, e poverta vergognosa," *Società e storia* 5 (1979).

30. AST, sez. 1, Materie Criminali, mazzo 13, Risposte personali di Giovanna Cattarina Rama, April 2, 1717.

31. For the definition of the total institution, see E. Goffman, *Asylums: Essays on the Social Situation of Mental Patients and Other Inmates* (New York, 1961). It might

well be asked if the prisons of the *ancien régime*—because of their incorporation in their urban fabric (with cells that faced out onto streets or courtyards, from which the detainees talked, exchanged messages, and so on among themselves, with passersby, and even with the people who lived in the adjacent houses) as well as because of the high visibility of former detainees (typical of a situation where criminality was based on a generalized notion of illegality and where large segments of the population had experienced periods of detention) and also characterized by continual communication with the outside world—should be seen as total institutions.

32. I use the terms "unprotected" or "not protected" to indicate the condition of an individual who has no social guarantees or assurances, *sans aveu*. Gutton, *La société* p. 10.

33. L. F. Soleri, "Il giornale di cose degne di memoria in Piemonte e specialmente in Torino," manuscript, Biblioteca Reale, Storia patria 230, annotation about April 7, 1717; L. Cibrario, *Storia di Torino* (Turin, 1846), p. 532

34. This program anticipated the prohibition of alms collecting, a progressive confinement of vagabonds and the expulsion of foreign vagabonds, the extension of the system of poorhouses, and the foundation of new institutions (for example, the Opera delle Partorienti and the Ospedale dei Pazzi). See A. Guevarre, *La mendicità sbandita col sovvenimento de poveri tanto nella città che ne' borghi, luoghi, e terre de' Stati di qua e di là da monti e colli di S. M. Vittorio Amedeo* (Turin, 1717). F. A. Duboin, *Raccolta per ordine di materia delle leggi, editti, manifesti, emanati negli stati di terraferma fino all'8 dicembre 1798, dai sovrani della Real casa di Savoia* (Turin, 1818–69), vol. 6, p. 267; vol. 12, pp. 280–83, 34–39, 79–92. G. Prato, *La vita economica in Piemonte a mezzo il secolo XVIII* (Turin, 1908), pp. 329–72. D. Carutti, *Storia di Vittorio Amedeo II* (Turin, 1897), p. 460. Quazza, *Le riforme*, pp. 313–19. P. Chierici and L. Palmucci, "Gli ospizi di carità in Piemonte: Appunti per una storia del fenomeno insediativo," *Storia urbana* 4 (1980): 27–57.

35. S. Cavallo, "Assistenza femminile e tutela dell'onore nella Torino del XVIII secolo," in *Annali della Fondazione Luigi Einaudi*, vol. 14 (Turin, 1980); Grendi, "Ideologia."

36. Cavallo, "Assistenza," p. 145.

37. AST, sez. 1, Materie Criminali, mazzo 13; Testimony of Lucia Giordano, April 14, 1717, Testimony of Cattarina Cuore, December 23, 1716; Testimony of Marianna Muratore, June 9, 1717, d. 4.

38. Founded in 1684, it was intended to offer a temporary refuge to women "fallen but not publicly dishonored." On these principles not being followed, see Cavallo, "Assistenza," p. 143

39. AST, sez. 1, Materie Criminali, mazzo 13, Testimony of Lucia Giordano, April 15, 1717, d. 22; Testimony of Clara Maria Brigida Ribolletta, May 3, 1717, d. 77.

40. For example, with the distribution of dowries and alms, people who were educated were explicitly selected over those who were not.

41. Ribolletta's version was confirmed by the treasurer and the Deposito's director Berlenda. AST, sez. 1, Materie Criminali, mazzo 13, Testimony of Clara Ribolletta, March 16, 1717, d. 18; mazzo 14, Testimony of the treasurer Berlenda.

42. AST, sez. 1, Materie Criminali, mazzo 13, Testimony of Clara Ribolletta, May 2, 1717, d. 76; mazzo 13, Testimony of Cattarina Cuore under torture, May 31, 1717.

43. AST, sez. 1, Materie Criminali, mazzo 12, fasc. 3, Atti criminali contro Gio. Antonio Boccalaro, Boccalaro's cross-examination, December 19, 1709; his confrontation with Boccalaro-Pern, December 20, 1709; mazzo 28, fasc. 4, Copia d'informazioni prese contro Carlo Faro, Bruno's testimony, January 12, 1726; mazzo 13, Processo contro C. Ribolletta, trial proceedings at Ivrea n. 23. C. M. Cantino, n. 26, M. D. Pavetto, n. 29, A. M. Caligaris.

44. AST, sez. 1, Materie Criminali, mazzo 13, Testimony of Clara Ribolletta, January 2, 1717, and March 17, 1717.

45. AST, sez. 1, Materie Criminali, mazzo 13, Testimony of Marianna Muratore, January 6, 1717, d. 99; mazzo 14, Testimony of Signore Francesco Domenico Berlenda, February 15, 1717.

46. On the question of confinement, see G. Assereto, "Alcuni cenni sull'assistenza pubblica genovese agli inizi dell'Ottocento," paper presented at the conference "Pauperismo."

47. Grendi, "Ideologia," and also Cissie C. Fairchilds, *Poverty and Charity in Aix-en-Provence (1640–1789)* (Baltimore, 1976).

48. AST, sez. 1, Materie Criminali, mazzo 16, fasc. 10, Atti criminali contro Francesco Gerolamo Freylino, Freylino's cross-examination, January 1718, mazzo 25, Atti criminali contro Martin Barro, Barro's cross-examination, March 6, 1724; mazzo 13, Testimony of Cattarina Cuore, March 23 and 26, 1717; mazzo 13, Testimony of Clara Ribolletta, January 1, 1717, and December 24–26, 1726; mazzo 14, Memoria del soldato di giustizia Serra, December 7, 1716.

49. Carlo Dionisotti, *Storia della magistratura piemontese* (Turin, 1881), pp. 361–70. Also relevant are the edicts of Carlo Emmanuele II (1673) and Maria Giovanna Battista (1675), in *Editi antichi e nuovi de sovrani principi della real casa di Savoia*, collected by Gio. Battista Borelli (Turin, 1681), book 4, title 9 and book 8, title 5.

50. Carlo Ginzburg, "Folklore, magia, religione," in *Storia d'Italia* (Turin, 1972), vol. 1, p. 660. Luisa Accati, "Lo spirito di fornicazione: Virtù dell'anima e virtù del corpo in Friuli tra '600 e '700," *Quaderni storici* 41 (1979): 650; English trans., "The Spirit of Fornication: Virtue of the Soul and Virtue of the Body in Friuli, 1600–1800," in *Sex and Gender in Historical Perspective*, Selections from *Quaderni Storici*, ed. E. Muir and G. Ruggiero (Baltimore, 1990), pp. 110–40.

51. Venturi, *Saggi*, p. 140.

52. AST, sez. 1, Materie Criminali, mazzo 13, Testimony of C. Cuore, December 28, 1716.

53. See Ginzburg's observations in *The Cheese and the Worms: The Cosmos of a Sixteenth-Century Miller* (Baltimore, 1980), pp. xvii–xix, about Foucault's edition of *I, Pierre Riviere, Having Slaughtered My Mother, My Sister, and My Brother . . . A Case of Parricide in the Nineteenth Century* (New York, 1975).

54. M. Perrot, "L'impossible prison," in M. Perrot, *L'impossible prison* (Paris, 1980), p. 62

55. AST, sez. 1, Materie Criminali, mazzo 12, fasc. 3, Parer sur la sentence criminelle par le Senat de Piemont le 27 janvier 1710. On the code of suffering as an integral part of punishment, see Foucault, *Discipline and Punish*, p. 37.

56. A. Dufour and F. Rabut, *Moilan prison d'Etat* (Chambery, 1879).

5 ⅋ The Florentines and Their Public Offices in the Early Fifteenth Century: Competition, Abuses of Power, and Unlawful Acts

by Andrea Zorzi

Perhaps more than any other crime, those of public officials, especially when they are seen as corruption, are subject to easy generalizations, which are derived from an anecdotal curiosity, if not from a teleological moralism.[1] There is no doubt that such crimes, as well as the moral tension and the laws intended to stop them, are physiologically part of every social and political organization that has a stable system of power and administration.

This does not mean that the crimes of public officials cannot present a specific problem, but if they are analyzed in a suitable social context, they can have a heuristic interest, especially if they are considered in a particular moment of transformation of the procedures of control and repression which reveals their social significance as a product of changed political perceptions.

This is the case, for example, of the Florentine republic in the first half of the fifteenth century when, because of the transition from a civic to a territorial orientation and because of the new bureaucratic system, the regime was looking for a new equilibrium that favored oligarchic closure and the concentration of power.[2] The distribution of offices, which was one of the most delicate issues of civil life within the regime [*reggimento*] and which was the means of expressing political identity and of directly participating in the *res publica,* was at the center of a vortex of tensions; therefore a confrontation about the honesty and integrity of public officials became one of the means

---

"I fiorentini e gli uffici pubblici nel primo Quattrocento: Concorrenza, abusi, illegalità," *Quaderni storici* 66 (1987): 725–51. Translated by Corrada Biazzo Curry.

of competition, an act that affected on several levels a large group of citizens who were qualified as officeholders. Through the activity of the new magistracy that was created with a special jurisdiction over the crimes of public officials, it is possible to discover, especially when repression vacillated, the social implications of the practice of corruption and the political discourse of a particular group of citizens. An approach of this sort allows us to reinterpret the struggle for public offices in terms other than those of institutional mechanisms for legal qualification and of the election systems. The crimes of public officials must be considered within a larger social and judicial context.

The documentation that has survived consists of a series of verdicts, which also contain mostly anonymous denunciations that had been reported to the magistrates. The particular configuration of the documents gives us the opportunity to discover the practices and behaviors that, even though they mainly refer to criminal cases, also reveal the conflicting relationships and the atmosphere of social competition in which they took place. The change of the means of control and repression produced the documentation that allows us to concentrate the sample from a relatively short period; this study does not pretend, in fact, to be more than an indication of some possible interpretations of a phenomenon that in the late communal period of Florence had other cultural and religious dimensions, which can be only alluded to in this paper.

⊰ The problem of how to face and how to stop abuses and civic corruption had persisted in the commune since the initial formation of political-judicial systems and administrative-financial organisms. Corruption had always been problematic to define because of the ambiguous distinction between governing and administrative functions and between the ruling class and the administrative class.[3] To solve this problem the commune of Florence, as well as the other Italian communes, had taken several measures: the commune issued a law against any action that could be considered contrary to the interests of the *res publica;* this law provided that public officials found guilty be permanently excluded from their offices and that they pay a large fine; sometimes such laws stipulated that culprits be subjected to humiliating corporal punishments.[4] Another measure enforced a short-term rotation system among the various offices and established an election system based on sortition, which was intended to prevent the formation of a permanent bureaucracy.[5] Finally, the commune resorted to controls on the office of syndic, which during the communal period assumed its defining characteristics.

The syndics, in fact, were established as a means of control over the financial activities and accounts of communal functionaries. More than just a guarantee of their legality and their responsibility,[6] the syndical office was extended to evaluate all the financial, administrative, and jurisdictional activities of the public officials.[7] Particularly in Florence during the fourteenth century, a highly articulated system had come into being: this system entrusted the political offices, judges, minor offices, and territorial offices to foreign judicial specialists who worked alongside citizen councils and, where necessary, Florentine bureaucrats.[8] This system, which represents a polycentric, multilayered, and inconsistent structure of control typical of the communal period, functioned reasonably well at least until the second half of the fourteenth century, when it began to show symptoms of a progressive decline of its repressive powers. This is shown in the judicial documents of the time: the few fourteenth-century statistics that have survived, in fact, show a diminution in the numbers of people charged with fraud and with other related crimes between 1352–55 and 1380–83;[9] in addition, these statistics show a low percentage of foreign communal officials who were convicted of crimes.[10] This paradoxical evidence may appear surprising at first, especially if it is considered in light of the enforcement capabilities of the regime and the continuous complaints about the decadence of public morals in contemporary literature[11]—complaints that undermine those who have celebrated the democratic legality of the commune[12]—and it undervalues the real dimensions of the phenomenon.

At the end of the fourteenth century and the beginning of the fifteenth, the office of the syndics became obsolete as a means of control for two reasons: on the one hand, the formal and public judicial procedures exposed the eventual plaintiffs to the possibility of retaliation and obligated them to pursue an accusation until the verdict was given;[13] on the other, the ideological bond, which had originated during the age of the commune and which entrusted judgments to the supposed impartiality of a foreign judge, weakened. During those years a very important transformation of the legal code was taking place. This transformation consisted of abandoning the administration of law by foreign judges and the tradition of basing it on old scholastic procedures in favor of new codes that, under the direct control of political authorities, entrusted committees of Florentine citizens with the task of administering more efficiently a kind of justice which was less bound to the rigidity of the statutes.[14] This institutional transition led gradually to supplementing traditional procedures with a new, more useful and incisive instrument of anonymous denunciations. After a few attempts to entrust the more strict enforcement of the public officials' obligations and the regulation of their conduct[15] to institutions that already existed, such as the executor of the Ordinances of Justice or the powerful Otto di Guardia, the magistracy of the Conservatori delle Leggi was finally instituted in 1429: this organism enforced public law and the laws concerning public officials' behavior during times of political discord.[16] The newest element consisted of the reliance on anonymous denunciations as the normal procedure for opening an investigation of an official under suspicion.

This procedure certainly opened up the possibility of the abuse of power, but since there were no criminal or social consequences for the anonymous accuser, it made possible the amassing of a large body of information, which was incomparably greater than what had been learned by traditional methods. This system made a real difference in the capacity to repress particular crimes and gradually deprived the syndics of authority: in fact, the syndics convicted a minuscule percentage of those accused (always less than 3 percent),[17] while the Conservatori delle Leggi from the first years of its operations sentenced more than 20 percent.[18] In the transition from the formalism of the inquisitorial procedure ex officio of the syndics to the vivacity and expressive richness of written denunciations (which were also called *tamburagioni*[19]), one can perceive a change in the quality of the prosecutions, the increased motivation for efficiency, and the compensatory functions of this particular social practice.

⁓ The creation of the Conservatori delle Leggi in February 1429 was determined by very grave political conditions. In fact, during the 1420s in an atmosphere of increasing discord, the oligarchic regime that had dominated Florentine political life since 1382 collapsed as a consequence of the almost continuous state of war, the languishing consequences of economic and financial crisis, and the deep social confusion that followed accentuated civic discords within the dominant group. Besides the progressive disunion among the political aristocracy, the business community, and the artisans, there was also a horizontal split among rival factions, which were becoming better defined and organized. This marred the political life and administration of the republic, inducing citizens to act more for their own interests and for their friends' and relatives' positions than for the public good. In order to avoid an incipient disintegration, the regime adopted in 1429 several coercive measures, attempting to reduce the sectarian tension and to reestablish civic harmony.[20] After the anachronistic episode on January 29, 1429, the members of the government publicly swore on the sacred books to abandon all sectarian feelings and to pursue only the good of the republic.[21] The institution of the Conservatori delle Leggi was created a few weeks later, mainly in order to make certain that the pact was going to be respected and to repress those citizens who held a public office and continued to prevaricate about their own personal interests in their public duty. The creation of this new institution was certainly meant to eliminate corrupt members of the regime, but in practice it gave the members of the ruling group the opportunity to settle accounts with their enemies and rivals.[22] In fact, the large number of denunciations presented to the Conservatori delle Leggi emphasized the prevailing atmosphere of defamation and discredit, of jealousies and reciprocal distrust. However, it was also true that the majority of the accused were never sentenced and that the most scandalous cases, which involved eminent figures in the regime, were undertaken and resolved in the traditional and ordinary courts.[23] There was, for example, the case of Giovanni Guicciardini, the Ten's commissioner in charge of the war with Lucca, who in 1431 was accused of making a deal with the enemy in order to provide food and supplies for the besieged; there was also the case of Donato Velluti, the standard-bearer of justice in July and August 1434, found guilty of "having sold off the right to collect fines for the commune" for a kickback of 2,350 florins. The acts of the Conservatori delle Leggi show a more general confrontation over the right to participate in the *res publica* within the group of citizens who were eligible for offices.

Many anonymous accusers addressed the Conservatori delle Leggi directly in their written denunciations, exhorting and sometimes threatening the members of the board, who belonged to the same social group as the officeholders, always warning them to keep their activities under control. "You are saints, saints in your principles. We want to tell you that the commune was in bad trouble and everyone could do whatever he wanted, but now you have created a good principle, so may God bless you for the future: it is up to you to continue." These few words, which opened one of the first *tamburagioni* addressed to the office, expressed the feelings, attitudes, and expectations common among Florentine citizens in that period. Besides the usual moral and spiritual positions of reproving immorality and invoking divine mercy, there was also a recognition of the need to change the penal approach in the face of the progressive degradation of political morals in those years. However, in the closing statement, "it is up to you to continue," one can also perceive a tone of skepticism about the concrete results of such an initiative that, even though it was innovative, was subject to future appropriations and compromises. The very same anonymous accuser exhorted the Conservatori: "[E]nforce the law ... and by providing a good example for the people who do inspections, prevent them from committing fraud. ... You are elected to a position of justice, do like the good Venetians who enforce their laws for the good of the commune and not for individual benefit."[24] This exhortation was found in the written charge against Filippo di Giovanni da Ghiacceto, accused of fraud during his inspections of soldiers when he was an officer of the army; he subsequently lost his eligibility for election to public office. The same accuser elsewhere referred to the Venetian model: "[N]ow, if it had been Filippo da Vinegia, he wouldn't be imprisoned more than once, while here he can be sentenced six times, but never receives punishment." (In 1425 Bernardino da Siena had also referred to the Venetian model, as "the way officers and rectors should behave."[25]) The anonymous accuser concluded his charge with an emphatic exhortation to the magistrates: "[Do] your duty and your job ... [or] will you abandon your city?"

Another accuser, instead, tried to flatter the Conservatori's sense of responsibility: "You know that you have been elected with diligence by the people of Florence, and you have been justly chosen from among a large number of citizens to enforce the law and especially so that your offices and the offices of other ancient and good citizens wouldn't be occupied by unworthy people"; while Filippo di Giovanni da Ghiacceto's accuser assumed an exhorting and resentful tone: "[D]on't look at the person and say he is a standard-bearer, because you must do justice to both important and unimportant people, and don't look more at the one than the other ... , because otherwise your laws and your rules will appear as a joke if they are not enforced, and this city will be worse than a den of thieves."[26] More impudent and blackmailing was the tone of the anonymous allegation against Leonardo d'Andrea di Francesco Bocchio, carpenter, who was accused of

not paying taxes and therefore of not being able to assume the consul-
ship of his guild: "And you must honor your office and not favor
[the person] who wants more power than city hall. We warn you that
we have made a record of this notification on the same day that we
notified you, so that if you do justice to the commune, you will be
honored. And, if this should not continue, we say to you that we will
protest, and if you should fail to do your job, you must give us reason
and an apology."[27] The above statements appear to be the most obvious
cases, but even among the panoply of *tamburagioni* sent to the Conservatori one finds many similar solicitations: "You must take care of
these things, because it is your duty to please everyone who asks you
for something"; "If you want honor, do justice and you will have great
honors; this will give you public fame, and if you should fail, you will
bring great shame to your office."[28] These are only a few examples.

Sometimes the addressee of this dialogue between authority and
society was a specific member of the Conservatori delle Leggi. The
anonymous accuser of Fruosino di Cece da Verrazzano, charged with
extortion and fraud while he was the governor of Anghiari, for example, complained about the presence among the ten officers of Rinaldo
di Maso degli Albizzi, one of the most important leaders of the regime:
"[T]he true Messer Rinaldo will do exactly like his father in 1383,
who wanted to seek revenge on all his enemies, and Messer Rinaldo
will do the same thing in this office." The *tamburagione* was in effect
annulled with the justification that it had been written "in order to
injure and defame the said Fruosino."[29] However, such charges did
not appear only in political cases or in cases involving important figures
of the regime, as is revealed by the skepticism of Bernardo del Benino
di Guccio's plaintiff, who concluded his accusation stating "[What I
have said is] true, if you want to believe it, but I have my doubts that
you will because among you there is someone who is in the same
guild, and to your shame he will not let you do justice."[30]

⁊ The access to public office, in fact, was becoming the object of
harder and more intense competition: trying to obtain an office without
the proper qualifications by relying on the ineffectiveness of procedures of verification and regulation must have become a common
practice in the decades before the institution of the Conservatori delle
Leggi. One cannot otherwise explain the large number of lawsuits
received by the new magistracy which complained about the lack of
one or more of the necessary requirements among citizens who had

been elected to public office: minimum age, legitimate birth, regular payment of taxes, the absence of charges pending for fraud, or, if nothing else, the possession of a specific dispensation from such prohibitions granted by the councils.[31] The plausibility of this type of accusation was often transformed into a way of discrediting someone or a form of social and political competition, even though statistics indicate that the number of people punished for this type of violation was very small, perhaps as a consequence, as we shall see, of the introduction of a system of age declaration.[32]

Not everyone, however, was lucky enough to hide his lack of qualifications. A personal enemy of Antonio di Piero Migliorotti, for example, brought to light his illegitimate birth, which had taken place before his parents were married, in order to prevent him from taking up the office of the Sei della Mercanzia to which he had been named: "[C]heck the marriage license and you'll see if he was born before or after; then you'll see that he is a bastard." Notwithstanding formal attestations and legal opinions, and having declared that the "hated" law instituted by the Conservatori delle Leggi, "which corrected common law, ought to be seen as having corrected common law as little as possible," Antonio was excluded from his office and forced to pay a five-hundred-lire fine because, according to the way the Conservatori interpreted the Florentine legislation, "the subsequent marriage was not sufficient" to legitimate the son. Speaking against Bernardo di Filippo Salviati, a rival, who "used to spend a lot of time at his house," reminded the Conservatori, "[H]is mother was pregnant with him in 1400 and then he was born . . . , and I can tell this for sure because I was there when his mother gave birth." Further investigation verified that Bernardo had actually been born in 1399, "when those who were popularly called the Bianchi came through [Florence]," so that when he accepted the office of the Otto di Guardia in 1428, he should not have done so because he was only twenty-nine years old. Taddeo di Ser Gabriello Guidi, who in 1432 had been elected consul of the guild of physicians and apothecaries, was charged by the court of the Mercanzia with "falsidionem testium" that cost him the loss of his office after many years in addition to a twenty-five-lire fine. Paolo Agostino di Paolo, consul of the bakers' guild, besides being accused of not paying taxes, was also accused of being an illegitimate child: "[H]e was at his mother's wedding." His accusers wanted to emphasize the fact that he belonged to a rival faction: "and he is that charlatan who has said bad things about Nicholo da Uzano and about us; he is the one who is always with Davanzati, a slanderer of all of us ... , and he said that the Conservatori delle Leggi was ruining Florence and that it would meet only twice, after which it would disappear."[33] On the other hand, other officers were able to justify the irregularity of their position using some legal points made possible by the contradictions and legal inaccuracies that characterized public law in that period. When Giovanni di Bartolomeo di Boldro, for example, was charged with illegitimate birth, he argued that the 1404 law, which disallowed bastards access to public office, did not explicitly mention the one to which he was elected (the officers of the tower); therefore he obtained an annulment of the charge. The Pistoiese notary Antonio Salvetti, who had not paid Florentine taxes, declared the legality of his office as an ambassador from Florence to the duchy of Milan, showing that such an office "nullatenus officium censetur," which therefore meant that the office could be entrusted to non-Florentines.[34]

The atmosphere of strong competition, which was revealed either by these illegal practices or by the usual tone of the charges, was made possible by the peculiar conditions of these years. On the one hand, since the last decades of the fourteenth century, the process of consolidating the administrative structure of the commune favored the creation of several new offices, especially territorial ones, which were doubled owing to the hegemonic expansion of Florence into a large surrounding area.[35] On the other hand, this multiplication of offices had not been followed by more open access to offices; instead, the contemporary process of oligarchic closure had restricted access to both political and administrative offices, increasing the requirements for eligibility to office and reforming the rolls from which names were drawn. These measures increasingly limited the representation of artisans in offices.[36] With the confluence of these phenomena, a deep transformation of the social order was produced which restructured the distribution of the wealth, exacerbated social competition, and encouraged new political conflicts.[37] In the struggle for the distribution of offices one perceives the competition for the honors and income that offices gave. This is not the place to discuss why holding a public office was so important for Florentines;[38] it is sufficient to say that the attempt to profit corruptly from a public office and the fervent prosecution of accusations of that sort of behavior reveal more about the preservation of a political identity and of a social privilege than the search for material gain.

There was an intense competition for minor and low- or nonpaying offices, just for the pleasure of sitting in an office, even if for a short period of time: the internal rivalry among the artisan guilds for the office of consul, for example, was very strong. Apart from a few episodes (like the case of Ser Iacopo di Giovanni di Andreozzo, who was accused of not having reached the required age of thirty in order to be a consul in the guild of judges and notaries),[39] we have the documentation of disputes and arguments within the guilds of black-smiths, carpenters, bakers, butchers, and locksmiths. The accusations were always the usual stereotypical ones about age, illegitimate birth, and tax evasion, only rarely colorful, as in the case of the baker Piero di Leonardo, accused of being a bastard "as he appear[ed] from the shape of his body," or the case of the "painter" Ambrogio di Monna Bandina, who was accused of being found "on a bench and nobody ever knew who his parents were, and Monna Bandina, who sold candles in Orto San Michele, found him and raised him as her own son." There was the case of Pazino, "who [was] called Niccholo," a clothworker, accused of being the son of "Ser Cristofano, who was a priest in the Church of San Piero in Quaracchi."[40] In the majority of cases the substance of these charges was contradicted by various witnesses and several documents, such as private diaries or fiscal records, revealing them to be nothing other than the fruit of anonymous slander. This was sometimes revealed by the Conservatori delle Leggi itself, as in the case of the seventy-five-year-old farrier Bernaba di Maso, who was accused of illegitimate birth and also of "practicing public sodomy . . . in spite of his wife, and this [was] well known by all the city of Florence." This man, however, was recognized to be the victim of an attempt to discredit him, "that the said denunciation was made in order to strengthen the discord and enmity that exist[ed] between the artisans of the guild and Bernaba."[41]

Besides the internal guild disputes, there were also manifestations of strong competition for most of the civic offices: here rivalry was expressed on the level of a personal relationship between acquaintances and called into question the ties of kinship, neighborliness, and some-times the system of alliance. Political antagonism is more evident in the case of Gherardo Canigiani, who brought a number of accusations against those who failed to meet the age requirements [for office] when he was elected to the Otto di Guardia and was reputed to be a member of "the faction that paid frequent visits to the Medici palace." There was also Messer Giuliano di Niccolò Davanzati, who was elected to the office of captain of Pisa and belonged to the Medici faction;

accusations were made against Niccolò di Biagio Degli Agli, officer of the monasteries, because his ancestors, according to the accuser, "used to keep glue in the house"; charges were also made against Ser Nicola di Mangieri di Castel San Giovanni, notary of the Dieci della Libertà, whose father "was admonished because he was a leader of the Ghibellines and persecutor of the Guelfs."[42] If these cases reveal a certain atmosphere of political factions, from an even larger variety of accusations emerge day-to-day rivalries with more narrow social features. Martino Schiavo, for example, was accused of holding two relatively modest offices at the same time, the office of bell ringer for the podestà and the office of messenger for the Bigallo, and of behaving "like a ruffian . . . so that he was very wealthy, since he had those jobs for a long time."[43] The anonymous accusations did not always hide the context of the relationships, the frequency of interactions, and the forms of sociability in which ties of friendship as well as persistent reciprocal hatreds could be found. We have already mentioned the case of Bernardo di Filippo Salviati, who was the victim of a denounce-ment by a person who stated that he had been present at Bernardo's birth. There was also the case of Cristofano di Antonio di Piero Guidi, consul of the leatherworker's guild, whose accuser called upon the neighbors to testify to the fact that his parents had gotten married five years after his birth—"they say that they saw him bringing apples to his mother when his father married her"—and the case of Andrea di Bonsi, who was accused of not paying taxes but who was helped by neighbors who testified in his favor.[44] In the same way, the accuser of Michele di Benvenuto, who was a swordmaker and consul of his guild, based the accusation of bastardy upon "what he had heard from the neighbors." The doubtful paternity of "Bartolomeo, son of Meo di Mona Chiappina, called Bartolomeo di Piero, armorer," was traced back to the gossip and rumors of the neighborhood. (The ambiguity of Bartolomeo's identity can be seen in the confusion about his proper name.) Again, the accuser of Ser Lorenzo Franceschi, notary of the Monte, referred to rumors from the street and was also trying to provoke resentment in the Conservatori delle Leggi by reporting, "[H]e has said in public that you are worthless men, saying that you are that thing found below the waist." Giovanni di Iacopo de' Bartolelli's accuser referred to gossip and rumors that he had many times held the office of standard-bearer of the militia without having reached the minimum legal age: "[H]e bragged about it everywhere he went, and . . . even his uncle confirmed it as well as other people who said that he isn't old enough; in fact, you can check this out in his father's diary; therefore send for his father's diary, and you will discover his true age."[45]

The accusations that questioned people's age allow us to evaluate the spreading practice of keeping a record in the so-called memory books of the main events in the lives of the family members and, at the same time, the legal and probative value that such private *ricordanze* assumed for public occasions, such as the qualification for a particular office: the annotations of the children's dates of birth, as well as the annotations of the dates when they were put out to nurse, were very useful to many citizens in countering slanderous accusations of not having reached the required age to accept office. For example, in May 1429, Giovanni di Miniato, leatherworker, presented his father's "long notebook" in which "there appeared on the first folio how this Giovanni was born on June 21, 1403," and on folio 62 it stated that on December 16 of the same year he was put out to nurse "to be breast-fed by Fie, wife of Paolo di Ponte in Grieve," showing in such a way that he had already turned 25, which was the necessary minimum age to hold office in Arezzo.[46] Like him, several other citizens brought their family *ricordanza* to the Conservatori delle Leggi to clarify their position. To resolve the question of age once and forever, the Conservatori delle Leggi was ordered in the summer of 1429 first to draw up for each quarter a register with the names of all minor citizens with an exact indication of their date of birth and then, since people were very reluctant to fill out a census, gather and approve the statements of age of all citizens who were "seen" by the officials.[47] Besides the registry office that, after considerable disputation, had been instituted two years after the inauguration of the *catasto*, there was now a sort of political registry office, the result of an additional stage in the long process of the statistical affirmation of the principle of organization in public affairs. However, the problems related to the exact determination of age were not completely solved, as is shown by the precision to which citizens were subjected. The legal problems concerning the exact determination of age did not disappear because most people only had an approximate knowledge of their own age,[48] as is shown by the case of Silvestro di Leonardo Pucci, who, although from his family diary he appeared to be thirty years old when elected consul of the wine merchants' guild, was convicted because in the official books approving claims of age redacted in 1429 he was marked down as younger and was therefore ineligible according to the strict terms of the law. It was of no use for him to argue that although the obligatory statement given to the Conservatori delle Leggi showed that "he would be younger than thirty, it was done erroneously and against the truth." However, after a few years, it was that book "in which was written the age of all Florentine citizens" which acquitted Giovanni di Iacopo Bartolelli from a similar accusation.[49]

Another component of office holding for which citizens fought strenuously was the profits and material benefits that many offices guaranteed. The strong ambiguities that characterized the so-called crime of fraud went back to this material conception of the *res publica*. First of all, the citizen approached his office with a certain directness: this directness implied that the honors and profits an office offered could help to redistribute public wealth and political power. Since a sense of public interest had not yet developed and a bureaucratic class was still being formed, which would eventually consolidate itself in part through corruption,[50] a detached conception of the different levels of government persisted. The ambiguous character of corruption, therefore, appears less obscure if we consider corruption as the reification of a conception of authority typical of a mercantile society. This relationship persisted through either formal and moral denial or tacit acceptance. This palpable ambiguity can be seen in the very education of the dominant class, as the precepts penned in the middle of the fourteenth century by Paolo di Messer Pace da Certaldo show: "Keep in mind," he warned his son, "[that] when you have to make a judgment, you must be just and honest; never forget this, neither for money, nor love, nor fear, nor kinship, nor friendship, nor factional loyalty"; later, after telling his son "not to accept any present ... sent by the participants," his advice turned on itself: "On the other hand, I tell you that, if you need the friendship of some lord or provincial rector, you can gain much from giving them presents."[51]

Therefore, one can understand how, as far as the jurisdictional confrontation about the crime of fraud is concerned, there was an ambiguous mixing of the roles of citizen, judge, and potentially judged; one can also better understand the substantial caution, the moderateness of the penalties, which always consisted of fines, the abbreviation of some procedures, and the reduction of some sentences which characterized the activity of the Conservatori delle Leggi. The rotation of jobs, which caused a fundamental ambiguity in the relationship between citizens and officials, could in fact produce at some future date an exchange of roles in the same type of judicial proceeding. The dense interrelations that existed among individuals who belonged to the same group, which we have already discussed in their most conflicted aspects, clearly emphasize the intimately political character of these crimes.

Citizens did not long as much for those offices that managed money, such as the *camarlingati,* for example, because they were highly regulated and subject to more systematic accounting procedures, as they did for those offices, such as those in the subject territories, which might offer the opportunity to add extra remuneration to the official salary. Iacopo Salviati, for example, noted in his diary all the profits that he earned from each territorial appointment he had filled: as a governor of Valdinievole in 1401, "[he] earned about 250 florins," and as podestà of Montepulciano the year before, he drew 100 scudi profit.[52] A territorial rector, in fact, was guaranteed in addition to his regular salary a percentage of a whole series of official imposts: on the collection of fines and taxes, on arrests, on attachments of collateral, and on confiscations; in addition, his notary could ask for compensation for each copy of a document he was asked to issue, as well as for the annulment of a sentence on an official register. The acuteness of the economic crisis Florence was suffering in these decades made these offices more desirable, even indispensable for some heads of families who belonged to ancient lineages in growing and unexpected financial difficulty.[53] In the same period, there were innumerable requests to the Signoria from common citizens for immediate employment in a territorial office without waiting for the regular sortition so that they could support their families: so the linen draper Iacopo di Zenobi di Cenni complained about being "burdened by a large family, [and] he did not see any way that, by his own efforts, he could support them with his small earnings," while Giuliano di Francesco di Andrea feared "the weight of having to beg . . . as he [was] a pauper and without any work . . . with a poor and unemployed family of large number."[54] We must therefore take into account this substratum of persons if we want to understand how conditions reached the point that citizens were willing to go beyond the limits of the law and take advantage of the possibilities offered by the abuse of power and the violation of duty in order to obtain additional compensation.

The most common practice was either to demand more money than was legitimate for official services or to ask for payment even for services that did not require one: the most frequent accusation was "taking a large amount of money in the name of right of office." This behavior was typical of city officials, such as Bernardo di Ser Cambio Salviati, *provveditore* of the Regolatori della Camera. He was accused "of taking money" for a service and "of having done the same to more than a hundred people." However, the majority of the accusations were made against the territorial officials, especially the rectors and their notaries. Discontent and protests rose against the "shearing" of the subjects of the republic by the Florentine representatives from the most peripheral areas such as Premilcuore in the Bolognese Apennines, where Ser Mariotto di Piero da Bucine, the notary of the podestà of Portico, was very powerful, to the areas close to Florence, such as the Lega del Galluzzo, controlled by Ser Bartolomeo di Antonio da Volterra,[55] the podestà's notary. Typical of some of these representatives was Ser Piero di Antonio di Pratovecchio, the notary of the captain of Campiglia, who tried to justify this procedure by declaring that he had accepted eight *grossi* "for certain damages . . . which were given to him for his predecessor who normally collected them." In contrast, others were like Ser Iacopo di Ser Filippo da Colle, notary of the podestà of Monte San Savino, Tuccio di Manetto Scambrilla, who tried to blame his superior for the consequences of his actions, confessing that he had accepted "illegally from many people certain quantities of money for briefs and documents . . . but that all the said money had gone to Lord Tucci."[56] It was very easy to move from extortion to violent intimidation in abusing a position of power, as Bernardino da Siena recalled in his Lenten sermons of 1425, which had left a deep impression in the uncertain moral climate among the Florentines in those years. He described the behavior of corrupt functionaries as a way of obtaining or refusing to do their job without receiving something in return.[57] The power of arrest was one of the most widely used coercive methods for extortion: Francesco di Rinaldo Gianfigliazzi, podestà of Ripafratta, for example, was sentenced for sequestering a goat, a horse, and a team of oxen which were worth thirty florins and belonged to Chiaro di Giovanni di Montespertoli, who had been arrested. Once Chiaro di Giovanni was liberated, the podestà of Ripafratta permitted him to redeem only the oxen for eighteen florins. Guido di Beste Magalotti, podestà of Modigliana, confiscated a hat, a belt, a cuirass, and two silver cups from Antonello da Urbino, taken in lieu of additional days in prison.[58]

There were numerous accusations of corruption: Antonio di Lorenzo Baronci, podestà of Prato, was accused of receiving from Vincio da Vinci "capons, turtledoves and quails, and a sack of peaches because Vincio had a case pending in the podestà's court"; in the same way, Cresci di Lorenzo di Cresci, podestà of Pistoia, while investigating Nanni di Simone because he had slaughtered some meat in forbidden places, "didn't want to see anything because Nanni di Simone had given him a wild pig he had killed"; the same Cresci "got lots of cheese" from some farmers to whom he had granted the license to use the pasture in the three-mile zone surrounding the city walls; even Iacopo di Piero Ottavanti, podestà of Castelfranco di Sopra, got forty pounds of cheese, "because he allowed some oil that was being sold illegally to get by."[59] The practice that was thrown in the face of Fruosino di Cece da Verrazzano, governor of Anghiari, was "of receiving lots of presents and not attending to business." This practice was very common among other officials, and it consisted in the collection not only of money but also of goods, especially food, such as fruit, fish, game, poultry, oil, wood, and hay.[60] The material profits that could derive from the authority of an office were so tangible that Piero di Manetto Scambrilla decided to have his wedding celebration while he was podestà of Castel Focognano, taking his wife and his relatives there and inviting the communes of the *podesteria,* which inevitably "gave him so many gifts that he got a lot worse in his greed." Doffo Spini, *vicario* of San Miniato, instead "married off one of his daughters while there and invited many men and women of San Miniato to the wedding celebration, and in order to have a rich banquet ..., he requested that all the communes of the area ... go hunting so that the *vicario* would have lots of game."[61]

Sometimes the exploitation of a position of power, which functioned through the fear of authority, was transformed into real coercion: Piero di Niccolò Gherardini, podestà of San Gimignano, for example, was accused of having taken "wood from his subjects violently and without payment." Bernardo Ciacchi, captain of Campiglia, received as a gift [*ex dono*] wild boars, capons, cheese, and forty pounds of linen cloth; in addition, "he several times ordered the men of Castagnieto ... to go hunting for him, without giving them bread or wine or anything, making them lose work time ... and finally he also ordered them many times to hunt wild pigs, and he did similar things to all the other communes in order to send five pigs to Florence, and salted more than 2,000 pounds of meat at Guardistallo"; and while in Guardistallo he claimed rights to free room and board: "[H]e stayed there all the time and bought neither bread nor wine nor oil nor salt;

in addition, every evening and every morning he sent his messenger now to this house, then to that, to get what he needed." Again, Amerigo di Niccolò Cavicciuoli, podestà of Montecatini, harrassed Monna Maria, Giovanni d'Ugolino di Montecatini's wife, confiscating forty-four pounds of salted meat and ten pounds of sausage, a pot, and "a nearly new blue jacket" that belonged to her, and at the end of his office did not even pay for the baking of his bread, and "he made fun of her without reason and justice." Ser Andrea di Ser Guido, a knight, friend of the captain of Livorno, was sentenced to return a pair of boots, a purse, several baking pans, dishes, majolica bowls, and an "ivory statue of Our Lady" which "he took, abusing of his power, ... when he went to write some things in the house of the teacher Domenicho da Serezana."[62]

In general the complaints about territorial officials sent to the Conservatori delle Leggi were rarely about individual incidents, but rather they constituted a proper list of problems created for the community by the mischief and abuses performed by the rectors and their assistants.[63] From the accusations made directly by subjects in the territory, one can deduce the history of the relationship between the central power and the subject community in order to evaluate the subordinate communities' attitudes toward the representatives of the dominating class and to reconstruct the image that these officials projected in the exercise of their functions. We have already seen how extortion of money or goods from people was typical of corrupt officials; in fact, the constant complaint against the notary or the podestà who extorted "lots of money and who receive[d] and [took] many different rewards and gifts" was that he was a "greedy wolf who haul[ed] away possessions and people."[64] Thus, the allegory of the rapacious and corrupt governor spontaneously inspired animal metaphors. Bernardino referred to the bad governors who [were] similar to "the locusts ... that [did] not leave a blade of grass alive, that is, nothing under their rule survive[d]."[65] The word play on *rector* and *raptor* was also very common.[66] If through the Conservatori delle Leggi Florence tried to strengthen its image as a dominating power that was willing to listen to the subjects' resentments, it is also true that the peasants, even if "they talked about how the citizens of Florence [robbed them]," sometimes explicitly expressed the powerless sense of their resentment. This was the case of the communities of Val d'Ambra and Montaio, which discussed the ways they corrupted Messer Giovanni Davanzati, *vicario* of Valdarno Superiore, in order to avoid having to contribute their own men to the mustering of crossbowmen for the Dieci di Balìa. The accusation against Amerigo Cavicciuli, podestà of Montecatini, said that "extortion [was] common, but the poor peasants [were] shy, and they [didn't] want to complain." Other accusations pointed out how Michele di Alessandro Arrigucci, podestà of Terranuova, "was able to operate so well ... that many people [did] not dare to tell the truth about him for allurements or for fear, because it [was] certain that there ha[d] never been in Terranuova a thief worst than him."[67] Thus, subjects refused to testify about very plausible accusations. There were different reasons for this reluctance: either because they lived too far away, or because they did not want to go through long and expensive procedures, or simply because they were used to the abuses of the powerful. In addition, the subjects' resentment was directed toward a single corrupt official without calling into question the entire Florentine administrative system. In other words, since criminal behavior was personalized, the state did not exist as a superior entity that was detached from the individual exercise of official functions.

Besides the cases involving extortion of private citizens, there was also the common practice of embezzling public property. Less numerous were cases of peculation of the public treasury. However, the posting of bond money and the civic audits of the books entrusted to specific organizations influenced the honesty of those officials who handled money.[68] Therefore, it is understandable why those few cases involving large thefts of public funds, such as the episode of Donato Velluti to which we referred in the beginning, were tried by the ordinary judicial bodies; in addition, those few cases that were sent to the Conservatori delle Leggi often revealed themselves to be only slander, such as the groundless accusation brought against Domenico di Francesco dei Sapiti, *provveditore* of the Camera del Comune, for embezzling 934 florins he had been sent to pay the troops in the field in the war against Lucca.[69] The most common practice involved the position of commissioner, an official with the extraordinary functions of a locum tenens in the military and diplomatic sector who had delicate and important duties, especially during wartime.[70] These duties could be very remunerative. One of the most common practices of war was the pillage of enemy territory, but according to a law issued in 1430, all Florentine officials who confiscated or received war booty during the war against Lucca had to turn it over to the Conservatori delle

Leggi, which was supposed to sell it at auction to add to the city's coffers.[71] Nevertheless, in practice, war booty went to those individuals capable of collecting it.

Representing the Dieci di Balìa in the field, these plenipotentiary commissioners functioned as the central command entrusted with the direction of the war and could dispose of booty as they saw fit. Thus, although many of them properly respected their duties, others diverted booty from its legal destination: Messer Bartolomeo di Giovanni Orlandini, for example, "sent several teams of looted oxen" to his Monterappoli farms instead of to Florence; Ser Iacopo Ricciardini sent another team "to his sister Monna Pellegrina ... to the house at Borgho a Buggiano"; Francesco di Rinaldo Gianfigliazzi, who, as we have seen, had extorted cattle when he was podestà in Ripafratta, added numerous head to his herds at Giogoli and San Casciano the following year by taking advantage of his term as commissioner in Valdelsa.[72] The pillage from fortresses and castles could be even more conspicuous, as was well realized by Taddeo di Giovanni di Masino Dell'Antella, commissioner in Garfagnana who managed to take possession of weapons, cuirasses, hardware, cattle, tablecloths, bolts of cloth, clothing, and even a feather bed, all of which were worth more than 100 florins and 150 silver *grossi*. In the same way, from the fortress of Castiglione in the countryside around Lucca, Antonio di Ser Tommaso Masi, after distributing to his soldiers 150 *sarcinas* of wine and large amounts of cloth and clothing, hauled away on the backs of oxen and mules seven sheets, two pots, two women's robes, ten sacks of wheat, and various iron goods. All the loot was worth about 150 florins.[73] Sometimes even Florentines had to suffer the commissioners' arbitrary expropriations. Two cloth merchants, Andrea di Giuliano Borghi and Teri di Lorenzo, saw some soldiers led by Antonio di Vieri Altoviti, commissioner in Valdinievole, take away 194 pairs of soldiers' stockings that they had temporarily left with the podestà of Borgo in Buggiano. The two merchants' comment on the episode was very bitter, since the commissioners "should [have been] sent to conquer the territory of Lucca and to defend the Florentine lands and not to steal the possessions of their own citizens."[74] Even the rectors of the areas that bordered the territory of Lucca profited from the pillaging. One of these men was Andrea di Niccolò de' Giugni, *vicario* of Pescia, who arrested the pillagers who came from the war zones and confiscated "all the things that had been stolen," that is, "oxen and other cattle, feather beds and other cloths." One of his assistants, Biagio di Pazzino da Montale, saw "on more than one occasion such things being carried out of Andrea's house and leaving Pescia." In the same way, the captains of Barga, Pisa, and Pistoia and the podestàs of Palaia and Ripafratta took possession of cattle, wine, bolts of cloth, iron goods, sheets, and weapons that came from the pillage of the territory of Lucca.[75]

❧ The picture that has emerged from this study creates a social portrait that, even though it has colorful characteristics, represents in its daily repetition a vision of normal life. In general, competition occurred especially for the secondary offices, which offered some remuneration, while the struggle for political survival was limited to guild offices. Monetary profits were modest, while what interested most people were goods, such as cattle and foodstuffs, wood, cloth and clothing, dishes, pots and pans, and iron goods. In short, they were all goods that certainly could not change the quality of life but which could raise its level for a time. Daily life during this period, in fact, suffered from a permanent state of economic crisis which especially affected, as we have seen, both the middle classes and members of old aristocratic families. The abuse of power which was practiced by civic officials was therefore related to the needs of society. The creation of the Conservatori delle Leggi represented a change in the repressive powers of the regime, but, in fact, these criminal practices were not actually repressed by the stricter legal procedures but were regulated as practices recognized to be inherent to the political and administrative system. By using a specific judicial institution, which also offered a fiscal advantage for the regime, since the sentences were limited to fines, authorities were able to control the dynamics of public corruption, singling out its real dimensions with more precision than had the previous judicial procedures. This was part of a more general and institutional process that had a moralistic purpose, involving in the first decades of the fifteenth century other criminal practices, such as manifestations of deviant sexuality, violations of monastic rules, overconsumption of luxury goods, and gambling. This last criminal practice was assigned to the jurisdiction of the Conservatori delle Leggi, perhaps because of the relationship between money and morals. In conclusion, this process began that complex pattern of discipline and repression which characterized legal procedures during the oligarchic regime of the Medici in the fifteenth century.[76]

Notes

1. Even the most recent work on the subject is not exempt from these interpretive schemes. See J. T. Noonan, Jr., *Bribes* (New York, 1984). For a historiographic analysis of these problems, see J. C. Waquet, *Corruption: Ethics and Power in Florence, 1600–1770*, trans. Linda McCall (University Park, Pa., 1992), pp. 1–18.

2. For an extensive bibliography of the period, which emphasizes the most recent studies, see G. A. Brucker, *The Civic World of Early Renaissance Florence* (Princeton, 1977).

3. On this problem, see A. I. Pini, "Dal comune città–stato al Comune ente amministrativo," in *Storia d'Italia*, ed. G. Galasso, vol. 4 (Turin, 1981), pp. 525–58.

4. See the analysis of the legislation by U. Dorini, *Il diritto penale e la delinquenza in Firenze nel sec. XIV* (Lucca, 1923), pp. 97–109.

5. For a detailed description of this system, see G. Guidi, *Il governo della città–repubblica di Firenze del primo Quattrocento* (Florence, 1981), vol. 1, pp. 99–355.

6. Historiography has traditionally emphasized the modern and democratic character of the city government during the age of communes, considering it as a means of reinforcing the principle of legality. See U. Nicolini, *Il principio di legalità nelle democrazie italiane* (Padua, 1955), pp. 130–48.

7. See the up-to-date contribution of V. Crescenzi, "Il sindacato degli ufficiali nei comuni medievali italiani," in *L'educazione giuridica*, vol.4: *Il pubblico funzionario: Modelli storici comparativi* (Perugia, 1981), tomo 1, pp. 383–529.

8. See G. Masi, "Il sindacato delle magistrature comunali nel secolo XIV (con speciale riferimento a Firenze)," *Rivista italiana per le scienze giuridiche*, n.s., 5 (1930); L. Martines, *Lawyers and Statecraft in Renaissance Florence* (Princeton, 1968), pp. 143–45; and Guidi, *Il governo della città-repubblica*, vol. 2, pp. 337–41.

9. Dorini, *Il diritto penale*, p. 106.

10. Masi, *Il sindacato*, p. 25; see also the statistics quoted in note 17.

11. On this subject, see L. Chiappelli, "L'amministrazione della giustizia in Firenze durante gli ultimi secoli del medioevo ... secondo le testimonianze degli antichi scrittori," *Archivio storico italiano*, ser. 4 (1885): 35–54 and 180–200.

12. These have been explained as "extrajudicial formations," "spontaneous compliances," and "temporary political opportunities." See Masi, *Il sindacato*, pp. 25–26, and Nicolini, *Il principio di legalità*, pp. 144–45.

13. Recognition of the problem created by threats and legal bonds can be found in the statutes of 1415, which attempted to solve the problem by allowing the private accuser to withdraw from the procedure. See *Statuta Populi et Communis Florentiae ... anno MCCCCXV*, 9 (Fribourg, *sic* Florence, 1777–81), statute no. 1, rubric 62, in vol. 1, pp. 72–75.

14. On this transformation, see Martines, *Lawyers and Statecraft*, pp. 119–69 and 387–404; M. B. Becker, "Changing Patterns of Violence and Justice in Fourteenth- and Fifteenth-Century Florence," *Comparative Studies in Society and History* 18 (1976): 281–96; S. K. Cohn, Jr., "Criminality and the State in Renaissance Florence, 1344–1466," *Journal of Social History* 14 (1981): 211–33; A. Zorzi, "Aspetti e problemi dell'amministrazione della giustizia penale nella Repubblica fiorentina," *Archivio storico italiano* 145 (1987): 391–453, 527–78.

15. See Archivio di Stato, Florence (omitted in archival citations hereafter), *Provvisioni, registri* [hereafter PR], 105, fols. 236r–237v, December 12, 1415, and PR, 106, fols. 164v–165v, October 23, 1416; and PR, 110, fols. 97r–99r, September 20, 1420, and PR, 111, fols. 71r–72r, July 8, 1421.

16. PR, 120, fols. 7v–11r, February 11, 1428 [Florentine style]/29.

17. One case out of 55 between 1400 and 1401, 5 out of 176 in 1433–35, 0 out of 88 in 1439, 0 out of 91 in 1476, 0 out of 84 in 1478. For the archival references to the sources, see my article cited in n. 14 above.

18. I discovered 45 examples of condemnations for abuses and fraud out of 195 cases between 1429 and 1434, the period in which I concentrated my analysis of the Conservatori delle Leggi. The sentences can be found in the series *Condanne proferite dagli Ufiziali intrinseci* from the collection *Giudice degli appelli* [hereafter GA], nos. 75, 77, and 78.

19. On the subject, see Dorini, *Il diritto penale*, pp. 230–32; Guidi, *Il governo della città-repubblica*, vol. 1, pp. 129–30; see also *Dizionario del linguaggio italiano storico e amministrativo*, ed. G. Rezasco (Florence, 1881), pp. 1162–63. The denunciation boxes of the Conservatori delle Leggi, where written charges could be deposited, were located in the churches of S. Maria del Fiore and S. Pietro Scheraggio. See *Miscellanea repubblicana* [hereafter MR], 117, fol. 24r, fragment of the copy notebook of the denunciations delivered to the office from August to November 1429.

20. On the events of these years, see Brucker's synthesis, *Civic World*, chaps. 7 and 8, and D. Kent, *The Rise of the Medici: Faction in Florence, 1426–1434* (Oxford, 1978). On the measures of 1429, see also *Commissioni di Rinaldo degli Albizzi*, ed. C. Guasti (Florence, 1973), vol. 3, pp. 163–72, commissions 51 and 52.

21. The text of the oath, with the names of the people who took it, is found in *Consulte e pratiche*, 48, fols. 54v–60v. The population had not used such a symbolic measure for about a century and a half.

22. This has been pointed out by Kent, *Rise of the Medici*, pp. 200–201 and 244–45. (Kent gives a list of officials involved), and by Brucker, *Civic World*, pp. 560–62.

23. For Guicciardini's case, see M. Antonelli Moriani, *Giovanni Guicciardini ed un processo politico del 1431* (Florence, 1954); for Velluti's case, see G. Cavalcanti, *Istorie fiorentine*, ed. G. Di Pino (Milan, 1944), pp. 299–300 (X, IV), and *Esecutore degli ordinamenti di giustizia*, 2257, fols. 17v–20r, September 1434, for the civic sentence.

24. GA, 75, fol. 304r–v, March 7, 1428–29.

25. "The Venetians, to their glory, do not do this, and they have a better reputation. In fact, if a vicar in their lands received a gift, he is ruined and dismissed from his office": San Bernardino da Siena, *Le prediche volgari*, ed. C. Cannarozzi (Florence, 1934) vol. 5, p. 15. On the origins of the "Myth of Venice" in the later Middle Ages, see G. Fasoli, "Nascita di un mito (il mito di Venezia nella storiografia)," in *Studi storici in onore di Gioacchino Volpe* (Florence, 1958), vol. 1, pp. 445–79, and F. Gaeta, "Alcune considerazioni sul mito di Venezia," *Bibilothèque d'humanisme et renaissance* 23 (1961): 58–75.

26. See MR, 117, fol. 29r, August 30, 1429, and GA 77, fol. 288r, April 5, 1431.

27. GA, 77, fol. 257r, March 12, 1430/31.

28. GA, 75, fol. 341r and fol. 408r.

29. GA, 75, fol. 467r–v, October 1429; another case of a direct charge, ibid., fol. 441v, September 20, 1429.

30. GA, 77, fol. 193r, November 13, 1430.

31. These are the main requirements of the founding legislation of the Conservatori delle Leggi: see PR, 120, fols. 7v–11r, February 11, 1428/29.

32. Only five out of ninety eight figure in the sample of 1429–34.

33. For the above-mentioned cases, see, respectively, GA, 75, fols. 306r–307r, April 6, 1429, fols. 341R–342v, May 10, 1429; GA, 78, fols. 401v–402r, June 16, 1432; and GA, 77, fols. 195r–196v, November 15, 1430.

34. See GA, 75, fol. 408r, August 22, 1429, and fol. 468r–v, October 12, 1429.

35. There has been no attempt to take a census of either internal or territorial

offices. For an initial approximation, see Guidi, *Il governo della città-repubblica;* Martines, *Lawyers and Statecraft,* pp. 220–44; and G. Chittolini, "Ricerche sull'ordinamento territoriale del domino fiorentino agli inizi del secolo XV," in his *La formazione dello stato regionale e le istituzioni del contado: Secoli XIV and XV* (Turin, 1979), pp. 292–352.

36. On these aspects, see A. Molho, "Politics and the Ruling Class in Early Renaissance Florence," *Nuova rivista storica* 52 (1968): 401–20; J. Kirshner, "Paolo di Castro on 'Cives ex Privilegio': A Controversy over the Legal Qualifications for Public Office in Early Fifteenth-Century Florence," in *Renaissance Studies in Honor of Hans Baron,* ed. A. Molho and J. Tedeschi (Florence, 1971), pp. 227–64; D. Kent, "The Florentine Reggimento in the Fifteenth Century," *Renaissance Quarterly* 28 (1975): 575–638; Brucker, *Civic World,* passim; in addition, for the period following 1434, see N. Rubinstein, *The Government of Florence under the Medici (1434 to 1494)* (Oxford, 1966), passim.

37. On these aspects, see R. Goldthwaite, *Private Wealth in Renaissance Florence* (Princeton, 1968); L. Martines, *The Social World of the Florentine Humanists* (Princeton, 1963); and D. Herlihy and C. Klapisch-Zuber, *Les Toscans et leurs familles: Une ètude du catasto florentin de 1427* (Paris, 1978), pp. 241–300, in abridged form in English as *Tuscans and Their Families: A Study of the Florentine Catasto of 1427* (New Haven, 1985), pp. 93–130.

38. See the examples used by Martines, *Lawyers and Statecraft,* pp. 190–91, and by G. Pampaloni, "Fermenti di riforme democratiche nella Firenze medicea del Quattrocento," *Archivio storico italiano* 119 (1961): 42–43 and 52–53.

39. GA, 75, fol. 354r–v, June 4, 1429.

40. GA, 77, fol. 309v, October 25, 1432; GA, 75, fol. 419r–v, September 5, 1429; GA, 78, fols. 116r–117r, September 15, 1431.

41. GA, 75, fols. 350v–353r, May 30, 1429.

42. See GA, 75, fol. 345r–v, May 21, 1429, fols. 369v–370r, July 11, 1429, fol. 458r–v, October 5, 1429, and fols. 330r–331r, April 27, 1429.

43. GA, 78, fol. 172r–v, October 17, 1431.

44. See GA, 75, fol. 350r–v, May 30, 1429, fol. 348r–v, May 28, 1429.

45. See GA, 77, fol. 730r–v, June 8, 1434, fol. 698r–v, May 5, 1434; and GA, 78, fol. 58r, July 28, 1431, and fols. 118r–119r, September 15, 1431.

46. GA, 75, fols. 337v–338v, May 6, 1429.

47. See the two provisions in PR, 120, fol. 251r–v, July 15, 1429, and fols. 271v–272v, August 3, 1429; see also the registers for each area in *Tratte,* 39, and for each family, in *Tratte,* 1093. New books, which were "approbationum aetatum," were published in 1457 by the Conservatori delle Leggi (*Tratte,* 41) and in 1485 (*Tratte,* 40).

48. See Herlihy and Klapisch-Zuber, *Les Toscans et leurs familles,* pp. 350–60, *Tuscans and Their Families,* pp. 159–69; a case of conflicting statements about age in the various compilations of the *catasto* can also be found in GA, 75, fol. 730v, June 8, 1434. On the subject of the *catasto,* see also Herlihy and Klapisch-Zuber, *Les Toscans et leurs familles,* pp. 17–106, *Tuscans and Their Families,* pp. 1–27; and E. Conti, *L'imposta diretta a Firenze nel Quattrocento (1427–1494)* (Rome, 1984), pp. 119–80.

49. See GA, 77, fols. 103v–104v, April 11, 1430, and fol. 373r, December 22, 1432.

50. Waquet has recently extensively discussed this as far as Grand Ducal Florence in his *Corruption.* On the embryonic bureaucratic nuclei in Florence during the late communal period, see G. A. Brucker, "Bureaucracy and Social Welfare in the Renaissance: A Florentine Case Study," *Journal of Modern History* 55 (1983): 1–21.

51. Paolo Da Certaldo, *Libro di buoni costumi,* ed. A. Schiaffini (Florence, 1945), pp. 109–11.

52. See I. Salviati, *Cronica fiorentina dall'anno 1388 al 1411,* ed. Ildefonso di San Luigi (Florence, 1784), pp. 182, 195, and passim.

53. See Brucker, *Civic World,* p. 503; during that same period, in fact, the phenomenon of shameful poverty was becoming very common. On the subject, see A. Spicciani, "The 'Poveri Vergognosi' in Fifteenth-Century Florence: The First Thirty Years' Activity of the Buonuomini di San Martino," in *Aspects of Poverty in Early Modern Europe,* ed. by T. Riis (Florence, 1981), pp. 119–82.

54. See PR, 109, fols. 243v–244v and 244v–245v, February 15, 1419/20. The first petitioner obtained the *podesteria* of Castiglion della Pescaia for a year; the second obtained the *castellania* of Montepetroso fortress for a year. These are only two of several examples that appear in the registers of wages during those decades.

55. See GA, 77, fol. 440r, March 31, 1433, fols. 72r–73v, March 27, 1430; GA, 78, fol. 262r–v, January 28, 1431/32; and GA, 77, fols. 498v–499r, June 20, 1433.

56. See GA, 77, fols. 146r–148r, May 26, 1430, and fol. 153r–v, June 9, 1430.

57. Bernardino Da Siena, *Quadragesimale de evangelio aeterno,* in *Opera omnia* (Quarracchi, 1950), vol. 3, pp. 326–27. In October 1424 a law was issued to determine in detail the duties and the limitations of the territorial governor's behavior. See MR, 78, fols. 10r–12v, copy in the vernacular.

58. See GA, 77, fols. 84r–85r, April 4, 1430, and fol. 355r, December 9, 1432.

59. See GA, 77, fols. 17r–18r, January 30, 1429/30; GA, 78, fol. 478r–v, June 20, 1432; GA, 77, fol. 312v, October 30, 1432.

60. See GA, 75, fol. 467r–v, October 12, 1429; for other examples, see ibid., fols. 421v–422r, fols. 440v–441r; GA 77, fol. 355v, fol. 709r; GA, 78, fol. 59r.

61. See GA, 75, fols. 477v–478r, October 19, 1429, and fol. 503r–v, November 4, 1429.

62. See GA, 78, fol. 476r–v, May 23, 1432; GA, 77, fols. 145r–148r, May 26, 1430; GA, 78, fols. 84v–85v, August 12, 1431; and GA, 77, fols. 406r–407r, February 10, 1432/33.

63. See some powerful examples in GA, 77, fols. 62r–71v, 218r–v, 226r–v, 355r–v, 374r–v, 381r–382v, 550r–551r.

64. GA, 77, fol. 185r–v, October 27, 1430.

65. San Bernardino Da Siena, *Le prediche volgari,* pp. 13ff.

66. It appears also in Bernardino, ibid. See also the literary examples quoted by G. Lumbroso, "La Giustizia e l'Ingiustizia dipinte da Giotto," in his *Memorie italiane del buon tempo antico* (Turin, 1889), pp. 13–14.

67. See GA, 78, fols. 478v–479r, June 20, 1432; GA, 77, fols. 271r–272v, March 27, 1431, and fols. 278r–281r, April 5, 1431.

68. See *Statuta Populi et Communis Florentiae [. . .] anno MCCCCXV,* statute 1, rubrics 19–20, vol. 1, pp. 33–35; see also Guidi, *Il governo della città-repubblica,* vol. 2, pp. 180–81.

69. GA, 77, fols. 286r–287r, April 5, 1431.

70. These duties were often inconvenient, as demonstrated in the above-cited case of Giovanni Guicciardini. See note 23. On the Florentine commissioners, see for the moment the few notes in R. Fubini, "Classe dirigente ed esercizio della diplomazia nella Firenze Quattrocentesca," in *I ceti dirigenti nella Toscana del Quattrocento* (Monte Oriolo, 1987), pp. 164–65. William Connell is currently working on this subject; see also O. Hintze, "Il Commissario e la sua importanza nella storia generale dell'amministrazione: Uno studio comparto," in his *Stato e società* (Bologna, 1980), pp. 1–26.

71. MR, 78, fols. 35v–36v, copy in vernacular.

72. See GA, 77, fol. 224r, January 20, 1430/31, fol. 225r–v, January 20, 1430/31; GA, 78, fols. 122r–123v, September 15, 1431. Other remarkable cases are found in GA, 77, fols. 183r–184r and 540r–541r.

73. See GA, 77, fols. 214r–216r, December 21, 1430, fols. 208r–212v, December 16, 1430.

74. GA, 77, fols. 269r–270r, March 27, 1431.

75. See GA, 77, fols, 124r–125v, May 2, 1430, and for the other cases, ibid., fols. 86r–87r, 93r–95v, 224r–225r, between April 4, 1430, and January 20, 1430/31.

76. On these aspects, see R. Trexler, *Public Life in Renaissance Florence* (New York, 1980), particularly pp. 379–82; idem, "La prostitution florentine au XVe siècle," *Annales E. S. C.* 36 (1981): 983–1015; M. S. Mazzi, "Il mondo della prostituzione nella Firenze tardo medievale," *Ricerche storiche* 14 (1984): 337–63. In addition, see M. J. Rocke's article published in *Quaderni storici* 66 (1987), and Zorzi, "Aspetti e problemi."

6 🦂 Feuding, Factions, and Parties: The Redefinition of Politics in the Imperial Fiefs of Langhe in the Seventeenth and Eighteenth Centuries

by Angelo Torre

On November 30, 1682, Gaspare Vaira, the son of Messer Giovanni, with a "squadron" of armed men kidnapped Maria Cattarina Merlo, grabbing her away from her mother while she was leaving the chapel at San Ponzo di Vernie, a village situated between Barolo and Novello in the region of Langhe. Gaspare and his men took the young girl to Barolo and from there to the high Langa, where the kidnapper's father, who led another "squadron," had preceded him to prepare several refuges in the taverns of the area. At the same time Maria Cattarina's stepfather, Messer Giuliano Pira di Novello, did not lose any time: with the help of a distant relative, notary Giuseppe Malacria, Giuliano gathered "followers" and hurried toward Serravalle, where, "with the help of God, these followers, and the people from the environs," he reached Vaira's squadron, "arrested" his stepdaughter, and secured her in the marquis Del Carretto's palace. Probably with the marquis's help Giuliano was able to capture the Vaira son and two of his supporters.

The two parties made a peace treaty in front of another member of the Del Carretto family, the marquis of Balestrino. Then they returned to Novello but "separately." It looked like Vaira had reorganized new "squadrons," composed of "Spaniards and the bandits of Mondovì." The peace was, in fact, only temporary: the next day Gaspare Vaira "called one of Pira's men and he told him . . . . that he did not want to live with such a shame . . . and that he had made peace only to get out of prison."

"Faide, fazioni e partiti, ovvero la redefinizione della politica nei feudi imperiali delle Langhe tra Sei e Settecento," *Quaderni storici* 63 (1986): 775–810. Translated by Corrada Biazzo Curry.

In perfect concord with this declaration, Gaspare and his father did not desist from their original purpose. The first step was to involve the justice of the peace representing the marquis Del Carretto di Monforte and Novello, lord of the place. The justice presented himself at the house of the Piras in order to take in Maria Cattarina and interrogate her at the castle. Her parents opposed this decision, saying that the members of the clan had already asked her so many questions and that the young girl kept denying her consent to the kidnapping. The justice, however, was not an impartial investigator, because not only was he a cousin of Messer Giovenale Moretti, Gaspare's uncle, but he was also the marquis of Monforte's brother-in-law and the marquis of Novello's uncle. Since Pira refused to allow Maria Cattarina to go to the castle, the justice levied heavy fines on the young girl's mother and stepfather. The two were therefore obligated to surrender, that is, to accept a new truce, first for two days and then for eight, during which time Gaspare continued to insult his rivals. However, this was a very uncertain truce. The local feudal lords, "instead of discussing a truce, began to consider a marriage"; in such a way, "tongues were loosened," and the feudal judge started menacing the Piras with obscure threats. The Piras answered first by resorting to the vicar of Novello and finally to the justice of the duke of Savoy, whose jurisdiction extended to nearby Cherasco beyond Tanaro. At this point, the Vairas complained of being threatened with death by the young girl's mother and asked for fifty doblas to forget about it. However, the rivals refused to pay and instead decided to make Maria Cattarina marry one of Pira's nephews.

The strife between the two families began to grow more bitter. On the day of Saint Ann in 1683, Gaspare Vaira attacked a follower of the Piras and beat another one; in exchange the next night he was shot at. In October some of Pira's followers "declared war" on a brother-in-law of Vaira's father; they surrounded his house, forced the women to flee, and then locked the doors from inside, as though they wished to cancel out that family from the list of Novello's living. They did not have to wait long for the response from the opposing side: on November 3, Maestro Michele Ferrero, Pira's brother-in-law, found forty of his mulberry trees cut at the base of the trunk. Four nights later, his son Francesco Antonio was killed by two bravos of Messer Giovenale Moretti, the brother-in-law of Vaira. One of the two bravos was killed in this encounter. The Piras reacted by attacking Vaira's father near his farmstead in San Ponzo di Vernie. Vaira's father was saved by miracle, and a few days later he responded by hiring someone from Barolo to kill Maestro Michele Ferrero.

Starting from this moment, the encounters became fiercer and fiercer: there were confrontations among "squadrons" of relatives, followers, and bravos which culminated in an assault on Pira's and Malacria's houses led by some ninety bandits from Mondovì, from the high Langa, and from the neighboring towns. Finally, in the spring of 1684, Vaira's father was killed while he was returning from Monforte accompanied by a Monregalese bravo.

With its few dead and its theatrical exhibitions of violence, the feud seemed to fade away around the middle of 1685, but it started again twenty years later, in 1704 and in 1705, with the murder of Giovanni Battista Vaira, Gaspare's young brother and the only surviving member of the family. This murder aroused a vendetta among more than 250 bandits, coming from all over Langhe and from the Monregalese, who attacked the houses and the people belonging to the Malacria family, which was one of the most powerful of the allies of the Piras, who were accused of the murder. Those few who were able to survive the raid, the burning of the houses, and the slaughter of the three generations who composed the clan permanently abandoned the town for Turin.[1]

This event, even though it was not exceptional for Langhe and kept the Turinese judges busy for years, effectively reveals the complexity of the institutional structure and of social relationships in this area during the seventeenth and eighteenth centuries. The interlacing of seigneurial jurisdictions, which were plagued by feuding, represents the most revealing aspect of the political configuration of the continuous overlapping of judicial prerogatives and systems of justice which characterized a vast area in Tanaro, Scrivia, and the Ligurian coast. In fact, imperial, Spanish, Piedmontese, Genoese, and ecclesiastical dominions frequently overlapped, contradicting the image of this territory as having already formed a relatively rational political system during the *ancien régime*.[2]

The protagonists of the feud were aware of the implications of this jurisdictional scenario: for example, the Vernie farmsteads, where Maria Cattarina's kidnapping took place, were under the jurisdictional authority of both the marquis of Falletti di Barolo and the marquis of La Morra, even though the most powerful landowners in the area were the Dominicans from Garessio, a center for trade with Liguria; to make matters even more complicated, these particular farmsteads belonged to the duchy of Savoy, which governed them from the nearby city of Cherasco, a proper military outpost that faced the uncertain areas of Langhe. Novello, an imperial fief and the home of the rivals of the Vairas, together with four other villages of the Monforte marquisate (Monforte, Castelletto, Monchiero, and Sinio), belonged to two branches of the Del Carretto family. In addition, Balestrino and Bagnasco were subject to other members of the Del Carretto family, imperial feudatories; Serravalle was entirely under Spanish control, while nearby La Morra was divided between Spanish and Piedmontese authority in an extreme jurisdictional hybrid. From this viewpoint, as we shall see, the feuding called into question several different systems of power.

The overlapping of so many heterogeneous jurisdictions cannot be considered as an inert residue of a political system that only today we see as inescapable. During the years of the Novello feud, in fact, imperial fiefs were particularly attractive to the Piedmontese, not so much to possess the infertile land as to control a politically and militarily strategic area. The imperial fiefs of Langhe, in fact, constituted a dusting of jurisdictions located along a military and commercial artery of primal importance in the communication lines between the Tyrrhenian coast and the Po Valley. If until the sixties the documents mainly emphasize the military importance of this Spanish corridor to Milan, part of the road to Flanders, and to the fief of La Morra,[3] in the following century the role of trade was more frequently emphasized, both in the sources of the central government (especially in Carlo Emanuele II's *Memorial*, which invariably associates the problem of Langhe with the problem of contraband[4]) and in the criminal sources, in which the growth of illegal trade clearly emerges.[5] The imperial fiefs were full of merchants, mule drivers, and apothecaries, natives as well as foreigners, who were attracted by the traffic that specialized in the export of grain and oxen to the Ligurian Riviera, in exchange for salt, tobacco, and oil, which were delivered to Milan, Monferrato, and the Piedmontese valley controlled by the dukes of Savoy.[6]

At first glance, feuding appears to have only marginally affected the flow of the trade; instead, it more directly complicated the problems of the jurisdictions and the prerogatives of justice within the imperial and immediately surrounding fiefs. These problems were crucial in the Savoyard strategy that for more than a century had tried to strengthen its political influence in those fiefs under its direct authority (Barolo and Vernie, for example) and to conquer important territory in the same imperial fiefs. In making political overtures to the imperial nobility, the Savoyards tried to obtain usage rights, the *dominium utile,* to the fiefs (the ultimate rights of *dominium directum* belonged to the emperor) by gradually purchasing jurisdictions from the poorest branches of the clans.[7] For example, in Novello by 1634 the dukes of Savoy had convinced various branches of the Del Carretto family to sell in exchange for pensions, offices at court, and jurisdictional and commercial privileges over the local population.[8] But this process produced ambiguous results, and during the entire seventeenth century the Savoyard presence was uncertain and ineffective, even in the jurisdictions such as Vernie which were directly controlled by Turin.

In 1666 Turin was not able to prevent a real "civil war" that began between two branches of the Falletti clan. This encounter was started by the La Morra side, which with the support of the Milanese Senate claimed some months of the annual division of jurisdictional authority from the marquis of Barolo, whose real sin was marrying a noblewoman from the Turinese court.[9] In 1682 Turin attempted to strengthen its authority by taking advantage of the tensions between the city of Cherasco and Carlo Ludovico Falletti di Barolo over the fiscal system of Vernie. This system, established in 1527 by an arrangement between the Fallettis and the city, required farmsteads to pay a symbolic tax of ten scudi, curiously undermining Turinese power.[10] Carlo Ludovico's fiscal immunity was the real target of the strife, and for the imperial feudatories of the area, it represented an unheard-of concession. Even though Carlo Ludovico had the imperial jurisdiction over some Monferrini fiefs and over La Morra, [11] which gave him the right to appeal to the judgment of the imperial representative in Milan and then to Vienna, he agreed to discuss the question in front of the Turinese Senate. In addition, in order to strengthen his position, he played upon the community's solidarity and called on the local peasants to testify regarding the fiscal immunities of Vernie and its properties in evidence against Turin's claims. Locally, this proposal was enthusiastically received.

It was at this point that Messer Giovanni Vaira sent his son Gaspare to kidnap Maria Cattarina. However, as our analysis will attempt to show, this decision was not a direct and necessary consequence of the social and political conditions of the time. In order to understand the peculiarity of Vaira's behavior, we must examine the origins and the development of the feud, identifying its characteristic elements. In such fashion, an apparently private episode of a violent conflict between kinship groups can reveal more general aspects of the social system and the ways of exercising power which characterized a "frontier" region.

In fact, Vaira's decision to stir up the feud was an oblique and very ambiguous maneuver that treaded water in midstream between the family tensions and the jurisdictional situation that we have described. We must closely analyze the logic behind the responses of both sides. The history of the Vaira clan represents a good point of departure. The Vairas were originally farmers from Vernie, and until 1670 they served as the stewards of the marquis of Barolo, but they did not limit themselves to managing the lord's interests: in 1653 the Vairas took a slice of the marquis's possessions, moving by a few meters the hedge and the road that came up from Barolo. In 1670 at the death of Messer Michele Antonio, one of the marquis's agents, the Vairas were accused of illegitimately operating one of the wine presses that belonged to the lord. Notwithstanding these conflicts with the marquis, the Vairas were very successful; in fact, between 1610 and 1660 the size of their landholdings doubled.[12]

The death of Messer Michele Antonio, the most powerful member of the family, represented an important turning point for the entire family's fortunes. In 1668, when the old man was about to die, the presumptive heirs tried to put pressure on him. Michele Antonio did not have any children, so the nephews Carlo and Antonio, his brother Michele's sons, and Messer Giovanni, orphan of the other brother Valerio, went to see their uncle one night in August at his farmstead, taking with them notaries and men who were able to persuade the old man. The strife that followed gives us a significant view of how aristocratic justice worked: at first Messer Giovanni tried to convince the judges that he was the victim, since he had seen some sign of shooting from the inside of the house. After a while, however, his cousins said they were forced to take action because Messer Giovanni, his brother-in-law who was the apostolic notary Giovenale Moretti di Novello, and some bravos had previously occupied their house. Giovanni's cousins also promised to return the wine press stolen from the uncle.

This confrontation had several consequences now that the Vaira family was split into two factions. Starting from this moment, Giovanni formed an alliance with his brother-in-law Giovenale Moretti, who had also been excluded from the inheritance by all the other Vairas. Giovanni moved to Novello, where he served several terms in the city council and became mayor the year before the conflict broke out between the Piras and the Malacrias.

If we consider these circumstances, the kidnapping that started the feud acquires a new meaning: the peasants who were asked to testify for the marquis of Barolo against the city of Cherasco were, in fact, the very Vairas who won during the strife of 1668, but rising to prominence along with them were some members of the Pira family, who at the beginning of the eighties had replaced the Vairas as stewards of the Fallettis.[13] From this point of view, the feud became a way to reinforce genealogical solidarity in order to impinge upon the patronage power of the marquis. The Piras had to side with the other Piras and the Vairas with other Vairas. In fact, with Maria Cattarina's kidnapping, Messer Giovanni Vaira managed to delay by more than two years the auspicious alliances of the marquis of Barolo. Only in 1684 was he able to obtain the witnesses in his favor which he needed.[14]

Therefore, the interlacing between family and power dynamics characterized the "political conjuncture" in Langhe at the end of the seventeenth century. The feud typically attempted to build binding ties: for example, the encounter of 1682 had emphasized building solidarity among brothers-in-law, and frequently the members of the same side had only distant and fragile family ties, such as those of brother-in-law or son-in-law, or they were simply political allies.[15] Despite their weakness, these ties were not a completely artificial construction but a selection from among more defused social relationships. As we have noted in the case of the Vairas, the inheritance practices caused a competition among relatives, which was often an open conflict among brothers or their sons, and this often led to a definitive fission among the various branches of a lineage. There was an extremely rigorous egalitarianism among the male heirs who remained living with their parents, while the daughters were definitively liquidated with a dowry and usually destined for exogamous marriages with respect to the community. In these cases, an alliance between brothers-in-law resulted from the competition for an inheritance and dowries for the sisters among blood kin.[16] However, the equality principle was often resolved through a delay in the conflict which started to emerge in the second generation: this is confirmed by the innumerable divisions among brothers and cousins, resulting in sordid hostilities that usually had peaceful conclusions, as borne out in the notarial sources of the area.[17]

In this particular aspect, the feud reveals its political nature, since it can be considered as an attempt to redefine social relations, a process of building alignments which tend to crystallize ties of preference and to firm up tentative commitments; the feud involves people, their property, and their other relations in a much vaster universe of dichotomous relationships. Everyone and everything, people and things, according to the logic of feuding, ideally belong to one of the two sides: they *are* either A or B. In this sense, as Jean Marcaggi intuited at the end of the last century, the feud is a language that intervenes in relationships, both those of kinship and of property, and reshapes them in a precise way. The logic never permits parity or balance: one can answer an offense only with another offense, and the debt is constituted by a condition of force. The advantage belonged to whoever had committed the most offenses and, thus, indebted others to him.[18]

In such a way, the feud continuously generates new relational and political resources, restructuring social communication. The fact that rivals "lose their voices" causes conflicts capable of growing with the establishment of a debt. In the case that we are analyzing, the conflict between, on the one hand, Vaira and Moretti and, on the other, Pira and Malacria transformed into positive resources things that were at first neutral and inert. This continuous creation of resources through the establishing of debts redefines the political game, adjusting it to new models of communication and social exchange.

The conflict impeded, in fact, the development of normal public life and the relationships that it encouraged, instituting instead new authorities and redefining the components of leadership at various levels of local political life, especially ceremonial life.[19] In the years preceding the feud, in Novello the two sides appear to have been equally represented in each of the four devotional organizations. The prestige of the entire dominating class, to which both sides belonged, required that alms, collections, pious donations, and tithes regularly go to each organization. But the conflict made it impossible for individuals who belonged to opposing sides to associate with one another closely. The confraternities thus assumed a partisan dimension with the consequence of reducing the size of popular alms giving. The income was reduced by half and was insufficient to buy candles for the altars.

Besides the contraction of alms receipts, the principle of ceremonial life was undermined, since with the feud religious ceremonies ceased to confirm the potential for peace among parishioners, becoming instead an object of conflict between the two sides. First of all, the feud began after a Mass celebrated at the chapel of San Ponzo, and later in the nearby chapels the assaults multiplied; the principals in the feud attended religious ceremonies surrounded by partisans and armed bravos. Consequently, a person's intentional absence from the ceremonies was an open declaration of hostility to the sponsors of the chapel. As Giuseppe Malacria said about his enemy, Giovanni Battista Vaira, during the second phase of the feud, "Vaira never wanted to attend the responsory" that was celebrated every Tuesday in the chapel of "the patron saints of the Malacria family." "All the population" assisted in this celebration, but "on that occasion he always ran away."[20]

In addition, the feud changed the meaning of the bonds sealed by religious ceremonies, particularly those of marriage and godparentage. If it is obvious that the conflict promoted marriages among the partisans, it is less so that there were consequences from the strife for the meaning of godparentage. Here, instead, the Novello feud penalized only some of the potential local godfathers. Let us take as an example the notary Malacria, an ally of the Piras: although during the previous forty years he had more godchildren than anyone else in the parish, during the years of the feud no one asked him to serve as godfather; on the other hand, the most active and numerous allies of the Vairas, the Belmondos, were very popular as godparents.[21]

The alteration of the patterns of godparentage constituted the most obvious manifestation of the ways in which the feud interrupted the regularity of public life, but in other respects opportunities were created for those who could take advantage of them. In the same way, the second consequence of the conflict was that the feud interfered with administrative life by interrupting the collection of taxes. In the spring of 1684, the city council stated that during the three years of fighting, "because of the poor information and conflicts that exist[ed] in this place between families, neither the taxes required for the last two years ha[d] been collected nor ha[d] it been possible to provide for the most urgent public requirements."[22] It was not just the physical danger that discouraged the tax collectors; the tax collector's fear became one of the weapons of the feud, a new resource created by the conflict.

To understand this crucial aspect of the feud, we must closely analyze the local tax system. In fact, despite its jurisdictional autonomy, the Novello marquisate was subject to the Savoyard state. Throughout the seventeenth century, its strategic location made it essential for any military operation, especially during the Thirty Years' War, and the annual military billets, either to protect or to punish the population, ruined the economic resources of the area. Much more dangerous than feudal burdens, which were always negotiable at some level, the military billets distinguished themselves for their unpredictability and their extraordinary and immediate demands upon local resources. Every military operation resulted in additional indebtedness by the communities to the local nobles, especially the Falletti di La Morra; to the religious orders, particularly the Dominicans from Garessio; and to the rich.

In other words, this system created a growing collective indebtedness toward a few creditors, who usually took advantage of the situation to keep the soldiers away from their own farmsteads with the excuse that they carried the burden of the unpaid debts of the "public." With time the number of local creditors multiplied, and this fact caused an administrative paralysis: none of the creditors wanted to pay anymore, demanding the repayment of previous debts before advancing any new moneys. However, every failure of the community to pay created new debts that led to the confiscation of the collateral of individuals, which could, in turn, be used to pad the communal accounts.

In 1677, the Savoyard monarchy had attempted to resolve this mess, entrusting Senator Richelmi to assess all instruments of credit held against the community of Novello and to liquidate the legitimate claims. The senator received nearly universal support, including that of the marquises Falletti, the principal creditors; the Del Carretto family, who possessed a fat file of unpaid loans; and even the Dominicans, who hoped that arbitration would lead to a voluntary resumption of payments. However, the Richelmi delegation failed because its calls for arbitration were suffocated by new arguments between creditors and debtors, as well as among creditors. Among the principals, the notary Giuseppe Malacria, who was one of the followers of the Piras, and the Moretti cousins, tied to the Vairas, refused to accept Richelmi's efforts, which at first they had accepted; thus the controversy began again.[23] The game was clear: to accept the sentence meant in some fashion to annul the feud because the peace and the requirement of reciprocal trust would not allow one to keep profits obtained through manipulations of the credit market.

This situation got worse at the beginning of the eighties. In fact, the feudal lords demanded the payment of the extant accounts, and the outside creditors exerted more and more pressure, while internally the dispute intensified to the point that in 1681 the two sides aligned in a confrontation that led to the feud of 1682–85.[24] The political options expressed by the opposing parties particularly tended to emphasize the notion of the "public." In fact, there was a side that wanted to emphasize the public character of the administration and the community's relationships; in other words, this side aimed to defend the community as an instrument of control open to personal family interests. The other side, instead, saw the community as a place where powerful citizens could legitimate their social superiority through public recognition of their tax-exempt status. Finally, some others wanted to keep the existing equilibrium, by taking advantage of the most desperate opportunities.

From our point of view, it is certainly surprising that in 1681 the main defender of the public interest was Messer Giovanni Vaira, who would instead choose private feuding the following year. At the beginning of 1681 he denounced corruption in the auctions for public contracts, such as the sale of salt, the provision of supplies, and baking. The participants in the auction had agreed "to keep this contract at a lower price, which [was] disadvantageous to the community." Messer Giovanni Vaira had a double proposal: he planned to increase the proceeds from the contracts, with a drastic elevation of the starting bid for the auctions; in this way he aimed to replenish the public treasury or at least to stop temporarily hemorrhaging debts. In addition, he proposed to consolidate all the contracts in one municipal monopoly, a proposal designed to eliminate private profiteering at public expense, and for this reason it was rejected.

The second option was proposed, in fact, by Vaira's brother-in-law, Giovenale Moretti, who claimed an exemption from all taxes because of the outstanding loans he had to the community, loans that he had inherited after the death of his cousin, the parish priest. Senator Richelmi had not been able to liquidate these loans in 1677 because they fell under the competence of the church. Thus, in January 1681, after his cousin's death, Giovenale with his brothers and relatives blocked the entrance into the parish church of the accountant entrusted by the community to manage the church properties until the coming of a new curate. On this occasion, Giovenale had excommunicated whoever came into the church to celebrate Mass. A few months later, he sent to the city council a copy of a letter that came from the Apostolic Chamber which prohibited "tax collection from any property that [was] claimed to be private property." However, this act, which would have stopped the recuperation of the land that had been so far exempted from fiscal contributions, was strongly opposed.

The third option, the preservation of the status quo, was proposed by notary Malacria, who was now willing to play the dangerous and hated card of relying on Savoyard justice to maintain his position of advantage. At first, Malacria seemed to yield to the pressures of the public interest, submitting himself to arbitration, but when his new tax bill came due, he refused to pay "because of the mistakes that had been made to his detriment" in the new arbitration.

Malacria's proposal was the only option that succeeded. Vaira was defeated in his attempt to reevaluate the idea of the "public" interest in local government, while Moretti was defeated in his search for fiscal immunity; however, a few months later they tried to solve the matter by force. Thus, those who wanted a collective control of private interests in 1681 decided to use force in 1682, in order to affirm private and family privileges, brutally destroying any hope of coordinating a consensus.

Maria Cattarina's kidnapping permitted Vaira to break those alliances that had been formed in Vernie with the marquis of Barolo's complicity and allowed Moretti to stop paying taxes. During these years Giovenale, as an archivist of the community, used to keep in his house all the documents necessary to allot the tax burden among the local population, papers that until the end of the feud he refused to let his enemies consult.

Malacria and Moretti, however, were not the only creditors of the community, and local financial pressures imposed a new demand for revenues to avoid further indebtedness: the marquises of Monforte and Novello kept insisting on having their feudal dues paid, the counts Falletti di La Morra had to collect the interest on the *censi*, and the justice of the peace had advanced a large amount of money to protect the community from receiving new military billets. Moreover, during the final phases of the feud, the salaried employees of the community (the town physician, administrator, schoolmaster, and chaplains) pressed for their wages.

If all these factors also lead us to search among the creditors for a silent but not idle "party of peace," another element suggests that it was the same dynamic of conflict which led to a proposal for a suspension of the feud. The restoration of the broken civil order and the renewal of normal social communication were paradoxically factors in the conflict. From this point of view, the feud became a resource to

exploit in order to guarantee one's prestige. Perhaps the most revealing aspect of the feud was its ability to transform the functions of
public institutions, since it implied the frequent presence of arbitrators, who were created by the feud and whose difficult work was
urged upon them by the very participants in the conflict.[25] As we
have already seen, the Piras turned to the marquis Del Carretto di
Bagnasco, while the Vairas relied on the marquis of Balestrino; and
as time passed, the marquis of Falletti di Barolo, the Del Carretto
di Monforte, the Novello, and even Savoyard justice either were
brought into the judicial cases or tried to impose themselves in
arbitrating the dispute. These arbitrators were hardly neutral observers.
In fact, if the marquis of Bagnasco represented Savoyard justice and
acted as the spokesman for the court in Turin and if the marquis of
Balestrino, as we shall show more fully below, represented the imperial
feudal interests of Langhe, then the marquis of Barolo constituted a
dangerous rival of the Novellos because he was their cousin and had
a rival claim to the marquisate. Finally, the Savoyards, with the help
first of the prefect and governor of Cherasco and then of Senator
Salmatoris, made their first incursion during the feud of 1682–85 into
the jurisdiction of the Del Carrettos, who as partisans of Savoy were
dexterously transformed into direct vassals of the duke. The conflict
ended with tightened reins on the marquisate. In the final stages of
the dispute the duke's secretary, the marquis of San Tomaso, personally
intervened as an arbitrator.

The feud thus revealed itself to be an attempt to redefine the politics
and composition of the leadership. It was certainly a result of local
rivalries and conflicts among kin groups, but a close analysis of the
exceptional events in Novello radically changes this image. The con-
tention was neither the result of psychological and cultural factors,
that is, the vendetta, nor the result of the pre- or antistate political
practices, but it was related to the social relationships proposed by
the state, which employed taxation policies and systems of credit to
mold the hierarchy of statuses. This interpretation considers the feud
as a way to redefine social boundaries, since it changed personal relationships by investing the arbitrators with political resources, which
enlarged the arena for competition. Twenty years later when the feud
started again, this competition between feudal jurisdictions and state
institutions caused such a radical change in the conditions of the
marquisate that even the means and ends of the dispute were completely changed.

᠀ The break in the feud did not mean an interruption of hostilities in the marquisate. Under the pressures of war they took new forms, but above all new conditions changed the meaning and relevance of the existing social resources and even created new ones. Local conflicts were not limited just to reflecting outside influences emanating from a new situation; on the contrary, such conflicts transformed local social relationships that in turn influenced the greater powers.

The most visible change came in the jurisdictional consequences of the feud: the political pressures of the Savoyards weighed heavily on the marquisate, although always with selective results. Thus, the excessive tolerance shown by Carlo Francesco, the marquis of Monforte, toward violence at the beginning of the eighties brought more and more attention from the central government. The Turinese government, after asking the marquis for clarification, discovered the disquieting news that during the revolt against Savoyard creditors, which was taking place in one of the marquisate's communities, an escape from the Monforte prison had probably been assisted by the offer of a generous reward.[26] The marquis was called to Turin, but sensing a threat to his jurisdictional rights, he refused to discuss controversial cases with the functionaries of the capital.

The behavior of Marquis Giovanni Battista di Novello was totally different: in fact, he had been dragged into mediating the feud by a powerful uncle, Count Solaro di Moretta, who exercised over Giovanni Battista the charm of a high noble of the court, elevated with offices and honors. Starting from this moment, the marquis of Novello began to move within his uncle's orbit and, probably in the hope of obtaining recognition from the court, took initiatives against the smugglers which nevertheless proved vain.

However, this remarkable difference in his interpretation of his governing role would not have been too important if it had not been for the preparations for the War of the League of Augsburg. Although the Savoyard alliances were now more directed toward Vienna than Paris, which after more than a century brought imperial forces back into Piedmont, Langhe did not draw nearer to Savoy; on the contrary, right before the war began, an edict issued by the baron of Neselrod[27] forced the vassals of the empire to renounce any alliance they had made for any reason with nearby "potentates." Carlo Francesco di Monforte and Giovanni Battista di Novello interpreted this decision differently: whereas the latter ignored the edict, Carlo Francesco prohibited his subjects from making appeals to Turin and his judges from recognizing the ordinances of the Savoyard Senate. The result was an unprecedented situation in which every two years the judges of the marquisate alternated the channel of appeals between the Senate of Turin and the aulic council of Vienna.

There were several good reasons for this radical choice. One reason can be found in the particular relationship between the son-in-law and his father-in-law, the one convinced of finding in the court the fulfillment of his own ambitions, the other being more attached to the regional nobility, that unstable vortex of the Del Carrettos and their clan. Among these nobles were the referendary Giacomo Alessandro de Magistris, the count of Belvedere, a good friend of Carlo Frances-co's, and his brother-in-law's brother, Francesco Giacinto. Carlo Francesco was, in fact, enmeshed through matrimonial connections with the imperial aristocracy of the upper Langa and the Ligurian Riviera, a group that included the Del Carrettos di Balestrino, their di Millesimo cousins, and the Calderas of Monesiglio.

Consequently, he favored their attempts to free themselves from interference by any of the territorial powers, whether Savoy, Monferrino, Milan, or Genoa. The attraction of this proposal for Carlo Francesco and others came from a peculiar interpretation of seigneurial rights of justice, which provided for the active and decisive intervention of the lord in the conflicts among subjects and between subjects and lord. The arbitrational function that the Vairas and the Morettis had promoted now had an institutional form that was impossible to circumvent.

In such a way, instead of being a dangerous weapon that could create unexpected alliances with destabilizing repercussions, the conflicts among the subjects became themselves a means of government. In other words, the lords took advantage of the conflicts between peasants and notables, emphasizing the active and biased character of the jurisdiction. In addition, the fact that in the case of the Novello marquisate the two lords were on opposite sides can only be explained by the strength of the factional alignments among the subjects of the jurisdiction. Among many examples, the quarrel between the Belmondo di Novello brothers around the end of the eighties can clarify this crucial transformation. These brothers belonged to the old peasant elite that in the second half of the century was divided among four branches of differing levels of prestige and wealth: a branch of notaries and judges, who were in decline after the sixties; one of innkeepers, who were ascendant; a lineage of peasant-merchants; and a branch that had fallen into penury.[28]

The conflict that broke out within the branch of the peasant-merchants between Giovanni and his brother, the Reverend Don Giovanni Pietro, was typical of this part of Piedmont at the end of the seventeenth century. In 1638, when Giovanni Pietro took holy orders, the majority of his relatives consented to give him a patrimony of about ten days' income per year from the family farm. In the fifties, when Giovanni Pietro obtained the position of parish priest at Salmour, a nearby village on the plain, he gave his ecclesiastical income to his brother Giovanni, who enjoyed it until the curate's death. At this point Giovanni's children started fighting over the income. This process, although similar to the Vaira episode, had an entirely different result. Giovanni's children came from two different marriages and split accordingly: the children of the first marriage had been legally emancipated by their father and through their own marriages found allies in the conflict in two local notables, one of whom was Francesco Antonio Ferrero, whom we have already met as a protagonist in the larger feud. He had now become a notary. The father was also looking for allies capable of guaranteeing him his continued possession of the patrimony, and he strengthened his ties with the most prestigious branch of the clan by betrothing one of his sons from the second marriage to a cousin, the daughter of the notary Giovanni Giacomo. The tension got worse between 1689 and 1692. On this deathbed the curate disinherited his brother in favor of the sons who had been emancipated, which led to the two sides to call upon their allies to testify about their respective legal rights. The first sentence of the courts of the march favored the sons, but the father appealed to the episcopal court in Alba. Finally the Senate of Turin intervened.

It was during this interruption that the Edict of Neselrod required Carlo Francesco di Monforte to abandon his support for Savoy, an act that he rather generously interpreted to prohibit appeals to Turin. Nevertheless, Giovanni Belmondo decided to ignore his lord's orders, appealing to the Senate, because Francesco Antonio Ferrero, the brother-in-law of one of his children, had become in the meantime the vicar of justice for Carlo Francesco in Novello, and the prospect of losing his land had become more concrete. The result of this asymmetry was evident, because while Giovanni had his allies testify that he was poor in order to convince the Senate, his children robbed their father of his possessions: the vicar of justice (the brother-in-law), some armed men (who were also in-laws), and some women and children began to pick their dead uncle's grapes in the dead of the night. Giovanni, after being attacked and beaten by the vicar, who was surprised as he was finishing the clandestine harvest, went to Turin to obtain a senatorial order that would stop the gathering of the grapes. After Giovanni returned, Carlo Francesco had him put in prison, and Giovanni responded, "Your Excellency well knows that I am very hard-headed, even if I have to find support wherever I can." After obtaining his freedom, he returned to Turin and was killed on his way home by persons unknown in a field at Moncalieri. Francesco Antonio Ferrero was able to dispel the Turinese judges' suspicions about his involvement.

This example shows how pressures that conflict among subjects exerted on a feudal lord can be interpreted. Even for the Turinese Senate, justice became a political resource, a way of mobilizing allies, a language for expressing relational distance and affinity, hostility and friendship. However, the Belmondo case with its ad hoc choice of allies by each of the contenders had a contradictory nature when compared with the feud of the preceding years: the Belmondos, especially Giovanni and his sons, had supported the Vairas' practice of sheltering bandits and had participated in the fight, creating memories of a consolidated alliance. Now, in the characteristic process of fission which we have already discussed, Giovanni turned to the Piedmontese courts, and testifying on his behalf was Gaspare Vaira, who a few years earlier had been decisively opposed to resorting to Turinese involvement. On the other hand, the supposedly "philo-Savoyard" Piras now sided with the jurisdictional claims of the marquis, and among their allies were at least two former allies and relatives of the Vairas.

The interactions between peasant conflicts and the lords' jurisdictional response produced mobility among the opposing parties. The configuration derived from this realignment was once again an example of fission within clans, but now the process created a temporary mobilization of allies who were not tied by kinship. The sides were formed according to a long chain of opposing political loyalties, generated by the jurisdictional definition of feudal power.

At the end of the eighties, the bipolar character of the Novello marquisate with its two different jurisdictional loyalties favored the presence of factions that supported the different jurisdictions, opposing them one to the other. The forms that conflict took varied according to the resources of the opposing parties. The first phase, immediately after Carlo Francesco's about-face, saw the success of an anti-Savoyard alliance. It manifested itself in forms of rebellion and coincided with the raising of taxes which characterized the preparations for war. On November 3, 1689, the peasants of Monforte refused to provide billets for the count of Vercellis's army and published a proclamation in which they reminded the duke of Savoy of the privileges of the marquisate and in which they refused to accept the intervention of the Savoyard ministers.[29] However, all of the community did not rebel. A few days after the mobilization, in fact, the peasants of the neighboring farmsteads armed themselves to meet the soldiers, but as soon as they left, the peasants surrendered to the local authorities. The philo-Savoyard captain Carlo Giuseppe Rinaldi (who had been living in town for many years with the task of fighting smugglers), his relatives, and his followers were besieged in the palace for more than two months until Carlo Ludovico Falletti di Barolo negotiated a ransom with the Rinaldis which enabled them to leave Monforte and to save their possessions from pillage.

The peasants were not alone: they had the support of Francesco Giacinto de Magistris and Carlo Costanzo Del Carretto, Carlo Francesco's eldest son. Other notables backed them up. Three years later, on December 18, 1692, when military conditions allowed the Piedmontese to repress the rebellion, the White Cross regiment went to the Monforte castle to capture Carlo Francesco, who had been held responsible for the revolt. The peasants and part of the notables resisted, but it is difficult to determine the victor of the battle. In strictly military terms, the peasants and notables seemed to prevail: after capturing forty-two soldiers and two officers, they despoiled them of their possessions, tied them together two by two, and took them over the snow to Langhe. Carlo Costanzo Del Carretto and several notables led them. However, the Piedmontese were able to capture Carlo Francesco and took him to the castle in Turin, where he died a few months later. The Piedmontese left devastation in their wake: Carlo Francesco's castle was looted, and his second son, Filiberto, was wounded in the head and eyes, surviving only by a miracle. Worst of all, the Piedmontese retaliation that followed was terrible. At the beginning of 1693, for ten days, five thousand soldiers put Monforte to fire and sword, not even sparing the parish church and the community archive. Following the capture of Marquis Carlo Francesco, the other communities of the marquisate divided into factions that appeared to be better balanced than those of Monforte. In Novello, for example, Francesco Antonio Ferrero rang the tocsin to mobilize the peasants against the Piedmontese, but he was stopped by Giuseppe Pira and was able to take part in the capture of the soldiers only with his own followers.

Confronted with the excesses of the peasants and notables, the Del Carrettos of Monforte attempted to use their authority to control the rioters. Thus, the first aim was to support the peasants' protest, since, as Count de Magistris said in front of his palace, which had been occupied by the "rebels" in 1689, "they were suffering very much and it was better to let them give vent to their anger." Carlo Costanzo organized a squad of guards, composed of his faithful followers, around the Rinaldi palace. He claimed that in 1692 he tried to remove the soldiers to Alba, saving them from the peasants' anger, but the roads were blocked. But there was something more precise, more calculating in his behavior: he went to Novello with some of the most influential nobles of Monforte to humiliate the syndics who had opposed him.

Subsequent events confirmed that Carlo Costanzo's intuition was right, even though it implied many risks. (He later died in prison in Ceva.) In fact, the factions could really be an efficient means for controlling behavior, since without the factions the feudatory would have been in a critical situation. After 1693, in fact, neither Savoyard nor imperial documents record any significant incidents. The factions seemed to have become unsustainable without the counterclaims of the jurisdictions: Giovanni Battista di Novello seemed to dominate the situation, since his young, weak, and retarded cousin Filiberto in Monforte was not able to propose an alternative form of government.

However, the absence of formal parties, instead of generating social peace, aroused conflicts much more dangerous to feudal authority. An exceptional document, a memorial redacted by Marquis Giovanni Battista in 1697 about the political life in Novello during these years, allows us to understand the new situation. In a hundred short paragraphs, Giovanni Battista sums up all the terrible things done by his subjects, including the violent competition for jurisdictional, administrative, and religious offices.[30] By looking at a series of extremely circumscribed conflicts, one discovers protagonistic groups of relatives, including fathers, sons, and sons-in-law, in a game of highly mobile alliances that continuously recomposed the playing field and which had the capacity, as did the factions of 1689–92, to make temporary alliances that were directed by the feudal lords. Philo-Savoyards and supporters of the empire thus became players on the field, employed when they were useful, but their involvement did not hide the diffuse character of the conflict.

Let us take as an example the two most important personalities in Novello, the notaries Giacomo Francesco Moretti, who was Giovenale's cousin, and Giuseppe Francesco Malacria. During the feud and the events of 1689–92, these two men belonged to two opposing parties: Malacria was exiled for three years for his behavior as judge of Carlo Francesco, while Moretti had boldly fought against Carlo Costanzo. Now the two became allies, the former to obtain the job for his son as town physician, the latter to have his loans honored, which had been challenged by Richelmi in 1677.

The reason that the conflicts took the form of a series of small, apparently irrelevant episodes with ephemeral groupings of allies who often turned against one another is related to the competition for offices during the nineties. The imperial, Piedmontese, and, briefly, French armies were encamped in the neighborhood, and each had the power to impose levies and other exactions. The imperial demands were the heaviest but also episodic and negotiable. Moreover, the imperialist authorities also levied a third from the feudal lords, but no one doubted that these lords would with time attempt to extract the levied funds from the communities in their jurisdiction through negotiation.[31] The Piedmontese military levies, in contrast, were allocated by community, thus fragmenting the feudal lords' power, and they were paid in kind by providing room and board for the troops, as we have seen was the case among the outlying farmsteads in Monforte in 1689. Here political negotiations were always possible, but those who were exempted were not always able to claim their rights. In any event, the policy consistently discriminated against the inhabitants of outlying areas, whether simple peasants or stewards of the great lords. In both cases, the levy was negotiated with the authorities, the Piedmontese on the spot and the imperialist authorities in Milan, creating the opportunity for frequent contacts among taxpayers on the one hand and between them and the government on the other hand. It was precisely this mechanism of negotiation which made offices in the community attractive. Participating in these negotiations translated into fiscal exemptions that consisted of paid missions with a fixed deduction to be taken from future imposts and from the number of days of lodging to be provided for troops. The immediate consequence of this policy was "an accounting of political commitment," which often meant a total exemption from levies.[32]

Faced with this mechanism, the marquis Giovanni Battista found himself in a blind alley. In the case of the imperial levy, the community of Novello proposed to pay his feudal share in exchange for an annulment of the dues owed him, obviously hoping to negotiate later with the imperial authorities over the exact amount of the share. In the case of the Piedmontese levy, the marquis could not avail himself of such exemptions on his lands that were not already immune from taxation because he could not hold public offices. He therefore decided to have the peasants give him back the money he had advanced to pay for the expenses of billeting, thus revealing the social processes behind Piedmontese taxation. However, the restitution was not paid in money but in "days of lodging": the peasants gave up the quotas that they could have presented to the tax collectors in order to have their share reduced and that could instead have been used by the marquis to reduce his own fee. Such practices, however desirable because they helped to reduce the fiscal burdens of the population (and are especially revealing of the workings of local social mechanisms), were blocked by the notables of the community.

Nevertheless, on this occasion the mechanism of peasant indebtedness was not yet in question: the *Memorial* that Giovanni Battista has left us focuses more on the measures taken by the author to protest his exclusion from collective decisions. Giovanni Battista, who was "disliked by this populace," was in fact kept in the dark about local matters, and he notes, "[One] can hear things said against my royal service." He was not allowed to take part in the city councils, whoever dared to talk to him was threatened, and his stewards were not favored in minor disputes. At first, Giovanni Battista reacted by asking the Turinese government for direct help. He asked to be named the official mediator between the community and the government "[The ministers should] receive news about that marquisate directly from the above-mentioned lord marquis. . . . The marquis will inform His Royal Highness about any turmoil that takes place in that community of the marquisate. . . . The marquis will also write to his Royal Highness on behalf of that community, in order not to alienate those people from the monarchy." Later, the marquis asked Turin to send him someone to whom he could confide information about the movements of his adversaries. However, when in 1695 the notary Malacria returned to town to make a temporary alliance with the notary Moretti, Giovanni Battista realized all too well that the conflicting alliances saw in him, the feudal lord, their predestined victim.

He says in his *Memorial*, "[I]f something is not done, I also will be forced to leave the service of His Royal Highness, since there is not a single person whom I can trust, and he who made me think he was going to help me is worse than the others." With their reciprocal hatreds all the notables of Novello "[could] be seen to be supporting one another." At the beginning of 1697 Giovanni Battista began some contacts with Vittorio Amedeo II to exchange fiefs. In 1699, he left the town for another imperial fief, leaving to his enemies the management of his property that had been confiscated by the duke. His old enemies, always at war with one another, thus gradually became stewards, contractors, and administrators of his farmsteads.

෫ The two different answers that Carlo Costanzo and Giovanni Battista Del Carretto gave to the problem of controlling local conflicts express ideas that characterized the factional traditions of Langhe for more than fifty years. These were different responses to the same problem, that is, two differing interpretations of the judicial and political values that would continue to typify conflict in the imperial fiefs and their immediately surrounding area.

The idea of an imperial party was not an invention of the nobility, even if it sprang forth from jurisdictional problems. It was born in 1666 when the curates of Monforte and Novello, four notables from Monforte, a tailor, and one of the members of the Del Carretto family from Torre Bormida asked the Spanish for military help against the collectors of the Piedmontese gabelles.[33] The authorities in Milan thought the request was crazy, but it forced a careful evaluation of the strategic position of the marquisate for reaching La Morra. The fief, which was half Spanish, was at the time being devastated by the "civil wars" among the various branches of the Falletti family, one of which had turned to Milan for protection. The Milanese government sent the podestà of Spigno to take possession in the name of His Catholic Majesty of the land in the five communities of the Novello marquisate, taking advantage of the deaths of Valerio and Aleramo Del Carretto, whose jurisdiction seems to have been ceded first to Alfonso Del Carretto from Finale and then to the Dorias. In order to stop the union, the seven curates and notables took an oath in a country chapel between Monforte and Novello, promising to act in total secrecy. Their objective was to strengthen ties with Milan after a long time of isolation due to the fact that most of the feudal lords had since 1634 been supporters of Turin. However, this attempt to free themselves from their isolation failed: at the time, Spigno determined that the the marquisate was still part of the duchy of Savoy. The new relationship did not go beyond "negotiations" with Milan, through the Spanish functionaries of Spigno, about staging a mass meeting of the population from the five communities with the podestà of Spigno and about sending the Milanese governor gifts that in the end were refused. Nevertheless, the conspirators' ability to mobilize the population must have been revealing when more than a hundred armed men escorted the podestà of Spigno into the Belbo Valley when suddenly he had to escape after being surprised by the Savoyard militia. Then, it seems, the contacts between the imperial forces and the Novello community stopped.

At the beginning of the nineties, the imperial ideal emerged with the assumption of the noble idiom that we have seen employed by Carlo Francesco. This idiom of government was based upon the autonomy of the jurisdiction: Carlo Costanzo in 1690 and Filiberto in 1718 claimed that in the marquisate "they heard cases in the first, second, third, and fourth instances."[34] This conviction revealed a noble attempt to manipulate justice for a complex series of reasons: besides the profit that he offered his lord, the feudal judge could in the lord's name orient the alliances and rivalries among subject families, as we have seen in the case of the Vairas and Belmondos. Above all, the jurisdiction offered its consent, at least in theory, to avoid conflicts over the amount of the fiscal immunity of the feudatory, and in this sense, the direct derivation of authority from the emperor tended to accentuate the legitimacy of the jurisdiction, in which authority was exercised without any bureaucratic intermediaries. The feudatory and his allies could thus talk to their subjects in a "direct" political language, which had the character of a populist language of free consent: the partisans of the empire presented themselves as "the party of the clothtrousers" [as opposed to doublet and hose], and their war cry was "forward comrades!"[35]

The peasants were able to contrapose symbolic images to this autocratic political idiom, using a carnivalesque institution, the youth abbey.[36] In Langhe this institution was one of the crucial elements in the political vocabulary. The head of the abbey had jurisdiction over street fights, at least for a limited time, and thus he was by virtue of his office an antagonist of feudal justice; in addition, he usually belonged to the community's elite, despite the youthful character of the institution. It is doubtful that the abbot could have exercised much real influence in settling quarrels, but the abbey was part of the symbolic conception of the community, which distinguished the abbey's authority from imperial ideology. It is therefore particularly significant that Giovanni Battista Del Carretto rejected, while Carlo Francesco accepted, its intervention in their capitulations. However, in the last quarter of the century, the abbey's rights were incorporated into the noble ideology of the government, and during the last half of the century the general approval of its statutes ended with the conflicts between the peasants and the lords. One of the imperial feudatories of Langhe, Gio. Antonio Caldera, count of Monesiglio, explained this principle to his heirs:

> These people must be kept happy. Having by nature a sharp, feisty, and unusual temper, they can be softened and sweetened by plea-sures; when they see that the master cooperates with them, they are moved emotionally; therefore, it is useful to tolerate joviality, games, taverns, and dances, which cheer them up greatly, keep them united, and prevent them from nourishing enmities among them-selves. It would not be bad to give even more freedom to the most respectable . . . and to grant privileges to the Abbey.[37]

It is difficult to say whether or not the nobles from the imperial fiefs considered this perspective of government through the abbey as anachronistic in the sense of being a true return to the past, but even if they did so think, they were conscious of what they were doing. Compared with the intrusive Savoyard politics, the imperial perspec-tive implied an understanding of the generations and their history. With his characteristic rough frankness, Carlo Costanzo said to the Novello notables "that he respected the duke of Savoy but that the duke did not have anything to do in this clan, and that even though his ancestors had sold some jurisdictions, they had not been able to tie the hands of their successors."[38] However, one cannot credit a similar proposal for going back in time by skipping over the immedi-ately preceding generations to find new ideals of government. This proposal was reported by a witness who was one of Carlo Costanzo's former allies in the 1689–92 conflict. This same principle can be found elsewhere, in the papers on Langhe preserved in Vienna, and in the formulation of a group of jurists who were hired by Gerolamo Del Carretto di Balestrino to pursue the rights of the vassals of Langhe against the duke of Savoy, who was later accused by Gerolamo of lese majesty. Many appeals were sent to Grozio and Pufendorf to maintain that the agreements made in the past between the imperial lords and the territorial princes could not be interpreted to grant additional rights to the princes. In fact, the agreement was a contract that lacked the moral qualities that demand personal obligation or the pledging of property. It was distinct from the *"potestatem a jure."*[39] On the basis, the imperial party distorted their appeal to history. The archives still preserve several examples of a persistent effort to search among the late medieval records, and the memory produced by these efforts is synonymous with a way of thinking that cannot in my mind be considered an anachronistic one.[40]

Nevertheless, how far did the rights of the communities go? Besides the preservation of social status and prerogatives, why did the feudal lords of Langhe defend the rights of communities that were quite capable of defending themselves, however poor? The Savoyards had no doubts: with a clumsy lack of restraint they trod over the sensitivities of the vassals of Langhe and in 1713 presented to the emperor a report on misdeeds of his vassals.[41] The Savoyard noose was too tightly drawn, and the extraordinary power that the emperor was determined to defend was in reality only a cover for abuses of power, judicial discrimination, and the protection of bandits and smugglers. In the Savoyard analysis all of these elements were closely connected: in order to protect smugglers, the vassals of Langhe gave refuge to bandits from Liguria, Lombardy, and especially Piedmont. The lords used them for the management of justice, which, when the lords' own agents were not directly involved, was entrusted to judges who were pledged to follow the lords' will, implicated in feuds, and involved in every kind of mischief. This picture is first of all incomplete, since all the evidence derived from blackmail and was also deliberately one-sided. In fact, the vassals of Langhe were under multiple pressures when they had to choose a "party": there were external influences coming from both Savoyards and the Milanese and above all internal ones coming from their own subjects. In 1700 Caldera wrote,

> This place, the fief of Monesiglio, is a mercantile center, which most of all freely trades in the kinds of merchandise forbidden in the states of His Royal Highness. The place is very useful for smuggling operations, is much desired by His Highness, and is highly valued by the Spanish ministers, because it supplies them more often than does the Royal Service and feeds the commerce of Finale. This commerce is conducted on three market days per week. It

takes lots of work, a fair administration of justice, and effective po-
licing to maintain the trade in such a condition. The subjects must
sustain this traffic by traveling to the coast, Cairo, Finale, and
Carchere to get salt and other merchandise. When they go through
the Savoyard lands, they risk being captured and taken to Ceva or
of being killed by border patrols even though this is clearly illegal
because according to the provisions of the Peace of Cherasco the
transit of merchandise cannot be disrupted. Therefore, either the
subjects take precautions to avoid the dangers, or, when it is necessary, they risk running the blockade armed with weapons in their
hands to resist harassment by the border patrols. Even though the
use of arms has been tolerated, especially since it has often been
very useful, it is necessary to keep arms under control, in order to
prevent fights among the populace and with their neighbors, which
would ruin the lord's reputation and compromise the government
of the community as well as the preservation of trade.[42]

The centrality of commerce in the region of the imperial fiefs was
a constant over the centuries, and certainly it was often used by the
lords to preserve and expand their own rights in a complex system of
reciprocities which encompassed the entire area between the Ligurian
coast and the Tanaro River.[43] During the seventeenth and eighteenth
centuries the lords obviously collected tolls, but we cannot now use the
record of these tolls to evaluate the extent of the Savoyard accusations
because, apart from the exemptions provided for reciprocity among
the different feudal jurisdictions, which are of limited value, the toll
accounts are lost. The only known fragment of a document covers
only two months in 1713 for the Millesimo transit station[44] on the
road to Savona, but the books only keep account of the trade going
to, and not that coming from, the coast. This document reveals in
every case a monthly transit of 8,556 liters, mostly of grain; it would
be reasonable to hypothesize return loads of oil, cheese, tobacco, and
lead bullets half-filled with salt.[45]

The existence of only one pass open for two months in the summer
does not allow us to evaluate the importance of the trade that took
place in western Liguria, but it shows us that use of this pass persisted
despite the legal road blocks on the plain. The Savoyard conquest of
Monferrato between 1709 and 1713 did not restrict employment for
the mule drivers of Langhe; rather, the conquest concentrated the trade
along the ridge line between La Morra and Millesimo. Evidence of
the route can be found in the official complaints that persisted for a

good part of the eighteenth century as well as in local reports. In 1720 Caldera di Monesiglio informed Milan about a Savoyard military billet in Saliceto, which prevented his subjects from passing through to La Morra, resulting in considerable economic damage.[46] There were innumerable reports of encounters between smugglers and gabelle collectors on the slopes of Langhe.

If it is true that the vassals of Langhe used to cover up all these clandestine trading activities, it also true that both the legal and smuggling interests of the merchants did not completely coincide with the nobles' aspirations. For example, between 1694 and 1720, contracts were negotiated between the Monesiglio merchants and the imperial authorities for the monopoly over trade in the "salt of Langhe."[47] These agreements guaranteed the Milanese and Viennese authorities an income of ten thousand lire per year without specifying the source of the money. Thus, within the shadow of the noble party appeared a mercantile party, which largely coincided with the former but differed in at least two crucial ways: in oppostion to the feudal jurisdictions, the mercantile notables made public proposals to the weak imperial government. For their part the feudal lords tended to defend their jurisdictional prerogatives from imperial interference and to discourage, therefore, contacts with the center of Milanese power except when requesting tax exemptions. For this reason nobles accompanied delegations of subjects on their trips to negotiate with imperial officials and bankers but did not go along when their subjects traveled on judicial matters.

During the investigation of contraband in 1713, the Turinese government held the feudal lords and their agents entirely responsible for smuggling as well as for the feuding, an accusation that gave hints to the local notables about who their allies were. Trade was also possible with the Turinese government, although under different forms, especially for salt. There were, in fact, other clandestine routes involving persons whose political leanings implied a philo–Savoyard position. At the beginning of the eighteenth century in Novello, which was by then fully under Turinese jurisdictional control, there were among the principal smugglers two former supporters of the empire, Francesco Antonio Ferrero and Giuseppe Francesco Malacria, who were now dukes and had direct contacts with Turin. The marriages they arranged reveal their orientation during these years toward the upper Langa of the smugglers: their daughters and sisters had married in Bossolasco and Monesiglio. At the same time, their close relationships with Turin reveal a refined sensitivity for knowing how to get along with the central government by combining overt respect for Savoyard regulations with the pursuit of profits made both by offering loans to the peasants at the time of tax collections and by smuggling operations. It was certainly not a coincidence that Giovanni Battista Vaira, shortly before his murder by the Monesiglio smugglers who were supplying Malacria, had, "blowing up with rage," asked the notary-apothecary, "Are you, perhaps, the marquis of Novello?"[48]

Nevertheless, these constant manipulative contacts with the central government dramatically altered the forms of local political competition. Starting in 1713 when the fiefs of Monferrato were definitively ceded to Turin, the imperial government began to pay more attention to Langhe. The Milanese plenipotentiary, Count Carlo Borromeo Arese, was convinced for good reasons of the strategic value of the fiefs and of the damage the Riviera trade could cause to Piedmontese finances.[49] The count was constantly solicited by the notables of the communities of Langhe, who often turned to him in local disputes. Borromeo discovered, as had others before, the central thread of the tangled skein in the operations of justice. Defending the jurisdictional autonomies drew him closer to the feudal lords, and giving judicial offices to the men most devoted to Vienna strengthened the party. At the same time, the increased possibilities for making appeals to Vienna and the dispatching of reliable judges to the location of the most serious cases guaranteed control of the local affairs. With the same objective in mind, Turin also began to pay its men on the scene.

The alternating of jurisdictions institutionalized the conflict. Judicial procedures were no longer simply in the hands of feudal clients but regulated by the counts. In 1716 in Novello, Francesco Antonio Ferrero, now a philo–Savoyard, had to return large amounts of the fines that as judge he had imposed on several communities of the marquisate whose citizens had been suspected of burning down his house. In the same way, two years later, the attorney Vittorio Felice Benevelli, auditor of justice within the marquisate for the emperor, was killed by the philo–Savoyards from Alessandria, who were his own brothers-in-law whom he had threatened with confiscations. In addition, the Appianos, a clan deeply divided over inheritance disputes, began systematically to eliminate one another. When Giuseppe Ottavio killed his teenaged nephew, some witnesses did not hesitate to identify as the motive for the murder the fact that Giuseppe Ottavio "was converting the nephew to the cause of the opponents," a reference to

the split between the philo-Savoyards and the philoimperial "optima-
tes." However, others maintained that Giuseppe Ottavio was also the
closest relative of the victim and that now he "had taken possession
of the nephew's patrimony." It was impossible for a foreign judge to
attempt to unravel all the personal ties, the allusions made by the
witnesses, and the meaning of local gestures. Again, Count Caldera
di Monesiglio wrote a letter to Borromeo in which he advised that
the judge be warned about the disquieting nature of the situation
before being sent to Monforte and Novello: "You should warn the
judge to be careful ... not to believe anyone if the proofs are not
more than clear because their goal is to make others appear culpable,
to dissimulate, and to make up everything to carry out their ideas and
their plans."[50]

⁊ What emerges from these events is the rapid transition from one
form of exercising power to another, albeit a form involving a small
number of actors on a relatively circumscribed stage. In addition, the
same individuals were able to pursue their political initiatives through
different political idioms, either by reflecting the interests of the "public" or by rousing private and family disputes. These individuals sometimes used local conflicts to legitimate their own power, and sometimes
they were used on a larger stage by the very persons they sought to
dominate as a strategy of government.

As a method of analysis we have deliberately concentrated on
following the various positions taken by the protagonists in the trivia
of daily affairs in order to show a complex political process, which
was of longstanding and crucial importance in understanding how the
political structures of an *ancien régime* society expressed and transformed themselves. This research strategy is not very common in the
studies on the development of the modern state, and it seems to call
into question some of the assumptions of such studies.

First of all, social alliances, in which a political struggle finds its
foundation and historiographic justification, appear here as true and
proper social constructs or as the projection of tensions rather than as
"structural" data. In other words, kinship, community, and institutions
were not biological, socioeconomic, and judicial facts, but they were
the fruit of an accumulation of choices, which were defined by behaviors put into relief by conflicts that produced the historical documents
we have to consult. This set of behaviors can be interpreted as an

idiom that had precise objectives, rather than as an expression of a structural order.

The result of this finding, thus, is a rereading of our categories of classification. For example, the feud was not the automatic result of kinship structures but a deliberate choice made as a way of establishing binding relationships. We can say the same thing for the community, which the political forces considered at various times as an arena for controlling tax collections, as a means of circumscribing feudal power, or as a place to affirm private interests. The same institutions—both central and peripheral institutions as well as those of justice and finance—can be seen as a means for controlling conflicts, controls that worked in various ways by using the offices of mediation for the constitution of political power. By considering these presuppositions, we can perhaps identify the precise spheres for political action among the nobility in the early modern period.

Finally, how the institutions were specifically used is revealing, since both the formal powers of the feudatories and the state on the one hand and the informal powers of the localities on the other were able to manipulate the institutions to serve their own ends. Thus, the evolution of a feud can be understood only in relationship to institutional activities. The factions were nothing more than the diffused response to a manipulative use of local institutions. The parties constituted the use of distant powers by forces emanating from "the bottom up." All of this paints, it seems to me, a portrait in all its complexity of "government" during the *ancien régime:* in the cases that we have presented, local dynamics raise several questions and generate pressures that the formal powers must convert into institutional actions. These actions, reverberating in the situations that generated them, constitute new interlocutors in the unceasing process of social communication.

Notes

1. This account of the feud is based upon the materials in the Archivio di Stato di Torino (AST), Sez. Prima, Feudi delle Langhe, Lettera V, Novello, m. 5, n. 8; m. 4, n. 1 and 2; m. 5, n. 4; AST, Sez. Riunite, art. 781, m. 2, n. 46, and in Archivio Storico Municipale di Novello, Ordinati, 1683–84.

2. On the Langhe fiefs, see A. Torre, "Elites locali e potere centrale tra Sei e Settecento: problemi di metodo e ipotesi di lavoro sui feudi imperiali delle Langhe," *Bollettino della Società per gli studi storici artistici e archeologici della provincia di Cuneo* 89, no. 2 (1983): 41–63. On the imperial fiefs in general, see K. O. Von Aretin, "L'ordinamento feudale in Italia nel XVI e XVII secolo e le sue ripercussioni sulla

politica europea: Un contributo alla storia del tardo feudalesimo in Europa, *"Annali dell'Istituto storico italo-germanico in Trento* 4 (1978): 51–93.

3. Haus-, Hof-, und Staatsarchiv, Vienna, Plenipotenz in Italien, Karton 1 and 2, in particular see the part entitled "Processus Langarum" (1626), which contains an account of a visit by the auditor Ottavio Villani in all the fiefs between the Ligurian coast and the Tanaro River; Archivio di Stato di Milano (ASM), Feudi imperiali, cartt. 360; 442, n. 1; 497, n. 15, "Apprehensio […] Novelli per Advoc. Fisc. Aloysium Cusanum" (1634; AST, Sez. Prima, Feudi delle Langhe, Lettera V, Novello, m. 2, n. 1, "Atti di visita dell'auditore generale di guerra Gio. Giorgio Bajardo" (1631–32); Istituto di Studi Liguri, Albenga, Archivio Del Carretto di Balestrino, Langhe, mm. 1–6.

4. See G. Claretta, *Storia del regno e dei tempi di Carlo Emanuele II duca di Savoia scritto su documenti inediti,* 3 vols. (Genoa, 1877), vol. 2.

5. See the material cited in n. 41.

6. On the Langhe contraband, see G. B. Pio, *Cronistoria dei Comuni dell'antico mandamento di Bossolasco con cenni sulle Langhe* (Alba, 1920; Cuneo, 1975); G. Prato, *La vita economica in Piemonte a mezzo il secolo XVIII* (Turin, 1908), pp. 325–27. As far as the Novello marquisate, the participation of the population in the transit and contraband activities is indicated in AST, Sez. Riunite, art. 781, m. 2, n. 45, also 36 and 37 (on this source see note 30). For the previous years, see ASM, Feudi imperiali, cartt. 352, n. 5; 442, n. 2, "Atti in punto del privilegio, e libertà di prender il sale ovunque" (1670); Archivio Storico Municipale di Novello, Ordinati, 1683–84: peasants such as Gio. Belmondo and Lorenzo Ferrero reported the confiscation of merchandise by Savoyard tax collectors on the Piedmontese plain (July 9, 1684). In addition, in AST, Sez. Riunite, art. 781, m. 1, n. 12, we find reports of the Novello community concerning the payment of the drafts for 1677–85.

7. On these aspects, see G. Tabacco, *Lo stato sabaudo nel Sacro Romano Impero* (Turin, 1939).

8. The contract for the sale can be found in AST, Sez. Prima, Feudi delle Langhe, Lettera V, Novello, m. 5, n. 4; for the privileges of the marquisate, see AST, Sez. Riunite, Patenti controllo Finanze, Reg. 1680 in 81, fols. 118ff. We do not have a history of the Del Carrettos' dominion in the Langhe imperial feuds. For a genealogy, refer to Jo. Bricherius Columbus, *Tabulae Genealogicae gentis Carrettensis et Marchionum Savonae, Finarii, Clavexanae* (Vienna, 1741). On the relationships between imperial feudatories and Hapsburg authorities, see G. Rill, "Die Garzweiller-mission 1603/4 und die Reichslehen in der Lunigiana," *Mitteilungen de Österreichischen Staatsarchivs* 31 (1978): 9–25.

9. On the civil war that divided the Fallettis in the sixties and seventies, see AST, Materie criminali, m. 5, n. 2; AST, Sez. Riunite, art. 599, Archivio Falletti della Morra, m. 4; see especially Opera Pia Bartolo, Turin, Archivio storico della famiglia Barolo, m. 217, n. 25, "Il vero, e succinto Racconto de fatti successi nella Morra dalli 11 novembre 1666 sino al presente" (around 1670), where the Spanish role is emphasized and clarified. S. Woolf, *Studi sulla nobiltà piemontese nell'età dell'assolutismo* (Turin, 1963), thinks that what motivated the civil war was pure economic interests.

10. Opera Pia Barolo, Archivio storico della famiglia Barolo, mm. 176, 177, 180, 181, 201, 202, 210.

11. S. Woolf, *Studi,* p. 45.

12. The reconstruction of the events involving the Vairas is based on the parish church documentation and on the Opera Pia Barolo, Archivio storico della famiglia Barolo, mm. 14–18, 177, 179, 180, 181, 185–202 (in particular, 201 and 202); Archivio Patrimoniale Falletti di Barolo, mm. 25, 67–70 (Minutari del notaio Pietro Paolo Patrito di Barolo).

13. This branch is different from the branch of Messer Giuseppe, who was Vaira's

rival in the feud: in fact, in 1682 the descendants of Odone Francesco became "tax collectors" in the name of Carlo Ludovico Falletti di Barolo.

14. Opera Pia Barolo, Archivio storico della famiglia Barolo, m. 201, fol. 87: the evidence was gathered between March and April 1684.

15. From this point of view, the two sides in the *faida* were very different. While the Vaira-Moretti side did not share any family ties and gathered people from Novello, Barolo, Monforte, and Serralunga (with the sole exception of a nucleus of kinsmen, the Belmondos from Novello, who all sided with the Vairas), the Pira-Malacria side had some members who were kinsmen: in fact, in 1621 the son of a brother of the great-grandfather of Giuseppe Pira married the widow of the cousin of Giuseppe Manescotto's great-grandfather; in addition, notary Malacria married his daughter to Giuseppe Manescotto in 1667. On the Pira-Malacria side, the central nucleus was composed of the brothers-in-law and sons-in-law of the leaders, but nine of the thirty-six followers did not have any family ties with the other allies. In addition, three people had different relationships: either they were friends with the leaders, enemies of the leaders' enemies, or relatives of members who belonged to the opposing party, but they worked as "bravos" for the Piras and the Malacrias. Analogous political alignments are emphasized by A. Blok, *The Mafia of a Sicilian Village: A Study of Violent Peasant Entrepreneurs* (New York, 1975).

16. The reconstruction of the genealogies has been done in the parish church archives of Monforte d'Alba, Novello, Barolo, Dogliani for the years 1580–1705. Between 1605 and 1715, in contrast to the median of 40 to 50 percent exogamous marriages in only seven years (1668, 1669, 1689, 1693, 1696, 1711, 1713), less than 20 percent of the marriages in Novello were contracted with foreigners. The only exception in Langhe to this matrimonial was the case of Castelletto Uzzone, as yet unexplained. See L. Carle, "Lo spazio definito dalle alleanze: Mobilità e immobilità sociale in una communità dell'Alta Langa dal XVII al XIX secolo," *Annali della Fondazione Luigi Einaudi* 17 (1983): 333–95.

17. These observations are based on the few notarial sources that have been found so far: Archivio di Stato di Cuneo, Notai Alba, notai Gio. Bartolomeo Lucio, 1668–1726; Guglielmo Vivalda, 1678–88; Agostino Bongiovanni, 1666–1712; Carlo Bongiovanni, 1676–99; Gio. Carlo Porro, 1680–1705; Gio. Francesco, Carlo Ludovico e Gio. Bartolomeo Viglione Porro, 1695–1754; Archivio di Stato di Alessandria, notaio Gio. Francesco Sitia, 1663–92; Opera Pia Barolo, Minutario del notaio Pietro Paolo Patrito; Archivio Storico Municipale di Novello, Minutario del notaio Gio. Domenico Daprà, 1655–64.

18. On the feud among the European sedentary populations, see J. Black-Michaud, *Cohesive Force: Feud in the Mediterranean and the Middle East* (Oxford, 1975) (see the bibliography there cited); see also J. Wormald, "The Blood Feud in Early Modern Scotland, " *Past and Present* 87 (1980) [now in *Disputes and Settlements: Law and Human Relations in the West*, ed. J. Bossy (Cambridge, 1983), pp. 101–44]; O. Brunner, *Land and Lordships: Structures of Governance in Medieval Austria* (Philadelphia, 1992). However, J. Marcaggi, *Fleuve de sang* (Paris, 1898), remains the most detailed study of the internal mechanisms of feuding Europe.

19. For the devotional practices in this area of Piedmont, see A. Barbero, F. Ramella, and A. Torre, *Materiali sulla religiosità dei laici: Alba 1698–Asti 1742* (Turin, 1981). Archivio Parrocchiale di Novello, Libro della Veberanda Compagnia del Santissimo Sacramento della Chiesa Parrocchiale di San Michele Arcangelo di Novello; see the same archive for the Carmine, Cintura and Suffragio, and the Santissimo Rosario associates; all the registers begin in 1681.

20. The allegation can be found in AST, Sez. Riunite, art. 781, m. 2, n. 46.

21. Archivio Parrocchiale di Novello, Liber baptizatorum, 1633–1705; during the period preceding the feud, notary Malacria and his relatives were requested to be

godfathers between eight and ten times per year. During the three years of the conflict they were never asked. Instead, between 1682 and 1684 the Belmondos, who in the previous fifty years had very seldom asked to be godfathers, reached the popularity of the Malacrias. However, the other lineages in the parish did not show any important changes. On the Belmondos see note 28.

22. Archivio Storico Municipale di Novello, Ordinati, 1683–84, March 15, 1684.

23. Archivio Storico Municipale di Novello, Ordinate, 1639–42, passim; these documents inform us about the devastations caused by the military billets of the previous decade; the costs of these devastations still left numerous debts in the community fifty years later. A report of the fiscal situation in the marquisate can be found in ASM, Feudi imperiali, cart. 443, n. 1, (probably subsequent to 1716); here we find the enumeration of all the taxes suffered by the five communities since the beginning of the seventeenth century. The Richelmi *"laudo"* of arbitration is in AST, Sez. Prima, Feudi delle Langhe, Lettera V, Novello, m. 3, nn. 18–20 (1677).

24. For the citations that follow, see Archivio Storico Municipale di Novello, Ordinati, 1680–81, January 5, January 12, May 12.

25. The arbitrational role of the nobility is confirmed by the correspondence with the court, which can be found in AST, Sez. Prima, Lettere Particolari. The survey for the two letters, D and F, which I have made suggests that the forms of violent conflict reached an apex between 1660 and 1680 on the Piedmontese plain. On the arbitration, see also R. Harding, *Anatomy of a Power Elite* (New Haven, 1978); N. Castan, *Justice et répression en Languedoc à l'époque des lumières* (Paris, 1980); on the Savoyard strategy, see Torre, "Tra comunità e stato: I rituali della giustizia in Piemonte tra 600 e 700," in *Problèmes de l'histoire de la famille,* ed. G. Delille and F. Rizzi (Rome, 1986).

26. AST, Sez. Prima, Feudi delle Langhe, Lettera V, Novello, m. 5, n. 4.

27. ASM, Feudi imperiali, cart. 500, n. 2, "Atti in punto della superiorità media concessa dall'Imperatore al Duca di Savoia sopra li feudi di Novello . . . , nonchè in punto dell'abuso fattone" (1634–1733). The edict is mentioned in AST, Sez. Prima, Feudi delle Langhe, Lettera V, Novello, m. 5, n. 4.

28. On the Belmondos, see ASM, Feudi imperiali, cart. 497, n. 8, and AST, Sez. Prima, Feudi delle Langhe, Lettera V, Novello, m. 4, nn. 9 and 10. The alliance with the Vairas was recalled in 1688 by Severino Belmondo's widow, who was entrusted to Messer Michel Antonio Vaira di Barolo, "since there was not any other woman in the house": Opera Pia Barolo, Archivio storico della famiglia Falletti e alleati, m. 15, n. 2. On justice considered as a political resource, see P. H. Gulliver, *Neighbors and Networks* (Berkeley and Los Angeles, 1971). On the significance of benefices in this area, see A. Torre, "Le visite pastorali: Altari, famiglie, devozioni, " in *Valli monregalesi: Arte, società, devozioni,* ed. G. Galante Garrone, S. Lombardini, and A. Torre (Vicoforte, 1985), 148–88.

29. Some reports of the revolt can be found in ASM, Feudi imperiali, cart. 500, n. 2; AST, Sez. Prima, Feudi delle Langhe, Lettera, V, Novello, m. 5, nn. 1, 2, 4, 6, 7, 9, 10; m. 6, nn. 1, 2, 3. On Rinaldi, see AST, Lettere Particolari, R, m. 38: his correspondence reveals very difficult tasks, such as the overseeing of the illegal transit of grain to Liguria, the recruitment of bandits for the wars, participation in local conflicts, especially during the civil war between the Fallettis in which Rinaldi recruited men for Carlo Ludovico di Barolo. The confession of Carlo Costanzo is contained in AST, Sez. Prima, Feudi delle Langhe, Lettera V, Novello, m. 6, nn. 1, 2, 3.

30. AST, Sez. Riunite, art. 781, m. 2, n. 45. This is a forty-page notebook that concerns the period 1692–97. The most relevant example of competition is represented by the rivalry between the Morettis and the Malacrias. These two families had been rivals during the feud, but now they went different ways. Notary Giacomo Francesco Moretti became administrator of the mint for Savoy in Alba, while Malacria worked

for the Del Carrettos and belonged to the philoimperial party during the revolt. Nevertheless, he was pardoned and decided to side with the Morettis against the feudatory; at the same time Malacria dealt in contraband (he was a notary and also an apothecary), and he had close contacts with both Turin and Milan. For an example of contacts with Milan, see ASM, Feudi imperiali, cart. 445 bis, with no date, besides the material quoted in note 1. Instead, at the beginning of the new century, the Morettis moved to Alba.

31. AST, Sez. Prima, Feudi delle Langhe, Lettera V, Novello, m. 5, n. 7, the testimony of Giovanni Belmondo, which is confirmed by Carlo Costanzo Del Carretto in his deposition, m. 6, n. 2.

32. Archivio Storico Municipale di Novello, "Reperto delle Consegne anotatte all'Incontro de nomi et Cognomi de Particolari che hanno respettivamente consegnato nel Libro delle Consegne dall'anno 1689 sino all'anno 1695 inclusivamente," where the political activity of each community member was considered thoroughly by the Savoyard delegate in order to determine tax allotments. The subsequent quotations are taken from the *Memoria* by Marquis Giovanni Battista, respectively at points 60, 1, 2, 4, 11, and on fols. 26v and 27r.

33. AST, Sez. Prima, Feudi delle Langhe, Lettera V, Novello, m. 3, n. 14. This is the charge brought in Turin on October 22, 1670, by a tailor from Spigno Monferrato, Messer Antonio de Benedetti. His testimony, which I had at first considered useless because it had probably been coerced by the Savoyard officials, was instead confirmed by the testimony of the notary Gio. Enrieto Benevelli some fifty years later. See ASM, Feudi imperiali, cart. 445, "Atti in punto dell'assassinio dell'auditore cesareo Avvocato Vittorio Felice Benevelli" (1718).

34. AST, Sez. Prima, Feudi delle Langhe, Lettera V, Novello, m. 6, n. 2; Haus-, Hof-, und Staatsarchiv, Vienna, Register der lateinischen Judicial Akten, 386, N. 8 (this trial had been brought in 1720 by the imperial representative in Italy, Count Carlo Borromeo Arese, against Marquis Filiberto Del Carretto di Monforte for lese majesty. The summary of the trial is in AST, Sez. Prima, Feudi delle Langhe, Lettera V, Novello, m. 1, n. 30.

35. AST, Sez. Prima, Feudi delle Langhe, Lettera V, Novello, m. 5, n. 7.

36. See A. Torre, "Tra comunità e stato."

37. AST, Sez. Prima, Archivio Saluzzo di Monesiglio, m. 15, "Libro in cui si vedran il stato, esser, beni mobili et tutto il sistema della casa di me Gio. Antonio Caldera di Monesiglio" (1700).

38. See note 35; testimony of Messer Giuseppe Pira.

39. Haus-, Hof-, und Staatsarchiv Vienna, Reichslehensakten, m. 28: this is the "Specificae Cronologicae Enucleationis a Dominis Administris Sabaudicis Evulgatae Excussio" (1712).

40. Istituto di Studi Liguri, Albenga, Archivio Del Carretto di Balestrino, Langhe, mm. 1–6 (see note 43).

41. AST, Sez. Prima, Feudi delle Langhe, Lettera II, mm. 3 and 4: Volume di diversi attestati comprovanti le ingiustizie, e delitti che si commettono nei feudi delle Langhe da Feudatari, ed abitanti in detti Feudi"; this contains eighty-four depositions carried out by merchants and smugglers between the month of October 1711 and the month of February 1712.

42. AST, Sez. Prima, Archivio Saluzzo di Monesiglio, m. 15.

43. An example of reciprocity can be found in ASM, Feudi imperiali, cart. 92 (Cairo), n. 13: Atti nella Causa della Comunità del Cajro contro il Feudatario di Novello in punto dell'istituzione d'un pedaggio lesivo delle convenute reciproche immunità pel transito delle merci sul rispettivo territorio" (1717). These reciprocities

go back to 1323, and they were found thanks to the archival work done by the imperial party.

44. AST, Sez. Riunite, Archivio Del Carretto di Gorzegno, Millesimo, cart. 107, n. 640: these are small volumes that contain the seals in 1713 by Cosseria mail; one of the volumes is entitled "Datio Generale del Monferrato oltre Tanaro."

45. AST, Sez. Riunite, Archivio Del Carretto di Gorzegno, Millesimo, art. 781, m. 1, n. 41, "Tariffe del pedaggio di Novello, 5 gennaio 1703."

46. ASM, Feudi imperiali, cart. 437 (Monesiglio), n. 2: "Atti concernenti gli attentati commessi dai Finanzieri piemontesi a danno dei Comunisti di Monesiglio con averli turbato il privilegio del sale, e merci sopra i territori di Saliceto, e Gottasecca" (1718–20).

47. ASM, Feudi imperiali, cart. 354, "Carte del Vescovo delle Cinque Chiese sul transito del sale per il marchesato del Finale" (1708–10); 355, n. 7, "Atti in punto della fissazione della qualità, e prezzo del sale" (1726). Previous testimonies can be found in Haus-, Hof-, und Staatsarchiv, Vienna, Feudalia Latina, Langae V, fasz. b, "Relationem über die Kontribution der Feude Langarum," and especially in "Akten über die Salzgewinnung Betreffend 1694" (a series of contracts stipulated by Monesiglio and Millesimo merchants in the nineties).

48. On the careers of notaries, see, Torre, "Elites locali e potere centrale." Vaira's phrase is reported in AST, Sez. Riunite, art. 781, m. 2, n. 46.

49. On the impulse given by Borromeo to imperial policy in the Langhe fiefs, see ASM, Feudi imperiali, Plenipotenza, cart. 2039 (correspondence with the imperial tax collector Gio. Tomaso de Quentell); Haus-, Hof-, und Staatsarchiv, Vienna, Plenipotenz in Italien, Kk. 1–4. This can be verified by looking at the appeals to Milan and Vienna; these appeals were particularly intense between 1716 and 1726, as far as the Novello marquisate is concerned. See ASM, Feudi imperiali, cart. 500, where the lawsuits discussed in Milan are reported; these records were destroyed during World War II. Other appeals are found in Haus-, Hof-, und Staatsarchiv, Vienna, RHR, Jud. Lat., 386. Borromeo's correspondence with the Milanese auditors, who had been sent to the place, is very lively: see ASM, Feudi imperiali; see especially cart. 352–60, which contain Borromeo's correspondence with auditor Martelli from 1718 to 1726.

50. ASM, Feudi imperiali, cart. 445 and bis (trial for the Benevelli murderer, 1718–21); 500 (Ferrero trial, 1716); Haus-, Hof-, und Staatsarchiv, Vienna, Feudalia Latina, K. 372 (1721). Caldera's statement is found in ASM, Feudi imperiali, cart. 437: the date of the letter is September 11, 1718, and it is addressed to Borromeo.

7 ᷜ Counterfeit Coins and Monetary Exchange Structures in the Republic of Genoa during the Sixteenth and Seventeenth Centuries

by Edoardo Grendi

It is a banal truism to state that we must take into consideration exchange structures in order to study monetary crimes. It is also true but less obvious that minting coins, clipping them, and spending counterfeit and prohibited money were common practices in the "relationships between states." This did not mean that these practices were the product of explicit state policies but simply that arbitrage or speculation on exchange rates among coinages was a universal practice both within countries and among different countries. Monetary counterfeiting was only a means for guaranteeing a favorable exchange rate among different currencies.

There is a good reason, it seems to me, to consider counterfeiters above all as people who performed or had someone else perform the fusion of base metals and melted coins, employing various folkloristic practices, and who at the same time were involved in the sale and distribution of other products. This was a refined art that was inspired by different cultural resources, such as books, orally transmitted "secrets," and practical knowledge, and it always involved groups of people of different economic and organizational abilities who also belonged to different social classes. Genoese criminal documentation between 1580 and 1650 shows frequent interclass cooperation, but also only specific social groups were capable of high-quality enterprises. Therefore, as we shall see, even the notion of the legitimacy of official coinage could be called into question. In every case, the sign that

"Falsa monetazione e strutture monetarie degli scambi nella Repubblica di Genova fra Cinque e Seicento," *Quaderni storici* 66 (1987): 803–37. Translated by Corrada Biazzo Curry.

these coins were counterfeit was the symbol of the mint, that is, the unauthorized insignia of the prince, which suggested the idea of an affront to regal majesty.

The first and fundamental items to be determined must involve the figures of monetary circulation, a phenomenon that was institutionally the responsibility of the Magistrato delle Monete, who served as a judicial authority but who above all was charged with periodically defining the rules of currency exchange.

Like all other early modern European states, the republic of Genoa forbade the circulation of particular specie, set the value of others, selected some on the basis of intrinsic value and for the needs of commerce, and divised schemes and projects in order to put an end to "a monetary disorder" that was intractable.[1]

If small foreign coins continued to circulate, despite their prohibition, this was due to the nature of commercial exchanges; if large coins were getting more expensive in relation to the money of account, this was due to the fluctuations of a demand that was structurally specific, that is, certain transactions could only be carried out in specific currencies. Around the second half of the seventeenth century, the awareness of this fact and of the connection between the value of small coins, which were always losing value, and the growing price of larger coins, which were intrinsically stable, was precise. Counterfeiting of large as well as small indigenous coins only added to the combustibility of the market in large coins, of that in small ones, and between the large and small coins.

Bankers, tax collectors, and cashiers of the magistracy were often denounced as practitioners of arbitrage; but all those who could, practiced it, and this put day workers, peasants, and retail buyers in a situation of financial inferiority.[2]

Using the language of that time, the prince, who was "considered to be the intrinsic" source of value, determined the face value of a coin (the *valutazione*), while "the consensus of the people," which was considered to be "the extrinsic" source, that is, the value determined by the laws of supply and demand, provided the estimate of its real value (the *estimazione*). Therefore, all that remained for the authorities was the work of containment: to withdraw coins that were compromised or devalued by speculation, to experiment with new issues of bullion, and to make sure that all the prohibitions and coinages were carried out. These acts took place within the arbitrage system that projected the future values of coins and which presented itself with the halo of the definitive result. Speaking of this process, Andrea Spinola used a medical metaphor: "I do not know what should be the true and appropriate cure for us. I will say, nevertheless, that among the variety of opinions expressed, we must follow the most popular one; and, if this does not work, we should not be ashamed to try another expedient, like sick people do when, while turning over from one side to another, they try to cause the least pain that they can."[3] The negative consequences of monetary disorder affected trade as well as the dispositions of the people. "Making the common people believe," Spinola went on, "that we do not want to find a remedy for this is wrong, because everybody should take responsibility for maintaining order." In fact, police enforced the laws especially on the common people, representing a state power that considered counterfeiting and the circulation of false coins as lese majesty, one of the most highly punished crimes of the time.

However, there is no doubt that monetary crimes were part of a common economic culture with the monetary policy that defined them as crimes and determined what penalties and sanctions should be applied to them. The prince could finally express his authority at a punitive level by employing his executive powers. His mark on the coin represented at the minimum a claim to jurisdiction. Therefore, authorities countered any attempt to frustrate their monetary policy with criminal prosecutions.

☙ The reality and workings of the two main currencies of the *ancien régime,* those of small and large coinages, have been amply documented. This distinction involved a schema of social dichotomies: in fact, whoever dealt with small coins not only suffered a loss in exchange but also suffered from a constantly deteriorating purchasing power over time. The principle of a "special purpose"[4] coinage must ultimately refer to the circulation of different kinds of coins, above all of large coins. Usually, merchandise purchased outside the borders of the state required the use of a particular coin. This was confirmed by the butchers who bought their cattle from the hinterland.[5]

An inquiry of 1612 clearly shows that the equivalency of gold and silver coins in florins was established by the Piedmontese merchants or by the Ghersi brothers who dominated the Coscia market (Sampierdarena). They evaluated the doubloon at thirty-three florins: "since they tell me," reported a butcher, "that this is how much it is worth, and I let the people who take the goods keep the account."[6] The preference of cattle traders for gold doubloons would become, as we shall see, the occasion for market cornering and coin clipping because of the poor judgment of the butchers, who were told to pay for their purchases in that coinage.[7] It was also necessary to pay for Lombard grain with doubloons or gold coins. Later, in Savona, foreign grain merchants refused Savoyard coins that they had introduced into the market themselves, and accepted only silver scudi and large Genoese coins; and the saying went, "Compatriots follow the sellers' wishes."[8] On the other hand, Provençal and English merchants desired reals for their grain. This coin was very important in the shipping business, but since it came to Genoa on Spanish galleys, its supply was irregular and subject to monetary variations. It was precisely this "economy of reals" which accounts for the lack of a policy of monetary reciprocity with the inland states.

Silver scudi were, however, required to buy Calabrian silk. A 1634 report on the forms of ducat accepted for payment in Genoa denounced the rapid pace upward of the Venetian ducat, "thus it was used for speculation"; the downward pace of the Genoese coin, "thus it emigrated"; and the corresponding devaluation of the others "thus there [were] few of them [ducats]."[9] There were, therefore, structural connections between merchandise, coins, and monetary mobility that were expressed in the exchange markets. The two main objectives pursued by the magistracy were exchange security with the project of a bank that could monopolize the most lucrative operations and a parallel concern for sustaining the convertibility of the coinage. Thus, it seemed a success that San Giorgio had to renounce the payment of gabelles in silver scudi alone and had to accept the other recognized large coins. Not only were the prescribed five-scudo coins accepted at the Piacenza fair but also reals and silver scudi. These appeared to be big steps toward the circulation of a coin that had a "universal purpose": eliminating the demand for a specific coin would stop its rise in value.

Nevertheless, this principle could not in practice be made more general. Certainly it could not be imposed on those merchants who did not have any choice in the coin acceptable for external payments. Therefore, the number of foreign coins that were traded on the Genoa market was not significantly reduced. When the currency speculation was excessive, the coin could be banned, as was the case with the Venetian zecchino; the same thing happened when the alloy content cheapened, as in the case of the *ongari* and the Mexican and Peruvian reals.[10]

This short account of the circulation of large coins gives us an idea of monetary offenses which is more complex than the one expressed in the criminal statutes under the rubric "*de monetis.*"[11] Persons who preferred to remain anonymous could well complain that "the monetary market was in the hands of a few people," but intensive participation in the exchange and cornering the market was never considered an offense, even less as an offense that could actually be prosecuted.[12] Notwithstanding the repeated denunciations by bankers and tax farmers, in every case the crime was identified at the moment of "estimation" rather than at the moment of "evaluation." In effect, the mint was directly managed or run by contractors,[13] and it served as a profit mechanism for those who wanted to transform for free their silver and golden bars for export to other mints outside the territory of the republic. They had a much greater interest in the money than just minting it. To search for prohibited or counterfeit money, the police had the right to enter houses and shops, even to search in the ceilings, to board ships, and to inspect mule packs. Many mule drivers, wine-boat owners at Darsena, and small businessmen habitually complained, while storekeepers and others escaped by paying bribes. Despite the legal complaints brought by many exasperated but anonymous persons, the police did not search the houses of the rich and the nobility, since the "the different qualities of people" were explicitly recognized in the criminal statutes.

The aristocrat risked judicial prosecution only if he counterfeited or clipped coins. In 1655 the state inquisitors thought that the nobility ought to "purge itself" of the infamy of adultering the currency.[14] This purgation was incomplete, since in 1666–68 the famous louis case broke open, an event that documents the characteristic mentality of monetary manipulators. This practice was first denounced through anonymous accusations and then officially confirmed in 1667.[15] The Monaco, Loano, Torriglia, Tassarolo, and Fosdinovo mints received a commission to stamp louis with the mark of the king of France, commissions that guaranteed them profits of 40 percent or more. Eugenio and Gio Maria Durazzo, Vincenzo Spinola, and Giacomo Grimaldi were certainly among those who made the commissions and who planned by using various channels, to transport the coins through the territory of the republic to Livorno for transshipment to the final destination of Smyrna.

Three theologians were asked to pronounce upon the licitness of the argument in defense of the commission, which stated that the coins had been minted outside the Genoese jurisdiction and that in any event they were destined for the Turks.

The theologians, citing papal decretals and imperial laws, unanimously declared that it was a case of the counterfeiting of money, "both in matter and in form," a case of lese majesty against the king of France. Moreover, the mintings had been commissioned by subjects of the republic, who, even though they were feudal lords, did not have permission to make counterfeit money. Finally, the theologians ruled that the trade involved transit through Genoese territory and thus compromised legitimate trade based upon the principles of "commutative justice," that is, the respect of laws and contracts. In 1668, the republic urged the merchants to make for their needs a new coin, the *giorgino*, upon which the face value would be stamped in both Latin and Turkish.[16]

The episode underlines the crucial role of monetary manipulation of peripheral mints, that is, the feudal mints that had always represented a threat to the health of coins in circulation in various states: for obvious reasons, these mints were a corrupting presence that spread the infection of counterfeit money among feudal nobility and others.[17]

The other "high" crime of exchanging money for a more highly valued currency found its ideological justification in the idea that coins were a commodity. In 1606 B. Costa argued that "it is different to spend coins than to sell and exchange them because, on the one hand, they constitute the price of a debt that one must pay, but, on the other, they serve as a commodity and as money that can willingly and with the mutual consent of the parties be exchanged for something else."[18]

These reasons constitute the rationale for the "consensus of men" on the value of a coin. A bit late the same magistracy, confronted with the influx of a mass of low-quality reals from Mexico and Peru, recognized that successfully prohibiting them was improbable, so it ordered that the real could be put into circulation only as a commodity, thus confirming the argument of the manipulators. One example of the coin as a commodity was debt, which was already subject to the principle of the "increase of the amount of money," even when it was negotiated in scudi of account in units of four lire.[19] Since frequently the buying and selling of specific goods required the use of particular coins, transactions postulated a monetary conversion, that is, a transaction of money and a commodity, which created the occasion for arbitrage in the markets. The motivation probably derived from the different exchange rates prevailing for the same specie in different markets.

The theory of coins as a commodity, which stated that they were not expendable, thus legitimated the universal practice, annulling the authorities' control of exchange rates.

  The problem of the circulation of small foreign coins in Liguria also appeared insoluble. First of all, official authorities had to issue small Genoese coins in sufficient but not excessive quantities: their availability was necessary for daily use, making them, therefore, a very important element in social policy. These coins were an alloy of silver and copper, and they were always stamped with a reduced face value in order to guarantee the economic viability of the operation. Since even these coins were subject to forgery, there were attempts to take them out of circulation by minting new issues. However, here the comparison with foreign money was more critical, since the balance of trade in the territory was governed by needs of the supply trade, especially in those areas such as the Levantine Riviera, which was characterized by a negative balance of payments.

The very same situation in the territory of the republic exposed the markets to a flood of Savoyard, Monferrine, Lombard, Parmesan, Piacentine, Lucchese, Corregiane, and papal coins, as well as those from Massa and Tassarolo. Repeatedly forbidden since 1584, these coins continued to dominate the markets at an arbitrary and hyperevaluated rate, which also created deformities in the rates of exchange with large coins, stimulating the arbitragers. In Genoa the food-rationing offices, which were structurally more likely to "take in bad money and to pay out good money," were full of these coins collected from consumers. As we have noted, the "strong" meat or grain seller determined the type of coin to be used in the exchange and was particularly interested in Genoese money, except for the purchase of salt.[20]

The "scandal" consisted in the fact that the excessive unilateral evaluation of coinage without any reference to the official exchange rates could not be eliminated through prohibitions without damaging trade. The podestàs' and captains' reports from Pieve, Savona, Ovada, Novi, Rapallo, Chiavari, La Spezia, and Sarzana were very explicit in this respect. They also denounced the way in which unbalanced negotiations distorted the ultimate transaction between storekeepers and daily consumers. For the same coin the rate for buying was always higher than the rate for selling. The alternative remedy of regulating the evaluation of foreign coins drove them underground, consequently making them rare.

In turn, monetary exchanges between the markets and the hinter-lands reproduced the asymmetry that existed between middlemen and consumers. The operation of buying and selling often implied the payment of a monetary interest of around 10 percent. Genoese coins were scarce, so much so that it was even useful to corner the small coins used for military payrolls, preventing them from circulating. In fact, this coinage had a higher intrinsic value, which made it useful for purchasing large coins. Therefore, the circulation of these coins went up, causing differences between the Genoese markets and those across the borders, between the markets in the provinces and Genoa. This was the situation in the sixteenth and seventeenth centuries. It was said in Savona that the prohibition of foreign money was like "rowing upstream": trade was threatened, people could not spend the coins that they were obliged to accept, and speculation on large coins increased.

In the end, the republic increased its coinage issues. During the period from 1575 to 1599 the issue amounted to only 45,339 lire; between 1660 and 1624 it grew to 552,861 lire; and between 1625 and 1649 it exploded to 1,668,207 lire. These are partial data, but one would not be wrong to postulate that they reflect the dramatically increased activity of the mint.[21] The problem now was that of imposing their circulation on the economy.

This implied a systematic conversion of coins, a losing proposition given the fact that it was very difficult to evaluate the value of foreign money. In Genoa, for example, the food-rationing offices for grain, wine, and oil were financially damaged, since they were considered to be the natural place for the circulation of the national currency, so much so that the general exchange bank was attached to the Ufficio dell'Abbondanza. The food-rationing offices would have had to ex-change quickly bullion coins for large ones, hastening the circulation of the bullion they stored, while the bankers would have had to absorb periodically a certain quantity of bullion coins in perfect harmony with the relationship between the Grain Office and the bakers.[22]

The disparity between the estimate and the evaluation made the administrative conversion of coinages highly problematic.[23] The dis-tance between small and large coins increased more and more: the price rise of silver required a change in the alloy of the national bullion coins, which competed with foreign money, a fact that was reputedly the principal cause for a monetary disorder. Moreover, the continuous presence of this debased coin was perceived as damaging to the prince's prestige, which was apparently not compromised by the circulation of large foreign coins. But the fact of the matter was that, independently of the circulation of foreign coins, once the amount of Genoese money increased, the balance between small and large coins constantly preoccupied the authorities charged with favoring the circulation of local coins in the territory. The task was delegated to the major officials, who acted as commissaries for the substitution of foreign money: in the Levantine Riviera the problem during the 1630s especially came from the sixteen- and twenty-*denari* coins and from the Parma and Piacenza *"vacchette."*[24]

An edict of 1638 issued in Rivarolo (an area for exchanges with the Ponent Riviera) provided for the conversion of foreign money, including Piacentine coins, the *cavallotti* and *soldini* of Massa, old two-florin coins, Savoyard *gianne,* and various Lucchese coins.[25]

Reports from the territory document yet again the classical problem: only a few people would ask to change their foreign money at a lower price, even if they had small Genoese coins. Such money instead flowed abroad, exchanged at a different rate. In the opposite direction, the interest for Genoese coins was tied to the possibility of exchanging them on the Genoese market for large coins, with the possibility of a more favorable local exchange rate, due to the systematically higher circulation of large coins.[26] The locally indicated solution was still that of evaluating rather than prohibiting foreign money: once its use was made inconvenient, the process of substitution became easier.

Because of the penetration of Genoese bullion coins in foreign territories, their decisive success was thought to be the result of the complementary efforts on the part of these states to accept the currency in their respective territories. Therefore, the action of the state was particularly felt at the small-coin level, following a political direction that can be compared to the administrative action taken against foreign beggars, since curiously the Magistrato delle Monete was charged with this task in 1625.[27]

In any event, the normalization process was especially related to exchange transactions along the borders. Again in 1644 Sarzana asked to be recognized as a frontier post under special regulations.[28] Notwithstanding such resistance, during this period the commissaries' requests for small coins seemed to indicate some success in the substitution policy.[29]

In the commercial centers of the Ponent Riviera and the area around Genoa, the coins that were circulating were mostly the ten-soldi Genoese coins, which had previously been forbidden but only partially withdrawn. In any case, the problem seemed to affect only the Levantine Riviera.[30]

In Genoa, monetary policy could be regulated by the courts of the magistracy, and the effect of the new issues was certainly felt more immediately. In 1650, the new difficulties of the Grain Office were related to the expensive withdrawal of the twenty-*denari* coins, the circulation of which had been compromised, like the five- and ten-soldi coins, by the counterfeiting of the mints on the borders.[31]

The controversies of the 1650s pertained to the issues of Genoese bullion coins, of submultiples of large coins, and of small copper coins for lower values.[32] In other words, the problem of the quality of small Genoese coins was a question of their "intrinsic value": people thought that lower quality favored arbitrage with the higher-valued coinage: "[M]ost of all there are people in the banks who watch over the arbitrage and who worship the bank ledgers all day long in order to earn a penny."[33]

Therefore, the cornering of small coins for exchange with large ones could be achieved in the same market, without requiring any differences in the exchange rates for the same coins on several markets, such as the cases we have mentioned earlier. The artificially high circulation of small coins in relation to monetary supply judged to be excessive created an opportunity for speculation.[34]

Obviously, people thought that a coherent mobility of the rate of evaluation for small and large coins was theoretically possible only with coins made of the same alloy. This type of issue, integrated with copper coinages, seemed to prevail at a certain point. At the same time, the monopolization of exchange mechanisms and the monetary regulation of commercial contracts again emerged.

There were multiple causes of the "monetary disorder": the pressure of the demand for this or that specie, the quality and amount of bullion in circulation, and so on. The idea of eliminating the money of account (from an imaginary value to one pegged to the real monetary unit of a sixth of a silver scudo) proved to be illusory. Disorder led to arbitrage, a transaction that caused evident social damage. Nevertheless, administrative corrections of the market, which were always possible, did not in the end lead to the demonization of anyone. The papers of the Treasury Office illustrate that the officials were perfectly aware of the objective reality and of the role of "the consensus of the players." Administrative or police interference could be absolute only in the prosecution for counterfeiting and clipping coins. Since the republic was unable to discipline the arbitragers and to affirm its monetary sovereignty over its own territory, it only struck at the small-time offense of counterfeiting.

This leads us into the realm of social affairs, a different terrain free from every pretense of objectivity, a necessarily pragmatic terrain of individual stories and of "collective conspiracies." I will attempt to take these social conditions into account in explaining the character of the circulation of money which I have reconstructed and to show how they constitute the rational principle for counterfeiting. Moreover, I will particularly emphasize those practices of fusion and coining which constituted the various forms of counterfeiting. But first of all we shall try to clarify the social culture of money in general.

&ent; What strikes us about the collective consciousness of the period was the sense of the individuality of each coin. A scudo or a doubloon was always recognizable, so that in a common judicial procedure, witnesses were expected to be able to recognize those coins that they had handled, and they quickly responded to requests to identify them.[35] However, the performance of identification was not completely neutral, since it often referred to counterfeit coins. With regard to this, the law required persons to cut up counterfeit coins or to report them and bring them to the mint.

The procedures for the evaluation of authenticity were obviously very differentiated: if a coin had a "bad appearance," whoever received it could bite it to prove its malleability or rub it to see if it became red. To make a definitive test, it was necessary to go to a goldsmith's shop in order to scrape the coin with a file or rub it on a polishing stone and then to test it under fire.[36] This practice is reflected in the testimony of a witness who stated, "One knows that coins are counterfeit when the third person does not want them; then, you can exchange them with the first person." This was a normal procedure when that person could be found.[37] And it explains the reason why the police and judiciary followed the itinerary of counterfeit coins: usually the surprised holder of counterfeit coins asserted that he had acted in good faith, that he was ignorant of the counterfeit, that it had been dark when he received the coin, or some other self-serving circumstance. It was clear that he had to find the person who gave him the coin, in the official language the "first person," whom the police were ready to detain. The "first person" could start the search all over again, but the responsibility was in his hands.

The prejudice in favor of the accuser's evidence was reinforced by the officially sanctioned and regulated practice of the anonymous denunciation. Thus, in 1611 a person who turned in prohibited money and already had a one-third interest in the funds seized also obtained substantial rewards for bringing charges for counterfeiting including impunity from punishment if involved.[38]

Later, the authorities organized systematic spying and resorted to using the safes of the mint and the state inquisitors for sequestered moneys. A 1642 proclamation, directed in particular against coin clipping, established rules to protect the anonymity of the accusers, even when they received a reward for their denunciation.[39] Therefore, anonymous charges became more numerous.

There is no doubt that in the common consciousness of contemporaries accusations were a very serious matter, and in the case of a direct charge the accused persons were subject to torture. The possibility of the abuse of the process of making accusations existed: sometimes rivalries between neighborhoods, soldiers, or factions motivated the accusers. In these latter cases, especially in the countryside, anonymous denunciations followed the judicial itinerary, with reports of the bribing of witnesses, threats against others, and the complicity of local authorities. In fact, the defendant could organize his defense and, when he had the means, could hire an attorney to draw up an apology.

Monetary offenses called for the death penalty, the confiscation of property, and the burning of the place where the offense had been committed, a standard of punishment which clearly recalled the crime of lese majesty. The practices that were prosecuted concerned gold and silver fusion, counterfeiting, coin clipping, and the possession of tools such as crucibles, punches, and scissors, that is, the material evidence, which were collectively called the "coin clipper's growth." The crime of lese majesty was certainly a judicial matter, and an offense against the prince did not have any mystical resonances. It was widely known how hard the punishment was, but less well known was the joint responsibility of people who passed counterfeit coins.[40] Once they discovered through tests that they had counterfeit money, these potential offenders could decide to throw the coins away.[41] Thus, when Francesco Percivalle was accused of coin clipping, he was instructed, "[I]f I confess, they will take me to the pier and cut off my arm, and if I do not confess, they will take me to jail."[42] A popular proverb that was very common in Genoa at the beginning of the seventeenth century went, "[C]ounterfeit coins bring the holy oil [of the last rites], and one must not deal with them." In addition, a young man who sold false coins was warned, "[Y]ou are training for the gallows."[43] The provincial inhabitants of small towns were probably the ones that needed instruction. This is how Abramo di Segre from Casale addressed one Lomellini: it did not matter if the doubloons were light, because the exchange broker would pay for the right value; what counted was that the doubloons should not be made of an inferior alloy, "in such a case he would not only lose the doubloons, but also his life."[44]

Nevertheless, sometimes this practice was the object of admiration: a Father Ippolito was defined by one of his friends in La Spezia as "a very talented man who [was] able to make a thousand doubloons." In 1607 in Monterosso on the Levantine Riviera, the encouragement to keep silent about certain coins was justified by arguing, "[S]ome people of high quality could be involved in this deal, and this could ruin our house."[45] The responsibility for judicial enforcement was in the hands of the Genoese magistrate, who usually charged the podestàs and captains with the responsibility to conduct the investigation, but he sometimes appointed ad hoc investigators even when the trial took place in Genoa. These were secret trials that allowed defense witnesses, and they were, nevertheless, centered on the use of torture, under a surgeon's supervision, who established how much the defendant could tolerate and for how long. Some defendants would be let go if they paid warranty on their future behavior, while others could be sentenced to exile or jail but rarely to death.[46]

❧ The various cases that we have mentioned must be related to the characteristic monetary practices, such as those of coinage and monetary circulation. However, monetary matters were dependent not only on the regional mints but also on a "metallurgical creativity," which was exercised by minters and goldsmiths but also by alchemists and generally by various people who had the expertise (the so-called secrets) or access to it and who experimented with minting coins with some success. These people were frequently priests but also convicts, soldiers (who moved about a great deal and were rich with experiences), notables, gentlemen, and even artisans.

In the specific case, the making of coins obviously involved the organization of its circulation, which was more important when the "manufacturing" was correlated to the larger productivity of a mint. In other words, it was necessary to market the coins, by spreading them out in different areas. On the other extreme was the fabrication of coins for direct use by the maker, often tied to a very experimental method of production. In the intermediary zone is the introduction of coins in a specific monetary exchange circuit, which is particularly interesting in the case of coin clipping.

Tangentially, in the territory monetary counterfeiting involved numerous notables from Ligurian and non-Ligurian villages. In Genoa, in contrast, this activity was more a popular one and thus more socially coherent, and perhaps it was less well organized. The relationships between center and periphery remained important.

Opportunities in the periphery were related to the mints and to the franking zones of the fiefs. For this reason, the magistracy forbade the republic's subjects to mint coins within forty miles' distance from the borders.[47] We have seen how the feudal mints had been mobilized by aristocratic Genoese speculators to make the louis coins.

We are also informed of fifteen thousand reals and piasters minted in Tassarolo, of small Genoese coins from Bozola which were then sold in the Sarzana and San Sebastiano areas, of counterfeit *cobianchi* from the fief of Rocca. In addition, the Seborga and Fosdinovo mints were overseen by the Genoese magistrate in the second half of the seventeenth century.[48]

Previously, issues of counterfeit coins had been made in Piacenza, Guastalla, Valoria di Provenza, and Camerano di Monferrato. The emphasis on feudal mints was new, but the phenomenon went back to 1588, when the Tresana mint (twenty-five miles from Massa in the Magra area) was famous for its "sad coins." Moreover, the Passerano, Desana, and Gazoldo mints were closed by the emperor's order.[49] In 1597 a minter from Tresana was in league with a merchant from Levanto and his agent in the coinage and selling of bags of four- and forty-*denari* counterfeit coins. Using a brother-in-law who owned six wine boats and who sold off twenty-five thousand loads in Darsena, Marco and Antonio Orlandini took on a supply of copper in Genoa for the Tresana mint. The coins were hidden in wine barrels, sorted out in Bollana, and from there transported in boxes to Lombardy, infecting the entire area.

Whoever was in possession of these four-*denari* coins was compelled to get rid of them for one *denaro,* and even the counterfeiters bought them up. Since they were protected by the Malaspinas, they were always able to hold justice in check.[50]

From the same mint at Tresana counterfeit coins were commissioned for dissemination in western Liguria. Gio Agostino Rivarola was associated with the Tresana and Sabbioneta mints, later becoming a contractor for the Massa mint, but he fell into disgrace and was imprisoned in Sarzana in 1605 when he was caught with counterfeit silver scudi.[51] Rivarola was also supplying patterns for a group of counterfeiters who were led by Father Giovanni Ruschi, vicar of Veppo. A few years later, Rivarola was sentenced to the galleys in Genoa, but again he got involved in counterfeiting. After working in the mint for eight years, he had become a real expert.[52]

At the other end of the region, Provençal minters were used, such as those minters from Nice who were recruited in 1599 by the Palmaro brothers from Sanremo to coin ducatoons and reals in the castle of Vingale, which belonged to the marquis of Dolceacqua.[53] These feudal options on mints and over specific areas of distribution often involved the cooperation of the same feudatories, not only as the proprietors of mints but also for more "experimental" initiatives. This was the case of Antonio Spinola from Montesoro and Gio Francesco Chiavari, who were involved in a complex affair in 1598 to mint counterfeit coins in Sampierdarena, Rigoroso, and Cassinelle near Cremolino. It seems as though Spinola had bought up some patterns that had been ordered from the goldsmith Domenico Basso, called Pizzo. Among the "experts" there was also a French captain called Guido, who had been sentenced to the government's galleys.[54]

This was also the case of Gaio Cesare Santamaria, who in 1607 took possession of many counterfeit coins that had been minted ten years earlier, and he was waiting to sell his part of the Moasca fief to return to his enterprise: "[O]ne cannot go on a voyage," he said, "without sea biscuits."[55] Metalworkers from the province, innkeepers, soldiers, and mule drivers mixed with these "poor" gentlemen in counterfeiting, making it possible for the Veronese Pietro di Pietrozanni, called the sergeant, to meet in the beautiful La Lomellina palace, three miles from Novi, a castrated Carmelite friar who was interested in making a deal.[56]

During those same years in the Ligurian Levant, Tomaso Landi, called the red priest, scoured the country followed by numerous armed men: sometimes not only the lords but also influential notables retained an armed retinue when they were minting counterfeit coins. In this rural context of factional struggles legal denunciations became a means of pursuing a rivalry: thus, the accusation of heresy, which was very popular some decades earlier, was replaced by charges of monetary counterfeiting. These two charges were decisive in making an enemy "get lost." In the little village of Bracelli, between 1608 and 1678, the main local sides were concentrated around this accusation made by a Roi against a Piaggio.[57]

The mountain lords' involvement in monetary counterfeiting was evident. It is interesting to note how in the Ligurian Levant monetary counterfeiting largely consisted of making small coins; in other words, it was a condition of the extent of monetary disorder in the circulation of bullion, which allowed a more capillary distribution. If the weak contracting parties paid a monetary interest in the exchange equivalent to 10 percent, what would the proportionate burden be when counterfeit coins came into play?

❧ At the other extreme, besides the more organized and speculative minting operations, there was also a more experimental way of counterfeiting, which we have called "usage" counterfeiting. We can thus distinguish between two aspects of counterfeiting, because the experimental form was largely self-contained. It is clear that the structures of production had some obligatory characteristics, mentioned in the criminal statutes. For example, in some cases cuttlefish bones were used instead of crucibles, and the use of powders played a special role.

The consultants of the magistracy were normally the minters, who were able to define "normal" operations. The same staff testified on the use of alchemists, mostly foreigners, who relied on the Genoa mint for their experiments.[58] It was probably a foreign magician, Adamo Centurione, who in the second half of the sixteenth century had been contracted under very stringent conditions for an experiment to make gold grow. The operation would be rewarded only if it had succeeded.[59] A century later, Ambrogio Pinello, who had been charged with "extravagant" coinage, defended himself by claiming to be a professional alchemist and bringing as evidence his manuscripts and a book on the transformation of metals. There was, in fact, a circle of Genoese alchemists, whose members included Gio Francesco Rebuffo, Filippo Doria, the Savonese G. B. Gavotti Guarnieri, G. B. Grimaldi q. Gerolamo (who had been active in Naples twenty-three years earlier), the knight Leoni, and Filippo Messini, a soldier from Orvieto, who was not an expert in melting "because," he said, "[his] profession concern[ed] chemistry and not alchemy." Filippo Messini reported on the mistakes of Pinello, who "wanted to stop the mercury and iron, transform it into copper, and scrape gold from some pieces of an old anchor."[60] These could be the practices of "a new man." Therefore, in the fluid relationship between alchemy and metallurgy, based on the common secrets that had been handed down or learned, alchemy was considered to be a legitimate activity, even though it was still somewhat suspect.

Let us move to the provinces toward the end of the previous century. In Triora in 1588, two apprentice counterfeiters, the tailor G. B. Oddo and Francesco Ferrando used cuttlefish bones to "make impressions for the coronets." According to the malicious testimony of their wives, the two friends had been together for two years, trying to make *cavallootti* with tin that the priest Marco Ferrando had supplied. However, they did not have much success, leaving their wives exasperated. When he was still denying it all, Oddo freely testified that he had two alchemy books in the house by Faloppa and Fioravanti. He evidently considered alchemy the best cover for his activities.[61]

Ten years later at Novi, Colomban de Barchi di Tortona, an illiterate goldsmith, moved into the house of Giovan Francesco Guidoboni, with whom he was implicated in a history of making counterfeit ducatoons. Colomban did not hide his knowledge of alchemy, which he had learned from "many friars and priests," particularly from a Monferrine friar called Gregorio. He testified, "I know how to stop mercury, and I am not afraid that this could harm me; I also know how to increase the quantity of silver with the use of other material such as copper or tin, but this would be too low in value, and gold has no equal." We note how in this testimony the alchemist's lawful acts are mixed with the metallurgist's unlawful ones. Less ambiguous were the activities of his friend Guidoboni, who thought he had the philosophers' stone, "since he had put certain things under the manure at the innkeeper's house at the White Cross Abbey in Tortona."[62]

It was still the search for the philosophers' stone which constituted the research for more than a decade of the apothecary Gerolamo Cappelletto in 1616. Cappelletto belonged to a local circle of intellectuals whose other members included the priest Giacomo Bertucci, a schoolteacher, the physician Santo Spontone, the musician Onofrio, and other priests who used to gather in the Piazza Conturla.

Cappelletto was a well-placed apothecary, but after he went bankrupt as a merchant in Naples, he had retired, trying to collect the money owed him and cultivating his passion for alchemy: thus, he distilled water for women and produced cancer ointments with copper powders, fir-tree oil, white incense, and other things, following a formula he got from an apothecary from Bollano.[63] In his depositions, Cappelletto frequently returned to his passion for the philosophers' stone, with a particularly defensive emphasis suggested to him by a notary friend.

Cappelletto said that, while coming into possession of his uncle Andrea's papers, he found in a book a "treasure," written in 1480, which revealed the way to make a compound of mercury and silver, making it possible to earn a hundred scudi per week. This teaching then disappointed him, since a foreigner who was passing by showed him the way to fix mercury with a stone. Once he had the formula, Cappelletto could not, however, repeat the experiment, since he did not have the necessary vermilion (i.e., "red sulfate"). He was not able to succeed, not even with the help of a Moor, whom he kept a house guest for nine months, and who escaped taking Cappelletto's money, naturally just at the moment when they were close to success. This story exposed Cappelletto to public ridicule.[64]

Santo Spontone was a young physician who had already practiced in Pammatone before being hired by the community of La Spezia: "[He] knows a lot about planets, the proper proportions in medicines, and when to draw blood at the right time, [and he is anxious] to meet a scientist, so that he can show off."

Father Giacomo Bertucci, a schoolteacher and well-to-do man who had been "financially ruined by his two brothers," took Santo Spontone to Carrara to meet the priest Ippolito of Garfagno, vicar of Vinca. The meeting was a big disappointment for the young doctor, who, having requested books of "curiosities," nevertheless obtained from the priest some "exotic books," including *De Misteriis Aegiptorum* by Tamblico, *Dialoghi annessi* by Hermes Trismegistis, and *Sulla magia naturale* by B. Napolitano.[65] Father Ippolito, "who had a gloomy and melancholic aspect that seemed to offend Spontone when looking at him," was wanted by the duke of Tuscany and by the bishop of Sarzana for his activities as a counterfeiter which had excited Father Giacomo's admiration.

When Father Ippolito was caught, he confirmed to the bishop of Sarzana that Father Giacomo and Cappelletto had asked him for help to mint some coins, so he had sent them to a goldsmith in Massa. In any case, Cappelletto's house was full of crucibles, stoves, and powders, even though Marco Aurelio had warned him that "those who practiced alchemy went to ruin." In 1620 Cappelletto was forced to renounce his search for the philosophers' stone, but his passion for alchemy was irresistible. Six years later, despite his protests to the contrary, material evidence proved that he was still practicing as an alchemist, and he was exiled to Sardinia for six years.[66]

The anonymous letter that accused him talked about some people who "made alchemy and counterfeit coins." This combination of practices was a constant: a successful alchemist would only make real coins, but of course such an alchemist did not exist.

The Triora tailor, the ensign Pacifico, and the fellow soldiers from Cairo who sold counterfeit reals in Savona in 1628 had a copy of the book by Fioravanti and an herbal, entitled *Il buon Procafaccia*. They had learned how to mint coins from these books and from a Venetian ensign who was a convict aboard the papal galleys. The informant made no distinctions: he who practiced alchemy was also trying to make money.[67] Even if the above-mentioned Santamaria failed to give any credit to an old Piedmontese, who knew how to make gold grow by 30 percent, it was true that two alchemists were involved in the counterfeiting operation, a Sergeant Pietro Veronese, who "[knew] how to convert copper into silver," and Andrea Laiti from Augsburg.[68] Indeed, alchemists, like goldsmiths, were experts in metals and powders, and alchemy was inconceivable without practicing it.[69]

Therefore, we should not be surprised if this practice, which was diffused on several social levels, played an important role in the falsification of coins. At a high level, alchemy was not very liable to suspicion, but at a lower level, where it lost its mystic halo, it became an indicator of criminal activity. Marginally educated people who were highly mobile were not tied to the theoretical and symbolic practice of research.

Now we shall compare the alchemists' procedures with basic monetary metallurgy, in other words, with how coins were actually made.

If the alchemical procedures were often unrewarding and research regularly frustrating, counterfeit metallurgic coining did very well. Its tools were stoves, flasks, crucibles, patterns, punches, files, scissors, metals, and various powders, which constituted the "material evidence" (obviously besides the possession of counterfeit coins) of counterfeiting.

Coins were made in different ways, varying the metals and the alloys. There were those who made fifteen doubloons out of thirteen, made four out of one, used copper or tin or "tin plate," transformed reals into ducatoons, coined *soldini* and *cavallotti*, minted scudi and doubloons, and simply lightened coins by clipping. Nevertheless, counterfeit coins were in general "cast" money, and the metallurgic process seemed to be common. Counterfeiters employed terra-cotta flasks that were filled with "crushed tiles softened with water" or with "ashes that were well sifted and mixed with egg whites and salted water." Once the paste was well pressed and warmed, it could take the shape of the coin to be minted. After extracting the coin used to make the mold, counterfeiters made the mold adhere again and poured the liquid alloy through a hole in the flask. This alloy had been previously melted in a crucible according to a ratio among metals which was determined by the desired result.[70] As it cooled, the fused metal adhered to the mold made from the original coin. For example, in order to have a ducatoon, one had to put in the crucible a four-reals piece and some copper and tin plate, so that it would weigh as much as a ducatoon; to make *soldini,* one used tin, which was mixed with iron to harden it. Now the problem was to whiten the coins, especially when, because of the copper content, they had remained entirely black. For this purpose, one put the coins to boil in a pot full of water mixed with bleach or "barrel residue." Once they were scraped and polished, the coins would become shinier. From another source comes the formula to whiten copper: "[F]irst you take ordinary but well-purged copper and melt it down; then in the months of May, June, and July (May is the best), take fresh ox shit and put it in a vase, then you pour liquefied copper two or three times over the shit, and in this way the copper becomes as white as silver, and if you cast it several times, it becomes whiter." This secret belonged to Battista, the vicar of San Pietro Oneglia, who was killed by the soldiers to whom he had revealed his formula.[71] This formula sounds as if it were an original one: the use of tartar and salt to bleach metals was the common method. The more sophisticated minter Rivarola argued that steel flasks lasted longer than brick flasks and recommended "boiling the coins three or four times in water with the flowers of fava beans."[72]

It does not seem that recourse to punches to mark the face was general because what counted was the rough reproduction of the imprint. Nevertheless, this was not the case of Santamaria di Moasca, who certainly worked with the higher metals and relied on the work of a German ensign to make "the letters on the coins."[73] Even Abramo Segre, a Jew from Casale who had been caught while selling counterfeit doubloons in Genoa, worked in terms of reducing the valuable metal content of coins, weighing down the golden doubloons with silver and then scraping off the gold that constituted the extra weight. However, he was not able enough in the execution of his "secret" to convince his rich cousin to entrust other doubloons to him.[74]

The employment of qualified minters and goldsmiths was obviously fundamental to the process. They were commissioned to fabricate the stamps, which were the preconstituted forms for the requested coin, coinages that could more easily take the imprint in the fused alloy. This process speeded up production time. Agostino Passano minted fifty ducatoons in eighteen days, while the minters from Nice who were hired by the Palmaros of the castle of Vinagale for fifteen days were able to coin 150 scudi of reals and ducatoons.[75]

Thus, there were at least two technological levels of counterfeiting: the more dilettantish one rendered singularly high profits by employing low-quality metals; the other, more speculative one brought together various specialized skills and assured circulation through preexisting channels.

A third level was represented by the commissions given to the feudal mints; and at this particular level, as in the case of the louis, an ideological self-justification was elaborated in defense of treating money as a commodity. There was certainly a considerable cultural dichotomy between the Genoese minters who were working as consultants and the dilettantes at counterfeiting. Could an iron grater or a particular powder be considered as material evidence of the crime? Like a goldsmith, the alchemist found himself in a fatally ambiguous position, since tools and powders could have different uses. Bright silver, for example, like nitric acid and alum, served to separate gold from silver. In his research scheme the alchemist wanted to make white silver, and for this purpose he used special oils, herbs, or even a toad, but these were also used by peasants to destroy lice. In another version the products of the alchemist's distillations could also be used as a health water for women and as a salve for gout. Equally ambiguous in its use was *feggia,* an unrefined bleach, which the beautiful Sicilian Angela, who used to frequent the Angel Tavern with the Neapolitan Gio Domenico Palombo, used to lighten her hair.[76] Tools, powders, and metals were all suspicious possessions and could become material evidence, a situation that created critical questions of judicial procedure. The exchange between alchemy and coining naturally went in both directions: in fact, a mysterious hermetic book found in the home of the gambler, coin clipper, and counterfeiter Andrea Viglieri was immediately handed over to the inquisitor.[77] However, it was rare to find a papyrus that explicitly explained the way to make counterfeit coins as happened in Novi in 1610.[78]

The "secrets," both written and oral, generally used a different level of language, or at least more general and positive titles. When a secret that had been handed down in written form corresponded to a common formula passed on by a wayfarer, the impulse to experiment became irresistible. However, the popular form of communication differed from that of alchemy, because the latter was based on a printed literature of "curious books" that could be found directly in the houses. Nevertheless, the "secret" as a more natural form of esoteric communication certainly embraced the two dimensions, in practice indistinguishable, of alchemy and popular metallurgy.

⅋ The range of coinage practices was so broad that they varied enormously according to the scale of the operation and the place in which the money was distributed. In Monterosso, the news of the circulation of counterfeit coins could provoke a public riot, but in Genoa, because of the density of the population, it was difficult to keep a large-scale operation hidden. In the city there were so many experts in the field (from the churches to the galleys and the goldsmiths' shops) that many counterfeiting operations that were conducted in the more discreet peripheral corners began in the city.

The contribution from the world of convicts should not surprise us, since sentences to the galleys were as common in the republic as elsewhere. People said that "vice was never lost" and that it passed from father to son, especially when the vice was an art that other people never forgot. Thus, a Bergamasque convict who had been a goldsmith confessed in 1593 that Gio Francesco Chiavari wanted to free him from the galleys "so that he could help Gio Francesco to make reals half of silver and half of copper."[79] The above-mentioned Gio Agostino Rivarola came to an agreement with Prospero Valeriano, another convict, "to soften steel in order to make molds."[80] And finally, the convict Vincenzo Ruschi, the son of a priest who had been a convict himself, was involved with Father Buttero and Orazio Schiavi, who was G. B. Doria's servant in 1612: once they helped him to escape, Vincenzo revealed the way to solidify bright silver by pouring it down a toad's mouth, a practice confirmed in other cases.[81]

When the galleys were in dry dock, the convicts had to make their own living through hawking merchandise, and this gave them considerable freedom to keep relationships open with the community.

The Mantuan Giovan Battista Gambatia, who was sentenced by the governor of Milan, was recruited to manage the gambling on the galley captained by Duke Doria by the German goldsmith Emanuele Valtemar, so that he could launder his counterfeit coins. The singular figure Valtemar, a goldsmith and innkeeper, was very familiar with the convicts who used to go to his tavern to play the trumpet.[82] Valtemar defended himself saying, "They are slaves and they can say anything they want." It was generally granted that a convict could not be a respectable person, but neither was a counterfeiter even if he were free. In Genoa it was said that counterfeit coins were minted aboard the galleys. To escape and find freedom in such circumstances was to search for subsistence.

Also searching for subsistence were the soldiers we have seen in Sarzana and Savona, who were willing to bargain away their *soldini* for survival. In Genoa, in 1624, some female bakers for the customs house in Piazza del Molo e del Fossatello gossiped about the soldiers' *soldini,* this time of copper. When the soldiers were denounced, the blame fell on Matteuccio di Orezza rather than on his fellow soldier, who was trained as a necromancer and counterfeiter. Matteuccio defended himself saying "[F]or a slug of wine these women would say that God is not God." The women, according to Matteuccio, had been stirred up by his enemies from Savona, who belonged to the company of Captain Muzio, with whom he was feuding.[83]

However, it is above all the story of Marietta Castella, "the charwoman," which gives us an insight into the atmosphere of the Olivella quarter, where everyone heard everything and where someone saw counterfeit coins being made in the first months of 1627. During the Christmas season of the previous year, Marietta's sister, Nicoletta, and her husband, Stefano Baitano, were starving, but a few months later, a neighbor saw them well dressed and well fed. The neighbor shouted to Nicoletta, "I don't live off counterfeit money."

The neighbor accused Marietta, who by now had a bad reputation, so much so that a woman named Massabò and the goldsmith Paolo threatened to put her in a brothel. Tools used to make counterfeit coins were found in Baitano's house, which led even Marietta's sister to accuse her of taking advantage of her hungry husband.

Having been abandoned by her husband, Marietta got pregnant

by Michele de Negri, Gerolamo Balbi's butler, who had taken her to live in his servant's room, but even he also threatened her to shut her in a brothel. When Marietta was caught and interrogated, she testified, "I have always been fascinated and inspired by counterfeiting ever since I was a little girl, and ... sometimes I fall into a melancholic humor." Her teacher was Giovan Battista Ravaschero, who had fled from Rome, and her accomplice was the goldsmith Tomaso Grasso, to whom Marietta handed over the silver shavings left over from coin clippings. In short, it was Marietta who had the competence and the connections. She brought the good coins (quarters of silver scudi and some thirteen-soldi coins) to those who clipped them and melted the remaining coins in a crucible. Marietta wanted "to work in turn for those who always gave [her] something to eat." She had known the witnesses well ever since she was little and explained why some of them were hostile to her: "Other people think well of themselves because they do not know their stomachs like I do mine."[84] In the same year (1627), Giacomo Castello, the son and brother of goldsmiths, was caught in Genoa in a house on the Piazza Sarzana, where many young men used to hang out. He was able to escape from his father, who, after having him temporarily sentenced to the galleys, had freed him and sent him to Corsica with thirteen doubloons and the tools of the trade. The judicial case provides a glimpse of the life of youths: Giacomo used to frequent late-night parties, carnivals, dance schools, and bathhouses; on the night of the feast of San Andrea he was with the sons of other artisans. For those who made counterfeit money life was free, they could afford fashionable clothes, and they spent their time amusing themselves. Now Giacomo had to serve eighteen years at the oars.[85]

Outside the city, networks of local solidarity were undoubtedly indispensable for extensive counterfeiting activities. The radical social discrepancies of the metropolitan center were reflected in the different activities of the aristocrats, who were involved in extensive speculative operations employing the feudal mints and were ready to defend themselves with the theory of money as a commodity. In contrast, the poor devils, such as the convicts, soldiers, or Marietta and the goldsmith's son, played with fire by trying to deal in "spendable coins" in a small and restricted market that was necessarily hostile.

In 1587 a series of anonymous letters denounced a miller from Voltaggio for passing counterfeit reals. The four other millers from the area immediately sided with him because these men dealt with grain merchants from Francavilla on the same basis.[86] The connection between counterfeit coins and trade in the provinces becomes clearer. During those years, one Nicheroso Barilaro became a partner in the agreements between the goldsmith Agostino Passano, the innkeeper Antonio Balestrero, and the priest Baldanè, who decided to transform reals into ducatoons during their transit between Genoa and Levanto: Barilaro's participation was clearly connected to a large-scale mercantile operation that involved transactions in many different areas. Nicheroso sold chestnuts for export with the payment in reals; then he increased his profits by transforming the reals into ducatoons and buying swine with these coins for markets in the interior. Thus, one can see that metallurgic operations found their rationale in the context of monetary exchange relationships.[87]

The local notables' involvement conformed to the logic of distinct economic spheres of activity: since it did not make sense to mint counterfeit coins to palm them off on one's fellow citizens, distribution was always directed outside the local economy toward the hinterland. The soldiers from Cairo, who attempted to circulate counterfeit coins locally in Savona, recognized that they had made a mistake in attempting to penetrate "an attentive market."[88] It was clear that the acceptance of various species of coins depended on the social variables of the specific territory.

The ubiquity of priests in the business of counterfeiting was quite extraordinary. What favored this role was the priests' education, their mobility, and especially their association with bandits, who often took refuge in churches. It was true that there were illiterate counterfeiters, but there were no solitary counterfeiters, who as a group shared their knowledge and resources. Mobility was also a very important factor, since, although most Ligurian secular clergy had local origins, many traveled around, if for no other reason, as one of them put it, than "to get something to eat besides bad chestnuts."[89]

Local benefices were limited and competition for them was too strong, so there were several reasons for priests to seek their fortune elsewhere. It was necessary to have a good inheritance to be ordained a priest, and this meant that priests generally came from well-to-do families and thus enjoyed the social capital of powerful personal connections. If a priest left home, this social capital could increase, since he could act as a mediator with the political center, frequenting the houses of nobles as well as the prisons. In addition, the priests' privileged judicial status gave them an undoubted prestige among the populace, which was obviously also extended to ecclesiastical spaces.

The monetary plot of Landi, Bianchi, and Opicino which was organized in 1587–88 is an example of a powerful local alliance of aristocrats. I have already spoken about the armed retinue of the priest Tomaso Landi, son of a counterfeiter who had died miserably in a stable. Landi distilled and prepared ointments and was protected by the bishop of Sarzana, whose gout he had cured. Even the vicar Tiberio Bianchi was suspected: he was the brother of Giulio Cesare, a very influential merchant with "three brothers-in-law who had eight sisters that had married in La Spezia." The merchant Agostino Opicino also had "many relatives," and they all worked hard for him because their financial condition was never solid.

The rumor was that the vicar Bianchi had convinced the priest Landi to resume his father's occupation and to mint coins in Ponzo and Marinasco. Landi escaped capture, and the vicar, interrogated by the magistrate with the permission of the bishop, defended himself by saying that friars and monks had spread lies about him and that he had made many enemies by bringing priests to trial. The trial did not have any result, because, as an anonymous complaint reported, "Opicino adorned himself with Your Highnesses' mantle and pretended to be a gentleman."[90] A similar alliance between priest-minters and merchants can be found in Veppo a few years later. Father Giovanni Ruschi reassured Father Camillo della Rocchetta, saying: "Do not worry, because lords and other people have their hands in this matter." This was the group that had contacts with the minter Rivarola.[91]

At the end of the century in the Sant' Agnese quarter of Genoa, another priest from Veppo, which was a feudal territory like Calice and Suvero, a Father Giovanni, and the priest from Zignago, Andrea Baldari, formed an alchemical group that was in contact with Agostino Passano. Even if the alchemical experiments regularly failed, Passano succeeded in finding a way to make ducatoons in a way that is reported by Antonio Balestrero, a velvet maker who had many debts and had been recruited by Father Baldari in Zignago. The priest reassured Balestrero that making counterfeit coins was not a sin "because it did not produce any profit, since the coins went from one person to the other one."[92] The counterfeiting operation, which appears to have been pursued casually, took place in the area around Genoa, Montale, Veppo, and Suvero.

So far, we have used only lay sources, but for the case of the priest

Lorenzo Buterio di Godano, chaplain of San Matteo in Genoa (the aristocratic chapel of the Doria), we have the copy of the trial conducted by the episcopal vicar of Sarzana in 1613. The priest was involved with the convict Vincenzo Ruschi and the servants of Giovan Battista Doria. Other priests were also involved in the deal: Father Pagano Buterio, who was a teacher in Adamo Centurione's house, and Father G. B. Andreoni from Varese, called "Barbassa," who taught at the Servite convent and who coined doubloons in Gio Domenico Spinola's house. The doubloons were sent to Pontremoli to purchase grain, sold in Bisagno, or pawned off on monks or nuns.

The priest Lorenzo, who was caught in Lombardy by a knight of Carlo Borromeo, did not hide his ambitions: he was called to Genoa by one of Godano's fellow soldiers and "had gone so that he could earn more money." After being tortured, Lorenzo changed his story, saying that he had coined only *piastrini* and accusing, in particular, Father Barbassa, who was sentenced to twelve years of rowing, while Father Lorenzo got a life sentence aboard the galleys.

The episode illustrates the typical kind of arrangements made among provincial priests, chaplains, schoolteachers, and servants of noble houses. G. B. Doria himself diverted suspicion from himself only by collaborating fully with the prosecutors.[93] In fact, the Treasury Office and the curia of the bishop of Sarzana actively collaborated in exchanging relevant information.

The same thing happened to the priest Ippolito Piccino, rector of Vinca, whom we met in the trial of Cappelletto. Father Ippolito was caught in Genoa, and it seemed as though, while he was being taken to Sarzana, his magic powers were so strong as to alter the ship's course many times between Portofino and the gulf. The priest was finally delivered to the bishop.

Torture was not a success, if it is true that Ippolito took back everything he had already freely confessed to the bishop. In fact, the priest was afraid that material evidence, the decisive element for the resolution of a counterfeiting trial, might never be found, and if such evidence was lacking, he ran the risk of facing even more serious charges.[94]

There were also doubts about the competence of the court. In practice, Father Ippolito was captured by the civil police and delivered to the bishop for trial, while the evidence was furnished by a lay magistrate, who also executed the sentence.

The controversy over the proper court of law only grew in later stages. The Carmelite Gerolamo Marcelli argued that the case should probably be considered as a crime of lese majesty, and as such, the prince should be the one to judge it, since it was his signature that had been forged. On the other hand, the Jesuit Father Gio Agostino Oldoino asserted that counterfeiting was not a practice covered by canon law, nor could it be considered as a case of first-degree lese majesty. He thought that the bishop should try the priest, divest him of his clerical status, and deliver him to the lay judge for the punishment. In reality this controversy followed the procedures that were typical of jurisdictional controversies. During the two short pontificates of Julius III (1552) and Gregory XIII (1572), ecclesiastical authorities did not agree at all on the matter of lese majesty: in fact, the second pontificate extensively limited the prince's jurisdictional sovereignty, while the first recognized it without reservations.[95]

There is no doubt that arresting someone in a sanctuary was illicit without the ordinary's consent and that, in any case, the ordinary should have been informed of a priest's arrest. It was, however, questionable whether or not counterfeiting constituted a crime committed in the priest's capacity as a subject of the prince. In the first decades of the seventeenth century, the relevant trial fell within the competence of the bishop, and the church and state searched to create the ways and means for judicial collaboration, as the Buterio and Piccino trials demonstrate. It is obvious that changes in this procedure can only be found in the episcopal archives. Our assumptions have taken us in another direction, illustrating in some detail the involvement of priests in the denunciations concerning counterfeiting and coin clipping.

⁂ It seems that coin clipping was, in contrast, a characteristically urban crime. To judge from the flood of anonymous letters, coin clipping increased dramatically in the 1640s as a consequence of the massive influx of unusually lightweight reals coming from Mexico and Peru, which seemed to indicate new possibilities for clipping older, heavier coins.

In October 1640 an anonymous person denounced Gio Andrea Morello, saying that forty thousand scudi' worth of eight-real coins were circulating in the city, "and this was due to the many people who lightened the coins in a similar fashion."[96] This offense was widely diffused among the aristocracy, such as G. B. Pallavicino, Orazio Morchio, Gio Domenico Chiesa, and others. Among the accused was the goldsmith Gio Stefano Assereto, who from a base in Recco had managed a recutting operation of every type of coin by buying low-quality coins and silver and by distributing them in the surrounding countryside and in the Piacentino. In 1626 the same goldsmith was involved in a similar deal with a group of used-clothing dealers who were all interrelated: Assereto loaned money to gentlemen gamblers against the collateral of clothes that he sold to the dealers.

One of these men, Francesco Trasi, denounced an association whose members included the minor clerk Ravaschero, Marietta Castella's male companion, and Assereto: this association had been formed to clip doubloons and reals. Each member put in some money and gained a profit according to the size of the investment, so that when Trasi invested sixty reals, he received a return of forty scudi. They exchanged light reals for doubloons at a loss and then bought good reals to clip. This meant that there was a high demand for light reals, and these kinds of market calculations seem to have characterized the clipping operations. The fraud was indirect in the sense that these people consciously sought out light coins. One could earn three or four soldi from the clipping of a single dobla. The clipped coins were presumably distributed outside the city. Some witnesses from the time reported that it was absolutely necessary to accept lightened coins in the wholesale transactions. In any case, the money changers established the value of these coins "at the rate" determined by their purchase value for the scarcest types of grain on the market. Thus, making a substantial profit was possible only by artificially creating and arbitraging differential exchange rates on the market, increasing the modest earnings obtained from the silver and gold that had been clipped off the coins.[97]

Later, an anonymous person accused Giovan Battista Pallavicino and his servant Gio Antonio Ponta of the same kind of operation. Suspicion came from the fact that although Pallavicino was very poor, he had lost one thousand scudi gambling.[98] The witnesses blamed the servant, since he "went around the city dressed like a noble and was well turned out, and his wife had beautiful dresses," so that the gentleman appeared to be the servant and vice versa. Some gentlemen testified that Pallavicino made a living running a gambling parlor in the house of Peirano, and occasionally he borrowed money from the goldsmith and from the shoemaker Ambrogio Casaregio, a singular character who was also a painter. Ponta, instead, happily gambled and lost his shirt: he had "a splint on his right hand and palm, which was as big as half a scudo and two splints on his left hand, on his forefinger and middle finger, which came from working with iron and similar things, and his hands [were] like the hands of artisans who [did] similar works with metals and other things."[99]

The group that included Battista Cocorno and the miller Lazzaro Maragliano bought ducats for between 5.6 and 5.8 lire each, clipped them, and recirculated them among millers and mule drivers from Bisagno, who in turn purchased grain in Lombardy: ducatoons were exchanged at between 5.1 and 5.2 lire each, at a time when their value in Genoa was between 5.4 and 5.5 lire each. In any event, the clipping of coins necessitated the marketing of the silver and gold remnants to a receiver, preferably a goldsmith, who in his turn melted them down. Assereto collaborated with the used-clothing dealers, Marietta with Tomaso Grasso, and Andrea Viglieri, as we shall see, with the goldsmith Ferrando.

Coin clipping was generally linked to particular trades in which sellers required that purchases be made with a specific coin: this was the case of the butchers, who were notorious for accepting only light doubloons to purchase meat from hinterland merchants. The buying up of these coins was therefore a way to make extra money. The banker Gio Paolo Sabino from Campetto took advantage of this situation by obtaining a commission to be the only duty collector for the meat market, thereby making a fortune from cornering the supply of doubloons. In this case the accuser was willing to sign his denunciation.[100]

In a parallel fashion, coin clipping seems to have also been connected with gambling. For example, Andrea Viglieri, who was tried with his sons in 1627, seemed to live off gambling, but in reality he cut and distributed counterfeit doubloons that he had minted with his cousin, the goldsmith Cesare Ferrando. When he was surprised with the clippings and the doubloons, he quickly hid them in his mouth. Ferrando was the servant of the gentleman Faustino Isola, who was also Viglieri's patron.

The search of the judicial investigators for counterfeit doubloons took them into all the gambling rooms of the city. Many people were interrogated about Viglieri's reputation, including Francesco Orengo, Gerolamo Granaria in San Siro, Ambrogio Lomellini in Banchi, G. B. Cavanna in Vico Lavagna, Aicardi in Sottoripa, and Alfondi at the Carroggio delli Negri.[101]

The officials found instead Gio Domenico Chiesa, who had not gone to work the day Viglieri was arrested. He was also a gambler. He used to go "where he knew there was a good game" with the Arpe and Centurione brothers. Chiesa managed not to get arrested (he had only made some loans to Viglieri), but later we again find him in the gambling rooms with Pallavicino and Ponta. The anonymous accusers had done their work, pointing out that for the players the gaming rooms were the places for the exchange of lightened coins.

Pallavicino was finally captured in San Pancrazio in 1646 and was sentenced to ten years aboard the galleys. Chiesa was also caught with some *piastrini* that he had just cut with a goldsmith's scissors. He was arrested and relegated to the fortress at Bonifacio. Andrea Viglieri, who had fled the year of the Pallavicino trial, was sentenced to decapitation.[102]

The judicial account, thus, furnishes us with only a few partial echoes of a phenomenon that must have been broadly diffused. In January 1628 it was reported that circulating in Genoa were many reals that had been minted in Spain and were not destined for circulation abroad. "Many people have weighed them and, finding them heavier than normal, have melted and reminted them, driving out all the other lightened coins and filling the city with these new lightened coins." The judge had condemned the enterprise of "weighing and arbitraging money."[103] This was not a clipping but a remelting operation, but the association between the two processes was interesting and explicit. The individuality of the coins implied differences in weight: remelting was a more radical and expensive operation than clipping, but it was certainly not illegal and was very convenient for large quantities of coins. It is known that the bank of San Giorgio had two scales: one to weigh the coins that came in, the other one to weigh the coins that went out.[104] Therefore, weighing became a way to speculate on the materiality of the coins, rather than on their circulation, but the one did not exclude the other. The clipping operation systematically inserted itself in a complex scheme of monetary circulation which included calculations about the differences in exchange value for the same types of coins on distant markets. Certainly such a practice introduced a singular handicap, but it is clear that the refusal of the receivers to go along would have ended the operation itself.

This was also true for monetary counterfeiting. The operative logic was that false coins circulated as a commodity but were also spendable; and it was significant that these coins were directed toward particular areas and that they were connected with structured transactions. In this sense, these monetary "innovations" were part of a system of currency differences which legitimated arbitrage as a general practice.

The risk was that the circulation of these coins would stop, that through the "consensus of the people" they might be refused. The juridical-political language referred to this situation as an offense against the prince which came from falsifying his imprint: this was a way of expressing the real circumstances on a symbolic level, that is, because of the debased alloy in counterfeit coins, their intrinsic value did not correspond to their normal face value. In such a way, counterfeiters overcame the threshold of the asymmetry in monetary exchanges, exercising pure fraud. This fraud represented one of the elements of the monetary disorder that gave priority to the arbitragers we have described. Nevertheless, we must insist on the fact that this "disorder" postulated a "prior" organization of exchanges based upon precise relationships between commercial transactions and species of coins.

The counterfeit louis coined for the trade with the Turkish were only the extreme case, in the sense of an organized fraud ring, of a process that was more general and systematic at a low social level, where small coins were coins of subsistence and universally recognized as such. To repeat, differential exchange rates among coins on different markets created special opportunities for counterfeiting and coin clipping. The tolerance within the specific exchange markets for light coins opened a field for transactional experimentation, which verified the passability of various "black coins" made with different intensities of false metals, but always appearing with the same imprint.

It is thus not the case that counterfeiting was a phenomenon of monetary circulation "with a special function" in the society of the *ancien régime.* On the contrary, what is striking is how well organized the enterprise was, how explicitly the rationale for monetary crimes followed the same structures of exchange as legitimate monetary operations. This interpretation also goes against the common assumption that coins had a "general exchange function," which is denied by the proliferation of various types of coins. In fact, it is enough to wonder why these coins circulated on the market and in what exchange situations they were useful. The advantage of the analysis of criminal records comes from their ability to create a situational focus through a series of case histories, which are less susceptible to abstract treatment derived from contemporary economic theories.

As we have seen, every case history has many facets, which cannot be simply reduced to the phenomenon of the circulation of money. Therefore, we have focused on the "folklore" of money, on the people involved, on the social categories, and on the different typologies of the enterprise. The matter is therefore larger, more pragmatic and dramatic, the significance of which was not merely episodic but individuated in the direction of the "general" view of monetary circulation. This double significance of the work, which derives from my agenda of studying crime and the violation of public norms, gives a privileged place to the study of a certain type of context.

Notes

1. In the edict of 1642 the evaluated coinages were the five face-value double coins [*doppie*, doblas, doubloons], that is, those of Genoa, Spain, Florence, Venice, and Naples, plus doubles from France, Italy, Savoy, Mantua, Piacenza, Parma, Massa, Milan, and Tassarolo, and gold scudi that conformed to the established rate; ducatoons from Genoa, Florence, Milan, Lucca, Savoy, Parma, Piacenza, Mantua, Venice, and Tassarolo; silver scudi from Genoa; eight-piece reals from Spain, distinguished from the reals coming from Peru and Mexico.

2. Some of the buyers were, for example, butchers and bakers, who bought meats and grain. Unfortunately, we do not know very much about the structures of this trade, so we cannot give more details on the imbalances of exchange.

3. *Ricordi*, s. v., "Moneta." Cited in the Biblioteca Universitaria di Genova, Manoscritto B VIII 27.

4. K. Polanyi, "The Semantics of Money Uses," pp. 175–203 in *Primitive and Modern Economies*, edited by G. Dalton (Garden City, N.Y., 1968).

5. Archivio di Stato di Genova (hereafter ASG), *Zecca Antica*, filze 43 and 45.

6. ASG, *Zecca Antica*, filza 32.

7. ASG, *Rota Criminale*, filze 80 and 82.

8. ASG, *Zecca Antica*, filza 54.

9. ASG, *Zecca Antica*, filza 36.

10. Ibid., and ASG, *Zecca Antica*, filza 39: the zecchini used to buy *doppie* [doubloons] were melted with a profit of thirty soldi per coin in 1637.

11. ASG, Manoscritto 138, Statuta Criminalia del 1557, chap. 31.

12. In 1606, a special investigation was set up against G. Stixella and others for exchanging doubloons above the normal value: ASG, *Rota Criminale*, filza 73.

13. G. Felloni, "Profilo economico della moneta genovese dal 1139 al 1814," in *Le monete genovesi*, ed. G. Pesce and G. Felloni (Genoa, 1975).

14. ASG, *Zecca Antica*, filza 43.

15. ASG, *Zecca Antica*, filze 43 and 48; *Rota Criminale*, filza 48. G. Rebora has studied the operation of louis.

16. ASG, *Zecca Antica*, filze 43 and 48.

17. ASG, *Zecca Antica*, filza 21, for previous cases. The most useful source of information about seventeenth-century mints can be found in F. and E. Gnecchi, *Saggio di bibliografia numismatica delle zecche italiane* (Milan, 1889), which covers Fosdinovo (mint of the Malaspina) for 1666; Seborga (abbatial) for 1660–71; Tassarolo (Spinola) for 1610–88; Torriglia (Doria) for 1665–70; Tresana (Malaspina) for 1571–1651; Bozzolo (Gonzaga) for 1497–1672; Monaco from 1512; Messerano (Fieschi-Besso) until 1685; Passerano (Besso) for 1560–98; Arquato (Spinola) for 1641–94; Borgonovo Rocchetta (Spinola) for 1669; Gazzoldo (Ippoliti) for 1590–1663; Loano (Doria) from 1548 to the

end of the seventeenth century; Massa (Malaspina); Compiano (Landi) for 1590–1630; S. Stefano d'Aveto (Doria) from 1668.

18. ASG, *Rota Criminale*, filza 73.

19. ASG, *Zecca Antica*, filza 21. For the 1637 law and the regulation of debts, see Felloni, *Profilo economico della moneta genovese*, pp. 211–15.

20. ASG, *Rota Criminale*, filza 71, report from Pieve di Teco.

21. The schedule of coins minted was published by Felloni, *Profilo economico della moneta genovese*, p. 282.

22. ASG, *Zecca Antica*, filza 33.

23. A typical problem came up in 1619: how could the grain office exchange a silver scudo with 4.15 or 4.16 lire of *soldini* or of four- and eight-*denari* coins, when the same scudo on the open market had a value of 5.2 lire?

24. ASG, *Zecca Antica*, filza 36.

25. Previous lists of confiscated coins or edicts that recorded forbidden coins are found in ASG, *Zecca Antica*, filze 39 and 40; in *Rota Criminale*, filze 74 and 75 point out the role of *gianne, oxelline*, or *bianche* from Monferrato.

26. From Sarzana, Varese, and elsewhere: ASG, *Zecca Antica*, filze 36, 38, 39, 40.

27. This happened before the institution of the Magistrato della Consegna in 1628. See ASG, *Zecca Antica*.

28. ASG, *Zecca Antica*, filza 39.

29. ASG, *Zecca Antica*, filze 39 and 40.

30. ASG, *Zecca Antica*, filza 40; for a "return" of Savoyard coins to Savona in 1692, see also *Zecca Antica*, filza 54.

31. ASG, *Zecca Antica*, filza 47.

32. ASG, *Zecca Antica*, filza 45.

33. ASG, *Zecca Antica*, filza 43.

34. We find a characteristic controversy with regard to this in ASG, *Zecca Antica*, filze 41–43.

35. ASG, *Zecca Antica*, filza 77: "I think that because it is marked by one bend in two places and by another one in one place."

36. The touchstone is a black and shiny stone upon which the scraped silver has left traces of a metallic luster.

37. ASG, *Rota Criminale*, filza 72. The liability of the people who received and passed on false coins was clarified in 1607. See ASG, *Zecca Antica*, filza 21.

38. The specific edict is found in ASG, *Rota Criminale*.

39. ASG, *Zecca Antica*, filza 38.

40. See note 37. The reference to false coins as a question of lese majesty was not very common among the jurists of the time. See M. Sbriccioli, *Crimen lesae maiestatis* (Milan, 1974).

41. These cases are cited in ASG, *Sala Senarega*, filza 1637.

42. ASG, *Rota Criminale*, filza 80.

43. ASG, *Rota Criminale*, filze 73 and 75.

44. ASG, *Zecca Antica*, filza 29.

45. ASG, *Rota Criminale*, filza 74.

46. The documentation on the jurisdiction is in Archivio Storico Comunale di Genova, Manoscritto 107-B-10.

47. ASG, *Zecca Antica*, filza 21, edict 1607.

48. ASG, *Rota Criminale*, filza 84 and filze 85, 88, and 89. *Zecca Antica*, filza 43.

49. ASG, *Magistrato Monete* 78/79.

50. ASG, *Zecca Antica*, filza 27.

51. ASG, *Zecca Antica*, Magistrato Monete 78/79.

52. ASG, *Rota Criminale*, filza 74.

53. Pietro Fabiamo from Sanremo paid forty scudi for the work: see ASG, *Zecca Antica,* filza 27.

54. ASG, *Sala Senarega,* filza 1637.

55. ASG, *Rota Criminale,* filza 74.

56. Ibid.

57. In 1608, the notary Clemente Roi was accused by Piaggio and Ravaschero, while in 1678, the accused was Bartolomeo Piaggio, and Giovanni Roi was involved as a witness. See ASG, *Zecca Antica,* filza 29, and *Rota Criminale,* filza 86.

58. ASG, *Rota Criminale,* filza 75.

59. ASG, *Notaio* . . . (I have not been able to rediscover the source).

60. ASG, *Rota Criminale,* filza 89.

61. ASG, *Rota Criminale,* filza 72. They refer to *Dei secreti naturali,* or to *Dello specchio di scienza universale,* by Leonardo Fioravanti, both published in Venice in 1564. As regards Gabriello Faloppio, they are probably referring to *De semplicibus purgantibus* (Venice, 1566) or to *De medicatis aquis atque fossilibus Tractatus ab Andrea Marcolino collectus* (Venice, 1564).

62. ASG, *Zecca Antica,* filza 27.

63. ASG, *Rota Criminale,* filza 79.

64. ASG, *Rota Criminale,* filza 76.

65. The reference is to Giamblico, a neo-Platonic philosopher and author of a classic text on hermeticism, and to G. B. Della Porta.

66. ASG, *Rota Criminale,* filza 79.

67. ASG, *Rota Criminale,* filza 80.

68. ASG, *Rota Criminale,* filza 74.

69. This expression belongs to Cappelletto. J. Read discusses how the conception of the philosophers' stone was alchemy's main inspiration. It motivated almost forty generations of alchemists. *Through Alchemy to Chemistry* (London, 1961). The main alchemical operations were calcination, fusion, sublimation, crystallization, and distillation. Historians have focused their attention on the great alchemists, such as John Dee and Sir Isaac Newton. The only work on criminal history I know which is dedicated to monetary counterfeiting refers to the end of the eighteenth century, and it does not mention alchemy. See J. Styles, "Our Traitorous Money Makers: The Yorkshire Coiners and the Law, 1760–1783," in *An Ungovernable People: The English and Their Law in the Seventeenth and Eighteenth Centurires,* ed. J. Brewer and J. Styles (London, 1980).

70. Detailed descriptions are found in ASG, *Rota Criminale,* filza 74, and *Zecca Antica,* filza 27.

71. ASG, *Rota Criminale,* filza 80.

72. ASG, *Zecca Antica,* filza 29.

73. ASG, *Rota Criminale,* filza 74.

74. ASG, *Zecca Antica,* filza 29.

75. ASG, *Zecca Antica,* filza 27. See U. Manucci, *La moneta e la falsa monetazione* (Milan, 1908), which emphasizes the same dualism between the imprint and the coin.

76. ASG, *Rota Criminale,* filza 80; for the lice, see *Zecca Antica,* filza 33.

77. ASG, *Rota Criminale,* filza 80.

78. ASG, *Zecca Antica,* filza 30.

79. ASG, *Zecca Antica,* filza 26.

80. ASG, *Zecca Antica,* filza 29.

81. ASG, *Zecca Antica,* filza 32: "they used donkey manure and rosemary, but when they put them on the fire, they no longer find either the silver or the toad."

82. ASG, *Rota Criminale,* filza 76.

83. ASG, *Zecca Antica,* Magistrato Monete 78/79.

84. ASG, *Rota Criminale,* filza 79.

85. Ibid.
86. ASG, *Zecca Antica*, filza 27.
87. Ibid.
88. ASG, *Rota Criminale*, filza 80.
89. Ibid., filza 84.
90. Ibid., filza 72.
91. Ibid., filza 74.
92. ASG, *Zecca Antica*, filza 27.
93. Ibid., filze 32 and 31.
94. ASG, *Rota Criminale*, filza 76.
95. ASG, *Archivio Segreto*, 1121.
96. ASG, *Rota Criminale*, filza 81.
97. Ibid., filza 79.
98. Ibid., filza 81.
99. Ibid., filza 82.
100. Ibid.
101. ASG, *Rota Criminale*, filza 80.
102. Ibid., filza 81.
103. Ibid., filza 80.
104. ASG, *Zecca Antica*, filza 42.

8 ঽ A Dream of Infanticide in
Fin de Siècle Vienna

by Ingeborg Walter

ঽ A Bourgeois Gentleman

In the spring of 1895, Mr. E. began treatment with Dr. Sigmund Freud, a still obscure Viennese specialist working on nervous illnesses. The identity of this patient remains unknown; in Freud's letters to his friend Wilhelm Fliess of Berlin, he is identified only with the initial E.[1] Freud spoke about him often in his letters, but very little has been learned about his life. Among the few details that are known is that at the time of his treatment he was unmarried[2] and that he was a member of an affluent Jewish family from Vienna. Everything known about him suggests that he was a bourgeois gentleman. Following a custom dear to the Viennese bourgeoisie, as a child he was entrusted to the care of a French nurse who played an important part in his life, and as his mother died when he was very young, even more so than normal. Louise was, as Freud wrote, Mr. E.'s "nurse and first lover," who taught him to speak French before German, his mother tongue.[3] Naturally, he attended high school and then the university. From associations to botany and zoology which he made in dreams, it can be deduced that he studied natural sciences or medicine, but it appears that he did not finish these studies. "He cannot get over the fact that later,

"Un infanticidio immaginario nella Vienna fin de siècle," *Quaderni storici* 66 (1987): 879–99. Translated from the German by Roberto Zapperi; translated from the Italian by Margaret A. Gallucci.

at the university, he failed to pass in botany," Freud wrote to Fliess.[4] After this setback, E. changed his field of study to jurisprudence, as is revealed in *The Interpretation of Dreams*, where he is described as an "intelligent jurist."[5] His elevated social status brought with it a love for the theater, where he habitually manifested the most important symptom of his illness. "The only new thing," Freud told his friend Fliess in a letter on April 11, 1895, "[is] the analysis of Mr. E. [*sic*], who perspires in the theater."[6]

Treatment began in the spring of 1895 and, contrary to the norm at that time, continued for many years. The case was followed with great interest and also a great deal of criticism within Freud's circle of colleagues and acquaintances. Freud himself referred in *The Interpretation of Dreams* to the fact that he had learned about the disapproval of a senior colleague who marveled that "the psychoanalytic treatment of one of [Freud's] patients had already entered its fifth year."[7] Essentially Mr. E. concluded his treatment only in April 1900, after five full years, celebrating his cure, as Freud told Fliess, with an evening at Freud's house.[8] This atypical ending taken together with other factors suggests that Freud and Mr. E. were friends and that perhaps their friendship was not a result of the long-term analysis. In fact, E. seems to have been a member of Freud's circle of friends, since Fliess also knew him.[9]

Described in *The Interpretation of Dreams* as the "patient of longest standing,"[10] E. played a central role in the development of Freud's thought. His cure fell in the very year that marked a decisive shift in Freud's theorizing, which had gone ahead for a long time concurrently with his own so-called self-analysis and indeed at times coincided with it. "He demonstrated the reality of my theory in my own case . . . providing me in a surprising reversal with the solution, which I had overlooked, to my former railroad phobia," Freud confided to his friend in a letter dated December 21, 1899.[11] E. gave his analyst moments of great triumph but also moments of profound depression. "It is as if Schliemann had once more excavated Troy," Freud wrote in the same letter,[12] even if he had to admit immediately afterward, "just when I believed I had the solution in my grasp, it eluded me."[13] And yet Freud made a fundamental discovery in his treatment of E.; his analysis taught him "that the apparent endlessness of the treatment [was] something that occur[ed] regularly and [was] connected with the transference."[14]

❧ E.'s Dream

In the course of his analysis E. had a dream that Freud not only recorded in his notes but considered worthy of writing about to his friend Fliess, since it seemed to confirm his thesis that every dream represented the fulfillment of a wish. The dream was transcribed in one of the manuscripts that Freud used to send Fliess with his letters from time to time. The manuscript accompanying the letter of May 2, 1897, also contained notes on closely related issues, like E.'s dream, sexuality, and love.[15] Freud described the dream in a crucial dialogue between analyst and patient:

> "I suppose that this is a wishful dream," said E. "I dreamed that just as I arrived at my house with a lady, I was arrested by a police-man who requested me to get into a carriage. I demanded more time to put my affairs in order, and so on."—"More precise details?"—"It was the morning after I had spent the night with this lady."—"Were you horrified?"—"No."—"Do you know what you were charged with?"—"Yes, with having killed a child."—"Has that any connection with reality?"—"I was once responsible for the abortion of a child resulting from an affair. I dislike thinking about it."—"Well, had nothing happened the morning before the dream?"—"Yes, I woke up and [we] had intercourse."—"But you took precautions?"—"Yes, by withdrawing."—"Then you were afraid you might have made a child, and the dream shows you the fulfillment of your wish that nothing should happen, as you nipped the child in the bud. You made use of the feeling of anxiety which arises after a coitus of that kind as material for your dream."[16]

As is evident, the dream was occasioned by the sexual encounter with a lady in the course of which E. took precautions to prevent a pregnancy. He did not wish to find himself a second time in the onerous situation in which he had found himself in the past with the other woman who had had to abort his child. Like that earlier relationship, this one, too, was an illicit one that he could not risk making public by making her pregnant. In Freud's interpretation, the dream was intended to reassure the dreamer, represented as the murderer of the child "nipped in the bud," that he had not created a child. In this way the dream represented his wish fulfillment, even though it was presented in a disagreeable form, which according to Freud derived from the anxiety associated with coitus interruptus.

Freud found an important proof of his thesis in E.'s dream and even included it in the fourth chapter of *The Interpretation of Dreams* dedicated to distortion in dreams.[17] For Freud, E.'s dream proved that even dreams with "distressing content" could very well be wish fulfillments. Dreams of this type, Freud explained, are linked to aversions about certain topics or particular desires that one cannot confess even to oneself. In each of these cases, "the dream is the (disguised) fulfillment of a (suppressed or repressed) wish."[18] If we analyze E.'s dream in light of Freud's theory, we come to this conclusion: wish fulfillment is presented in E.'s dream in such a disagreeable form because in addition to his memory of the abortion, the type of contraception he used caused feelings of anxiety. Thus the desire to prevent pregnancy appeared to the dreamer so unacceptable that it had to be repressed.

Compared with the first version of the dream, included in the manuscript attached to the letter to Fliess, the second version of E.'s dream, published in *The Interpretation of Dreams*, contains many variations not so much in its content as in the range of associations made by E. as well as in the information and explanations supplied by Freud himself. Above all, the dreamer was no longer designated by an initial, and the dream was specifically attributed not to a patient but to an acquaintance, described as an intelligent jurist. If that were the case, his identification as E. would no longer be tenable, since at the end of 1899, when *The Interpretation of Dreams* was published,[19] E. was still in treatment. This clearly was an understandable manipulation of the data motivated by the desire to maintain E.'s anonymity, but it seems to have been prompted even more by Freud's desire to anticipate a possible objection to his theory. In fact, Freud was afraid that his colleagues would reproach him for deducing exclusively from dreams of "neurotics" theories and inference that could not then be extended to normal people.[20] If the dreamer had indeed become an intelligent jurist in the end, it is impossible to know. It is clear, however, that Freud's dialogue with the dreamer reveals precise juridical knowledge.

A Viennese Ring-around-the-Rosy

In the second version of E.'s dream his love affair was given more significance. To Freud's query "And what were the circumstances in which you had the dream? What happened on the previous evening?"

the dreamer answered: "I would prefer not to tell you. It's a delicate matter." Only after Freud pressed him did he respond: "I didn't spend last night at home but with a lady who means a great deal to me." Freud still seemed unsatisfied: "Is she a married woman?" he asked. The answer was "yes" and thus clarified why E.'s contraceptive precautions were so important to him. Pregnancy, E. added rapidly, "might give us away."[21]

The abortion involving the other woman from E.'s past came up in their discussion only at the very end. After Freud interpreted E.'s dream as a wish fulfillment ("this dream gives you a reassurance that you had not procreated a child, or, what amounts to the same thing, that you had killed a child"), Freud asked him again, to have further confirmation of his theory, "Incidentally, your reference to infanticide has not been explained. How did you come to light on this specifically feminine crime?" Only at this point did the dreamer reveal the experience that could justify his imaginary arrest in his dream better than his use of withdrawal as a contraceptive method: "I must admit that some years ago I became involved in an occurrence of that kind. I was responsible for a girl's trying to avoid the consequence of a love affair with me by means of an abortion. I had nothing to do with her carrying out her intention, but for a long time I naturally felt very nervous in case the business came out."[22]

These two women—the lady who appeared in E.'s dream and the girl from his past—make an interesting group of women contacts along with those that Freud had already mentioned to Fliess in his letters: first, there was the French nurse who played an important role in his own childhood and adolescence, whose image was intertwined with his mother's image;[23] then there were the actresses with whom, Freud noted, "he normally sought only intercourse"; and finally, there were the young ladies designated by E. pejoratively as "silly gooses" who made him blush and sweat in the theater because he always fantasized deflowering them.[24] These brief excursions into E.'s erotic fantasies take on greater meaning if we compare them with the erotic fantasies of other young bourgeois men who were contemporaries of E.'s in the same city. The women who are indistinct in E.'s dreams and memories suddenly become recognizable not as individuals but as members of particular social classes, and their exact sentimental place in the love life of young bourgeois gentlemen in *fin de siècle* Vienna becomes clearer.

Married women and actresses, girls from "good" and not-so-good families, nurses, misses, and teachers also appear in the autobiography

of Arthur Schnitzler and become part of the repertory of stock characters in his plays and novels.[25] Schnitzler, the son of a noted doctor, was
a member of a haute bourgeois Jewish family from Vienna. Through his
father he had contact, even if distant, with Freud.[26] In his autobiography, which was published posthumously at his request, he recounted
the erotic experiences of his youth with surprising openness and subtle
irony.[27] There it is evident that his categorization of women had the
same parameters as did E.'s. Thus the nurse Louise corresponded to
Schnitzler's French nurse who seduced him as a high school student.[28]
The married woman loved by E. corresponded to the beautiful Olga,
wife of the owner of a famous hotel for holidays on the Semmering,
whom Schnitzler loved passionately even if their relationship, by his
own admission, was "not very sinful."[29] Actresses entered Schnitzler's
life because he was a writer.[30] The young women from the petite
bourgeoisie which he wrote about help one understand better E.'s
relationship with the girl who was forced to have an abortion.[31] And
finally, the young ladies at the theater who made E. blush, were they
not just like the woman whom Schnitzler presents as his potential
wife? Young ladies from good families, with whom he could only
innocently flirt, since, in addition to a dowry, they had to guarantee
their potential spouses the indispensable requirement of virginity?

At the end of his memoirs about his youth, Schnitzler asked himself
why he had not been able to decide to marry a young lady named
Helene Hertz. He concluded that it was certainly not because of
Jeannette, "and the others were even less likely to hold [him] back
from that path ..., certainly not Olga, the adventure of [his] life ...
not Adele, that devilish goose ... not Mitzi Rosner, that voluptuous,
tactless, spiteful girl ... and even less the fact that Helene was not
rich enough for [him]."[32] Here the whole range of categories appears:
from the young lady from a good family who could be considered
for marriage, through all the other women with whom a bourgeois
gentleman, following social convention, could have "intercourse" but
who were excluded from the possibility of marriage from the beginning.

ᐁ Debasement in Love

The morality of the period, or, to use Freud's words, "civilized"
sexual morality, condemned all forms of extramarital sexuality. But,
as is well known, it allowed men a "degree of sexual freedom only

with reluctance and under a veil of silence,"[33] while women were supposed to submit themselves completely to marital discipline. All aspects of upbringing were directed toward this end and used, according to Freud, "the most drastic measures." As a result, "not only [did] it [the morality of the period] forbid sexual intercourse and set a high premium on the preservation of female chastity, but it also protect[ed] the young woman from temptation as she [grew] up, by keeping her ignorant of all the facts of the part she [was] to play and by not tolerating any impulse of love in her which [could] not lead to marriage."[34]

This description refers above all to women of the upper classes, to those young ladies whom the youthful Schnitzler courted more or less passionately and who made E. blush because of his illicit fantasies about them. The lady from E.'s memories probably did not belong to this social group, since otherwise how could she have had a love affair with him and gotten pregnant?[35]

At the turn of the century Vienna offered young bourgeois gentlemen like E. many opportunities to have sexual experiences before marriage, especially with women of modest social status, who presented the most attractive possibilities. Schnitzler gave literary form to these women in his figure of "süsses Madel," who lived, in Vienna as did similar women in other large European cities, in the suburbs outside the city walls rather than in the city center, which was reserved for the upper classes.[36] This literary figure, as has been rightly noted, does not correspond to reality, which was much harsher, but rather to the fantasy of a young bourgeois gentleman, constructed "within the context of the morals and pleasures of the dominant."[37] Even the real woman whom Schnitzler writes about in his autobiography corresponds perfectly to the fantasies of a bourgeois gentleman: she gave freely of her love; she made neither financial nor emotional demands; she did not harbor hopes that he would marry her, being perfectly aware of the distance between them socially. All this did not spare her from being judged according to the moral values of these bourgeois gentlemen whose attractions so easily led her astray. In the eyes of their lovers, these women were always perceived as inferior both socially and morally. Almost certainly the woman who had an abortion from E.'s past belonged to this category. This hypothesis will be confirmed by what follows.[38]

In his essay "On the Universal Tendency to Debasement in the Sphere of Love," Freud studied the problem of psychological impotence. He explained that retarded psychological development prevented the "affectionate" current, directed in infancy toward the mother, from combining with the "sensual" current that was awakened in puberty. As a result, the link between "sensual love" and "the highest psychical valuation of the object," indispensable to normal love, was impossible. "The whole sphere of love in such people," Freud wrote, "remains divided in the two directions personified in art as sacred and profane (or animal) love." Freud could not hide the fact that this psychological split characterized his whole period. He argued, in fact, "[T]here are only a few educated people in whom the currents of affection and sensuality have become properly fused; the man almost always feels his respect for the woman acting as a restriction on his sexual activity [and thus needs] a debased sexual object, a woman who is ethically inferior."[39]

The ethically inferior woman, that is, the woman who transgressed the prevailing morality, however, was also at the same time socially inferior, as Schnitzler noted. Thus, the psychological split corresponded to the social hierarchy. On the one hand, there were the women who could aspire to "the highest psychical valuation," like mothers, sisters, and potential or actual wives; on the other hand, there were the "debased sexual objects," women who were of low morals and low social standing, like the nurses and servant girls who worked in bourgeois households, or the women from the petite bourgeoisie or working-class women from the suburbs, "worthless female material" to use Freud's expression,[40] who were at the disposition of the sexual needs of bourgeois gentlemen.

Traces of this split are also evident in E.'s dream. The anonymous woman who had an abortion evidently did not enjoy the "respect" of her lover; nor could she expect any respect even after she got pregnant as a result of their love affair. E. felt, to use Schnitzler's words, "completely without responsibility" toward the "debased sexual object." His feelings toward the married woman were quite different. Although she did not conform entirely to prescriptive moral behavior, she seemed to fit nonetheless into the sphere of those women who could aspire to be respected. E. cared a lot about her, enough for him to want "to take her to his house," that is, to marry her.[41] This feeling of respect is also evident in E.'s actions: he willingly took the responsibility to practice withdrawal in order to prevent a pregnancy. And yet it is precisely this aspect that was troubling to him and caused his dream.[42]

⁏✤ Juridical Questions

In the second version of E.'s dream, published in *The Interpretation of Dreams*, the first question that Freud asked E. was: "Do you know what you were charged with?" This time E. did not respond with the rather vague, "with having killed a child," but instead specified, "Yes, for infanticide, I believe." He used a term that in juridical discourse defined a precise crime. The term was understood by Freud in that context, for his next question was: "Infanticide? But surely you're aware that that's a crime that can only be committed by a mother on a newborn child?" Freud clearly was referring to the Austrian penal code that discussed infanticide in Article 139 and defined it as the killing of a newborn by the mother during childbirth. A treatise on the penal code then in effect read: "The perpetrator of this special type of crime can only be the mother . . . anyone else who kills the newborn child during childbirth commits homicide."[43] In his dream, therefore, E. accused himself of a crime that, according to the law, he could not have committed because he was a man.

The question about the relationship of the dream to reality was also now answered differently. The dreamer no longer made a reference to the abortion; instead he immediately began talking about his love affair with the married woman and the nature of his sexual relationship with her. To Freud's query of whether he practiced normal intercourse with her, he confessed: "I take the precaution of withdrawing before ejaculation." Immediately with this admission Freud explained the secret of the dream as the wish fulfillment of not "having procreated a child." The originally ignored abortion was considered, however, at the last. Freud had to admit that "[E.'s] reference to infanticide" required a better explanation. To this query the dreamer finally remembered having been "involved in an occurrence of that kind." But now he was referring to abortion, not infanticide. E. confessed his guilt, even as he denied being in any way directly involved. Evidently he meant that he had not taken the same precautions in his relationship with the young woman which he had taken with the married woman. Upon closer examination his preoccupation with declaring himself extraneous to the abortion becomes less innocent than he portrayed it. The dreamer had a significant reason to deny his involvement. Austrian law defined abortion as a crime and punished it with harsh penalties: from six to twelve months in prison for merely an attempted abortion, and one to five years of hard labor for a successful one.

These penalties were applicable both to the woman who sought an abortion on her own and to those who helped her procure one at her request. The natural father "guilty of complicity" was threatened with a yet "harsher" penalty.[44] Denying any complicity was a necessary precaution in a work, like *The Interpretation of Dreams*, which was destined to be read by legal authorities.[45] Yet the complicity, which could not be admitted publicly, was expressed in the dream, when E. was arrested by the police officer for his crime.

Ten years after E. had his dream a follower of Freud publicly took a stand on the issue of abortion. Doctor and writer Fritz Wittels published the essay "The Most Serious Crime in the Penal Code (The Prohibition against Abortion)." It appeared in the February 22, 1907, issue of Karl Kraus's magazine *Die Fackel* under the pseudonym Avicenna. The article's title foreshadowed Wittels' conclusion and argument, which called for the cancellation of articles 144–46 of the Austrian penal code on abortion. Wittels wrote that from a biological perspective the fetus was not yet a human being and at most should only be considered potentially so. Its development took place in such an imperceptible manner "that all of experimental psychology [was] not able to discover the boundary [between fetus and human being]." Thus, from the perspective of criminal law it was not possible to commit a crime against something that was not yet a human being. According to Wittels, the prohibition against abortion ended up, paradoxically, directly encouraging infanticide, understood in a broader sense than the term had in the penal code. In fact, Wittels was referring to all the intentional negligent acts with which mothers and fathers, constrained through material or moral necessity, ended their children's lives without having to fear the rigor of the law.[46]

Undoubtedly, Wittels had taken a courageous stand in the campaign headed by Karl Kraus against the moral hypocrisy that pervaded all aspects of society and, first and foremost, the judicial sphere. Wittels dreamed that his article would influence the jurists who were then revising penal codes, but that was not the case. In the treatise published in 1910 by Carl Stooss, one of the most famous criminal lawyers of Freud's time, whom Kraus had scathingly attacked on several occasions,[47] there is not the slightest hint of any opinion on the issue of abortion which diverged from the official line. For infanticide, Stooss supplied bibliographic references to a discussion that had taken place among the jurists at a slightly earlier time, but he did not accept any of their conclusions.[48] We do not know even how the article in *Die*

Fackel was received in the weekly Wednesday meetings held at Freud's house, which Wittels joined only a few months later. However, it may be possible to ascertain Freud's personal belief on these issues by studying how he interpreted E.'s dream.

?⇨ Biological Data, Medieval Controversies, and an Insurmountable Philosophical Problem

In the second version of E.'s dream, which appears in the form of a dialogue, Freud added a summary of a conversation which introduced important new material. Freud wanted to help the dreamer to understand the unusual connection made between infanticide and contraception by indicating "the intermediate links" between the two separate concepts. In the conversation, which he reported that they had had several days earlier, they had talked about "marriage difficulties" and the "inconsistency" in the fact that contraception was permitted while abortion was considered a crime. They had reviewed the medieval controversy "over the exact point of time at which the soul enters the fetus," and Freud then had remembered Lenau's "gruesome" poem "in which child murder and child prevention are equated." Although this summary is brief, it helps to reconstruct the line of thought revealed in the conversation.

The charge of inconsistency, directed at "legislators," clearly was based on a biological perspective on the issue. Freud most likely was thinking along the lines of Wittels' later arguments, primarily that from a biological point of view the boundary between a person, whom the law was supposed to protect, and the fetus, which as only "spermatozoa and ovum" was at most only potentially a person, could not be exactly determined and thus was decided by law only "arbitrarily."[49] The medieval controversy was also caught up in a similar question of boundaries, with the crucial difference that medieval thinkers believed that the charge of homicide could only be made after the fetus quickened and certainly not after simple fertilization took place. The divergence of opinion rested solely on the moment at which quickening occurred.[50] Law and theology posited a boundary that neither the dream nor Lenau's poetry was able to pinpoint. In this context perhaps it might be useful to take a look also at Lenau's poem.

James Strachey believed that the Lenau poem indicated by Freud was "Das tote Gluck" and mentioned this title in the edition of *The Interpretation of Dreams* included in the *Standard Edition* and as a result in all subsequent editions.[51] That is unlikely; the seven-strophe poem "Das tote Gluck" never mentions an equivalency between contraception and abortion. The poem that most likely merited Freud's judgment of "gruesome" was the longer ballad "Anna."[52] As Johannes Bolte has already shown, this ballad reelaborates a folklore motif widely diffused in the period which Lenau knew from a Swedish version of the tale.[53] The story runs like this: Anna, who is engaged to a cavalier, is convinced to accept a magic spell of sterility because she is afraid that she will lose her beauty after she gets married and has children. On the advice of an old woman, she throws seven grains of wheat, which symbolize her unborn children, through her engagement ring into a mill; while grinding the mill for each grain, she hears a moan as the mill crushes each child. Her punishment soon follows. Anna is repudiated by her spouse, and only after long suffering does she obtain the forgiveness of her unborn children and is freed from death.

This story clearly is a Christianized version of an old folklore motif, given its overlapping with church doctrine. An ecclesiastical tenet espoused in the *Corpus Iuris Canonici* still in effect in Freud's day defined sterility procured though magic, or *venena sterilitatis*, as homicide.[54] The analogy is clear. Popular Christian traditions like E.'s dream condemned voluntary sterility as infanticide, the only difference being that popular beliefs, unlike the dream, placed all the responsibility on the woman. In their conversation the two men in the dialogue discussed fully the issues of contraception, abortion, and infanticide, without coming to a clear conclusion. They did not find any biological criteria that could have justified criminal sanctions, but they certainly concurred that, according to popular perceptions revealed in the poem, preventing fertilization was equivalent to murder. Can we really argue that Freud was actually convinced of this? Was equating contraception and infanticide so obvious to him that he somehow shared this point of view?

The first topic the two men discussed concerned "marriage difficulties," even if it seems curious that they did so in the context of a dream which was deliberately focused on extramarital love affairs. Freud had already studied marital issues in two published essays, which makes it easier to see the context of his argument.[55] The "marriage difficulties" he discussed in those essays were sexual and centered on a Malthusian issue: the necessity or desire to limit the number of children in marriage through contraceptive practices. These practices, however, were deemed harmful to one's health, since they hindered the complete satisfaction of sexual desire and provoked a particular neurosis, classified by Freud as "anxiety neurosis."[56] Thus a married couple found themselves caught in a vicious cycle. If they wanted to remain healthy, they had to practice "normal" intercourse and were therefore confronted with the inescapable consequence of unwanted pregnancies. Thus Freud asked physicians to use their energies to find a comfortable and safe contraceptive method that did not hinder sexual pleasure.[57]

It has been noted that Freud gave a great deal of attention to the issue of contraception for personal reasons as well, reasons that are apparent in his letters and enclosures to Fliess.[58] The rapid growth of his family and the subsequent burden this caused him and his wife especially concerned him. To avoid the problems he had himself argued existed, he opted for abstinence. By his own admission this was a solution that compromised his psychological health as much as if he had used contraception. This choice, then, must have had other motivations and may well have resulted from his equating infanticide and contraception as evidenced in E.'s dream. Freud rejected withdrawal in marital intercourse[59] for scientific reasons because he felt it caused serious harm to health. But he did not know that these reasons were not at all scientific; in fact, he did not know and he did not want to know, for when his pupil Wilhelm Steckel discovered the nonscientific nature of this belief in 1912, he did not want to hear about it. The ancient ethico-religious prohibition on masturbation found in the Bible had been passed off as science. The scientific term derives from Onan's sin found in Genesis (38:7–8) and centers on his wasting his seed on the ground in order to prevent conception, a sacrilege for which Onan was punished with death by the Lord. That biblical passage furnished traditional Jewish morality with the scriptural foundation for the coitus interruptus prohibition which was then associated with masturbation.[60]

Although Freud recognized his profound ties to Jewish tradition, he nonetheless always professed he was a man of science and not a man with religious faith. And yet he found in science a condemnation of masturbation because it caused serious damage to one's health. In 1760 the Swiss physician S. A. Tissot described the pernicious effects of masturbation in a celebrated book on onanism reprinted many times and translated into numerous languages. The presumed effects of masturbation on the nervous system were held to be a true and indisputable dogma of nineteenth-century psychiatry, one that Freud did not dare question.[61] On the basis of this false scientific doctrine, Freud did not hesitate to claim that coitus interruptus was the physical cause of E.'s anxiety; he did not even suspect that E.'s anxiety could have been caused instead by a contemporary moral scruple linked to the ancient religious prohibition against onanism.[62] This pseudoscientific doctrine, which provided the cornerstone for the ethico-religious prohibition against coitus interruptus in Christian society, explains the curious discussion between the Jewish physician and the patient, also apparently Jewish, on whether it was legal to attribute the responsibility of a "specifically feminine" crime, like infanticide in the judicial sphere or like contraception in the popular sphere, to a man. Infanticide and contraceptive practices were exclusively feminine crimes only in the Christian tradition, however, not in a Jewish one, since the biblical precedent put the responsibility for coitus interruptus on Onan, the man, and not on the woman. It is interesting to compare Mr. E., who accused himself in his dream of infanticide when he really only practiced coitus interruptus, with a woman, the mother of a patient of Freud, who convinced her daughter that contraceptive precautions destroyed "the living seeds" of divine will. Freud recounted this story in a section entitled "Mushrooms" cited significantly in the manuscript that contained E.'s dream.[63] The woman's mother, probably a Christian, put the responsibility on the woman, while Mr. E., who was probably a Jew, put the responsibility on the man. The question posed by Freud evidently came from superimposing on the conscience of a Jewish scientist issues drawn from a scientific tradition which were conditioned by a juridical ethos of a Christian nature.

❧ Some Considerations Called a Conclusion

If, as Freud believed, E.'s dream was not an abstract product of his fantasy but rather drew its material from the concrete experience of the dreamer, then his dream was a historical document and must be read and interpreted as such. E.'s dream, as we have seen in fact, gives new meaning to the historical and cultural context in which it was produced. His dream is a document that not only reveals information about an individual but also reveals thoughts and motivations that are usually repressed and suppressed.

It is evident, however, that the dream per se reveals little about its context and takes on meaning only in light of the successive dialogue and Freud's comments. These three parts together form an interpretable text. The fact that this text is preserved in two versions is particularly useful, since it is precisely the differences between the two—omissions, changes, additions—which allow the dream to take on greater historical meaning. If Freud had limited himself to analyzing E.'s dream as a wish fulfillment in order to illustrate his previous work on dreams, then the historian, using the few references in the text, would discover that the wish expressed by the dream was closely linked to the regulation of socially conditioned sexuality. In addition, one would discover that the entire dream resulted from an implicit religious prohibition of which the dreamer was unaware; this prohibition conditioned his attitude toward sexuality and the issue of procreation—an attitude that, as we have seen, the interpreter of the dream shared with the dreamer.

In his essay "Sexuality in the Aetiology of the Neuroses" Freud wrote that the discovery of contraceptive methods that did not harm one's health would surely have a profound social impact.[64] He did not specify what that impact would be, but we can speculate that he would not have seen it as entirely positive. The separation of sexuality from reproduction which such a discovery entailed threatened not only ecclesiastical prohibitions and ancient traditions; it would also allow women to escape the compulsion to procreate by controlling reproduction and thus overcome the social strictures linked to it. But it was precisely this area of control which threatened men, as both the dream and its interpretation demonstrate, since controlling births was considered homicide (to E.) or else damaging to one's health (to Freud). If in his dream E. identified with the woman who committed infanticide, he did not do so because he felt as guilty as she, but rather this identification expressed his deepest conviction that this type of control—either through contraception, abortion, or infanticide—was not acceptable. Infanticide, which he accused himself of in his dream, was practiced in his time only in exceptional circumstances, and yet it always represented a "specifically feminine crime." To E. infanticide, a feminine domain where women tried to control their own sexuality and childbearing capabilities, had to be legally punished.

Nearly a century has passed since E. had his dream and Freud interpreted it. In the meantime, as a result of the profound social changes that have taken place, the regulation of sexuality has changed. Nevertheless, the polemics surrounding the issue of abortion still rage.

Notes

1. S. Freud, *Briefe an Wilhelm Fliess, 1887–1904*, Ungekürzte Ausgabe von J. M. Masson, Bearbeitung der deutschen Fassung von M. Schröter, Transkription von G. Fichtner (Frankfurt am Main, 1986), hereafter cited as *Briefe*; Eng. trans., *The Complete Letters of Sigmund Freud to Wilhelm Fliess, 1887–1904*, trans. and ed. Jeffrey Moussaieff Masson (Cambridge, Mass., 1985). Mr. E. is mentioned in the following letters: April 11, 1895; January 24, 1897; December 29, 1897; February 19, 1899, ff; December 21, 1899; January 26, 1900; March 11, 1900; April 4, 1900; April 16, 1900, ff. All translations from the letters are taken from this text.

2. Freud, *Complete Letters*, February 19, 1899, p. 345. The allusion that Freud makes in *The Interpretation of Dreams*, vol. 2 ("It was the patient . . . who had decided to get married immediately [after] the treatment was finished," p. 450), surely refers to E.

3. Freud, *Complete Letters*, December 29, 1897, pp. 290–91.

4. Freud, *Complete Letters*, February 19, 1899, p. 346.

5. *The Interpretation of Dreams*, vol. 1, p. 155. [All references are taken from the English translation version of James Strachey, *The Standard Edition of the Complete Psychological Works of Sigmund Freud*, in collaboration with Anna Freud and assisted by Alix Strachey and Alan Tyson, vol. 4 (1900): *The Interpretation of Dreams*, vol. 1 (London, 1953); and vol. 5 (1900–1901): *The Interpretation of Dreams*, vol. 2, and *On Dreams* (London, 1953).]

6. Freud, *Complete Letters*, April 11, 1895, p. 124. On the particular importance of the theater for the Viennese bourgeoisie, see C. E. Schorske, "Politics and the Psyche in *fin de siècle* Vienna: Schnitzler and Hofmannsthal," *American Historical Review* 66 (1961): 934ff. (reprinted as chapter 1 in id., *Fin de siècle Vienna* [New York, 1980]). The "theatermania" of the Viennese is also described by S. Zweig, *Die Welt von gestern* (Frankfurt am Main, 1970), pp. 29ff.

7. Freud, *Interpretation of Dreams*, vol. 2, p. 436. The senior colleague was probably Josef Breuer. The identity of the patient mentioned by Freud along with E. is in his letter to Fliess dated December 21, 1899, *Complete Letters*, pp. 391–93.

8. Freud, *Complete Letters*, April 16, 1900, p. 409.

9. Freud, *Complete Letters*, December 29, 1897, p. 290 ("Mr. E., whom you know"), and February 19, 1899, p. 345 ("our friend E., whom you know"). Fliess seldom went to Vienna. He only knew his wife Ida Bondy's circle of Jewish friends. Members of this group included the pediatrician Oscar Rie, Bondy's brother-in-law and a very good friend of Freud's, and Josef Breuer, who introduced them. The fact that Fliess knew E. leads me to believe that E. was part of Bondy's group of Jewish friends from Vienna.

10. Freud, *Interpretation of Dreams*, vol. 2, p. 438.

11. Freud, *Complete Letters*, December 21, 1899, p. 392.

12. Ibid, p. 391.

13. Ibid, p. 403.

14. Ibid, p. 409. According to Ernst Kris, this "is the first explicit sign of the role of transference in psychoanalytic treatment" (Freud, *Briefe*, p. 449, n. 2). This quote is not contained in the English translation of the letters. Therefore, we refer readers to the German edition cited above, from which the reference is taken, or to E. Kris, Anna Freud, and Marie Bonaparte's edition of the Freud-Fliess correspondence, Sigmund Freud, *Aus den Anfängen der Psychoanalyse: Briefe an Wilhelm Fliess, Abhan-*

dlungen und Notizen aus den Jahren, 1887–1902 (The Origins of Psycho-Analysis: Letters to Wilhelm Fliess, Drafts and Notes, 1887–1902, trans. Eric Mosbacher and James Strachey; intro. by Ernst Kris (New York: Basic Books, 1954).

15. Draft L., in Freud, *Complete Letters,* pp. 241–46.

16. Ibid, p. 242.

17. Freud, *Interpretation of Dreams,* vol. 1, pp. 155–57.

18. Ibid, p. 160.

19. *The Interpretation of Dreams* was begun by Freud in the summer of 1897. Most of it was written in the summer of 1899, and it was published in November 1899, not in 1900 as is indicated on the title page. See *Editorische Vorbemerkung* about the German edition in S. Freud, *Studiennaugabe,* vol. 2 (Frankfurt am Main, 1972), pp. 13, 16, 19.

20. Freud, *Interpretation of Dreams,* vol. 1, p. 104

21. Ibid, p. 155.

22. Ibid, pp. 156–57.

23. With the word *Marienkafer* ("ladybug") associated by E. in his treatment with his mother Marie, a symbiotic relationship was revealed with his French nurse, referred to as *netter Kafer* ("beetle"). Freud, *Complete Letters,* December 29, 1897, p. 290.

24. Freud, *Complete Letters,* February 19, 1899, pp. 345–46.

25. The multiple configurations possible in love affairs are the theme of Schnitzler's famous comedy *Reigen (Ring-around-the-Rosy),* which caused a great scandal. The "young gentleman" in this work was involved in an affair with a "servant girl" and a "young lady", that is, a married woman. The play *Liebelei* and the scene "Weihnacht-seinkaufe" in the comedy *Anatol* showed the "young bourgeois gentleman" in affairs with both a married woman and a peasant woman. Especially in *Liebelei* the gentleman revealed his different attitudes toward these two categories of women. While in his relationship with the married woman Fritz was deeply involved psychically and was killed in a duel over her, the peasant girl was only an object for his fun and pleasure. The heroine of Schnitzler's last novel, *Therese: Chronik eines Frauenlebens,* in A. Schnitzler, *Das erzählerische Werk,* vol. 7 (Frankfurt am Main, 1979), was a teacher. Schnitzler's works seem more useful than those of other Viennese writers because social reality was described with much greater detail in his works. Helpful information about the relationships between the sexes in *fin de siècle* Vienna is found in M. Pollak, *Vienne 1900* (Paris, 1984), pp. 155ff.

26. A. Schnitzler's father was the noted specialist in laryngology, Johann Schnitzler (1835–93). About him and his scientific significance, see E. Lesky, *Die Wiener medizinische Schule im 19. Jahrhundert* (Graz and Cologne, 1965), pp. 417–19. A. Schnitzler's brother, Julius, also a specialist in laryngology, sometimes played tarok with Freud (*Complete Letters,* p. 55, n. 1). On the relationship between Freud and Schnitzler, see M. Worbs, *Nervenkunst, Literatur, und Psycho-analyse im Wien der Jahrhundertwende* (Frankfurt am Main, 1983), pp. 179–258.

27. A. Schnitzler, *Jugend in Wien, Eine Autobiographie,* ed. Th. Nickl and H. Schnitzler (Frankfurt am Main, 1981).

28. Ibid, p. 84.

29. Ibid, pp. 215–314 (citation p. 236). Olga Waissnix was a member of this haute bourgeois Viennese family. Her letters to Schnitzler are published in A. Schnitzler and O. Waissnix, *Liebe, die starb der Zeit* (Vienna, Munich, and Zurich, 1970).

30. The actresses who played an important role in Schnitzler's life were Adele Sandrock, who starred in his first plays, Marie Glumer, and Marie Reinhard. On the social status of Viennese actresses in the nineteenth century and their role as objects

of erotic fantasies where they were considered free but corrupted women, see Pollak, *Vienne 1900*, pp. 164ff.

31. As is evident from his autobiography, Schnitzler had numerous relationships with women of the lower social classes. Anni of the petite bourgeoisie was typical of these women; their affair began when they met and danced together in a tavern outside the city walls. As Schnitzler himself wrote, Anni was a girl who belonged to "that group of people who deserve compassion and are condemned to live from one month to the next alternating continually between unconcern and fear" with respect to unwanted pregnancies, while he, by his own admission, felt "completely without responsibility"; *Jugend in Wien*, pp. 146ff. See also H. Scheible, *Diskretion und Verdrangung*, in *Arthur Schnitzler in neuer Sicht*, ed. H. Scheible (Munich, 1981), p. 212.

32. Schnitzler, *Jugend in Wien*, pp. 315ff.

33. S. Freud, "Civilized Sexual Morality and Modern Nervous Illness," *Standard Edition*, vol. 9 (London, 1959), p. 195.

34. Ibid, pp. 197–98.

35. J. Breuer, in his *Studies on Hysteria, Standard Edition*, vol. 2 (London, 1953), written in collaboration with Freud, suspected that the attitude of women from the lower classes (peasants and laborers) toward sexuality was different from that of women from the upper classes whom he knew through clinical treatment.

36. R-P. Janz, "Zum Sozialcharakter des 'süsses Madels,' " in R-P. Janz and K. Laermann, *Arthur Schnitzler: Zur Diagnose des Wiener Burgertums im Fin de Siècle* (Stuttgart, 1977), pp. 41–54, also p. xv.

37. Ibid, p.44.

38. Schnitzler refers to his lovers Anni and Jeannette Heeger as prototypes of his literary figure of the "süsses Madel," *Jugend in Wien*, pp. 146, 274. Their bourgeois lovers reproach them above all for their "unconcern," their lack of moral fortitude. See Janz, "Zum Sozialcharakter," pp. 50–54.

39. Freud, *Contributions to the Psychology of Love*, vol. 2, "On the Universal Tendency to Debasement in the Sphere of Love," *Standard Edition*, vol. 11 (London, 1957), p. 185. The essay was published in 1912 but takes up issues Freud had studied earlier.

40. This expression is used by Freud in a note entitled "Rolle der Dienstmadchen" ("The Part Played by Servant Girls") in Draft L, which also contained E's dream. According to Freud, his young female patients associated theft and abortion with servant girls. *Complete Letters*, p. 241.

41. According to Freud, this was a corollary wish fulfillment in E.'s dream.

42. J. L. Flandrin, *Familles, parenté, maison, sexualité dans l'ancienne société* (Paris, 1976), pp. 212ff. [in English, *Families in Former Times: Kinship, Household, and Sexuality*] showed that coitus interruptus as a contraceptive method was the man's responsibility and that consequently the woman had to have enough power over him to make him practice it. According to Flandrin, ladies of the French courts described by Brantôme in the sixteenth century had this power, as did wives with increasing frequency from the eighteenth century on. In his studies on anxiety neurosis Freud found that on more than one occasion a patient said he practiced coitus interruptus in order to respect his wife's wishes. A note written down by Freud in 1893 seems to describe E.'s situation: "Rarer cases of anxiety neurosis outside marriage are encountered especially in men. They turn out to be cases of *congresses interruptus* in which the man is strongly involved psychologically with women whose well-being is a matter of concern for him. In such circumstances this procedure is even more harmful for a man than coitus interruptus in marriage, for this is often corrected, as it were, by normal coitus outside marriage" (Draft B, *Complete Letters*, p. 43).

224 *Ingeborg Walter*

43. A. Finger, *Das österreichische Strafrecht* (Prague, 1891), p. 37.
44. Arts. 144–46 of the Austrian penal codes of 1852. Women were deemed the only perpetrators of this crime. According to this code, the person who carried out the crime was considered a "co-defendant" following article 146, which meted out the same penalty as for the woman but "a harsher" one if the father was the "co-defendant."
45. In the authoritative *Archiv für Kriminalanthropologie und Kriminalistik*, a certain Paul Nacke published two fairly positive reviews of *The Interpretation of Dreams by Freed* (sic!), and yet he could not help noting that the author, who recounted people's intimate experiences, allowed "suspect things" to come out (*Freuds Traumdeutung Frühe Rezensionem, 1899–1903*, ed. G. Kimmerle [Tübingen, 1986], p. 58).
46. Avicenna [F. Wittels], "Das grösste Verbrechen des Strafgestes (Das Verbot der Fruchtabtreinbung)," in *Die Fackel*, nn. 219–20 (February 22, 1907), pp. 1–2 (citations pp. 49, 10). The author became a member of Freud's "Wednesday Society" on March 27, 1907, after his article was published. He published thirteen articles in the *Fackel* which generated lively debate in the society reunions. Wittels was a sort of *trait d'union* between Freud and Kraus and was also the cause of their falling out (Worbs, *Nervenkunst*, pp. 149–77). In 1903 Kraus had already attacked two verdicts that were made in abortion trials (*Die Fackel*, n. 149, pp. 8–10).
47. Stooss's prohibition on abortion was grounded in his belief that the mother had a duty, which was not well defined in his analysis, to conserve the life of the fetus; in C. Stooss, *Lehrbuch des österreichischen Strafrechts* (Vienna and Leipzig, 1910), pp. 249–51. The Swiss Carl Stooss (1849–1934) was a professor of criminal law at the University of Vienna from 1896 on. Kraus attacked him many times, reproaching him for, among other things, using his Swiss criminal law bill to advance his own causes, which were centered "on the subtlest nuances in relationships between the sexes," and for wanting to use criminal sanctions to threaten "any deviation whatsoever from the path of virtue" (K. Kraus, "Sittlichkeit und Criminalität," in *Die Fackel*, n. 115, 1902, p. 87; Ital. trans. ed. B. Cetti Marinoni, in id., *Morale e criminalità* [Milan, 1976], p. 55). In their *Einführung in das österreichische Strafrecht* (Vienna and Leipzig, 1923), pp. 159ff., L. Altmann and M. L. Ehrenreich emphasize the "bloody battle" then taking place to abolish criminal sanctions on abortion, although they declared themselves to be against it.
48. A. Amschl, "Das Verbrechen des Kindesmordes nach österreichischen Recht," *Archiv für Kriminalanthroplogie und Kriminalistik* 30 (1908): 71–117, in particular pp. 78ff. A proposal made by Hanns Gross (1847–1915), a professor of criminal law in Graz, considered the founder of scientific criminology, was under discussion (about him, see *Österreichisches biographisches Lexikon, 1815–1950*, vol. 2 [Graz and Cologne, 1959], p. 74). Gross criticized considering the mother's "confused mental state" at childbirth as a motive for infanticide. From the eighteenth century on, under the influence of the Enlightenment this had been adopted as an extenuating circumstance to reduce the penalty against women who committed infanticide, although it had little consensus. Even Stooss, chided by Kraus as a Swiss philistine, wrote in his *Lehrbuch* that maintaining this motive was *"pia fraus."*
49. [F. Wittels], *Das grösste Verbrechen*, p. 3.
50. Gratian wrote in his *Decretum*, "Non est homicida qui aborsum procurat ante quam anima corpori sit infusa" (*Corpus Iuris Canonici*, ed. E. Freidberg, vol. 1, *Decretum Magistri Gratiani*, II, c. 32, q. 8 [anastatic reprint, Graz, 1959]), without indicating an exact moment. On this whole issue, see J. Demaille in *Dictionnaire de droit canonique*, vol. 1 (Paris, 1935), cols. 1536–61. Wittels commented in his pamphlet: "The juridical problem was connected to the protection of the supposed human soul of the child-to-be-born and thus is terribly confused right up to the present. In fact the Church does not want to preserve the State from depopulation nor preserve the embryo's life

and even less the mother's life; the Church wants to baptize the soul to save it from damnation. This is theological metaphysics which must be kept separate from the legislator" (*Das grösste Verbrechen*, pp. 8ff).

51. Nikolaus Lenau, *Sämtliche Werke und Briefe*, vol. 1, ed. W. Dietze (Frankfurt am Main, 1971), pp. 25ff.

52. Ibid., pp. 352–65.

53. J. Bolte, "Lenaus Gedicht Anna," *Euphorion, Zeitschrift für Litteraturge-schichte* 4 (1987): 323–33.

54. X, V, XII, I, entitled "Homicida est qui facit vel dat sortilegia vel venena sterilitatis" (*Corpus Iuris Canonici*, ed. E. Freidberg, vol. 2 [anastatic reprint, Graz, 1959]).

55. These are two articles published by Freud in 1895 and 1898, respectively, "On the Grounds for Detaching a Particular Syndrome from Neurasthenia under the Description 'Anxiety Neurosis,' " *Standard Edition*, vol. 3, and "Sexuality in the Aetiology of the Neuroses," *Standard Edition*, vol. 3 (London, 1962), pp. 259–85. The same point of view is expressed by Freud in a manuscript sent to Fliess in 1893, Draft B, *Complete Letters*, pp. 39–44.

56. For a definition of this concept, see J. Laplanche and B. Pontalis, *Enciclopedia della Psicoanalisi* (Bari, 1981), pp. 337–39. Also M. Krull, *Freud und sein Vater*, (Munich, 1979), pp. 25–37.

57. Freud, *Sexuality in the Aetiology of the Neuroses*, p. 277.

58. See in particular the letter to Fliess dated August 20, 1893, in *Complete Letters*, pp. 53–55.

59. Draft B, in *Complete Letters*, p. 41.

60. See the articles "Sexualhygiene der Juden" and "Abtreibung" in *Jüdisches Lexikon*, ed. G. Herlitz and B. Kirschner, IV, 2, cols. 383–87, and I, cols. 59ff, where it says: "homicide of a man . . . or woman capable of reproducing is considered the indirect destruction of human beings; the same is held for preventing contraception."

61. On this issue, see my introduction to D. G. M. Schreber, *L'educazione totale* (Rome, 1981), pp. 19ff, which also contains bibliographic information (p. 31).

62. This anxiety is confirmed in the data found by researchers on Jewish demographics, who discovered that Jewish families adopted Malthusian practices even before Christian families. See M. Livi Bacci, "Ebrei, aristocratici e cittadini: Precursori del declino della fecondità," *Quaderni storici* 54 (1983): 915–25 and the bibliography. This anxiety is obviously a consequence of this behavior.

63. Draft L, in *Complete Letters*, p. 241. We should also recall Freud's conversation with a young Jewish traveling companion in *The Psychopathology of Everyday Life*, *Standard Edition* vol. 6 (London, 1960), pp. 8–11. The young man forgets a passage in Virgil; Freud explains that the slip was caused by his anxiety that his lover was pregnant. It is significant that in his series of associations the young man mentions Saint Simon of Trent, a child whose murder in the fifteenth century occasioned a ritual homicide case that was brought against several Jews.

64. Freud, *Sexuality in the Aetiology of the Neuroses*, p. 277.

Afterword: Crime and the Writing of History

by Edward Muir and Guido Ruggiero

It is perhaps fitting that this volume begins and ends with articles that turn on death because what societies label crime usually represents perceived ruptures or breaks in the ties that bind people together, the little deaths of social life. These moments of literal destructuring usually have a history because they warranted a defensive response in the form of "justice," which often left extensive records. As we have seen in the preceding essays, such responses have the potential to reveal at numerous levels the fabric and the texture of life in the past. Thus, like Bakhtin's portrayal of the medieval vision of the physical world in which death was merely the beginning of life, we might see in the many deaths of the criminal record new beginnings that are full of lively and rich possibilities for the writing of history.

Traditionally the history of crime has focused on crime itself and how crime was defined, disciplined, and perceived in the past. The essays in this volume follow that tradition. But what is most interesting about them is the way in which they do a great deal more, for like much of the new work on the history of crime they use the richness of judicial documents to move beyond events themselves to look at their effects and contexts in the broader society and culture. From that perspective, crime opens many windows on the past.

First, a crucial aspect of most crimes is the way that they create records of behavior, not just the obviously central deeds of perpetrators and victims, but also the behavior of witnesses, neighbors, family, supporters, enemies, and the authorities responsible for dealing with crime. As a result the historian discovers in such records traces of behaviors that are invisible in other sources, behaviors emanating from various levels of society and viewed from multiple perspectives. In

addition, when a crime is prosecuted, it intersects with legal and bureaucratic structures that are frequently highly articulated and complex
(and difficult to decipher for a historian). That interaction can be
most revealing about the interrelationship between law, institutional
structures and procedures, and social values. The impressive work of
historians who have studied legal traditions as an evolving system of
thought can be rendered highly problematic when one turns to other
issues such as the law's relationship to social values, political and social
structures, and human deeds. Baptizing dead babies, for example, was
against the law of the church, and the false miracles that accompanied
them, as Fra Antonio Dall'Occhio saw immediately, were also illicit
given long-established theological traditions. Yet the key to the story
is how popular beliefs and local power relationships rendered the
apparent givens of the legal code and theological tradition moot. The
interactive nature of crime tests meanings and often reorients well-
studied aspects of the past such as law and bureaucratic structures.

    Another revealing aspect of crime develops from the way in which
crimes generate responses from those in authority. To a great extent a
crime that is investigated, prosecuted, and punished creates a recurring
drama that turns on the relationship between authority and deeds that
are perceived as undermining or threatening it. Needless to say, such
moments speak as much about authority as they do about crime. In
fact, one could well argue that they say more about the former than
the latter, since many criminal deeds remain unreported (or if reported,
unprosecuted), but those that clearly appear to challenge authority are
the most likely to be pursued and thus recorded. Sabina Loriga's article,
"A Secret to Kill the King," examines some of the possibilities such
a confrontation can create for the historian, even if the crime that is
at the center of her analysis may appear to modern eyes as so unlikely
as to be hardly worthy of study. Yet from the crime's apparent unlikeli-
ness, the historian begins a process of rethinking the nature of political
power at several levels from the meaning of kingship and sovereignty
to the impact of "total institutions" in the relationship between authority and relatively marginal members of society. That rethinking is at
once destructuring of more traditional political interpretations and
suggestive of alternatives.

    At a more abstract level crime is also intimately related to the
classificatory systems by which a society orders itself. In the identification of a particular action as a crime, one encounters the social and
cultural system defining itself. Giovanna Fiume's old vinegar lady

comes immediately to mind. Her crime in her portrayal of it fits within the context of magic, but unfortunately for her, her classification scheme was no longer shared by the authorities who prosecuted her. As a result her magic was reclassified as murder by poison, resulting in her execution.

The classification of the action is just the beginning, however, for there is a reciprocal relationship between deeds and labels, and both can be seen as products of changing social, cultural, political, and moral values. The resultant "discourse" is an extremely rich mix that is often spelled out with deceptive simplicity in law, prosecution, or contemporary accounts of crime. The extremes that complexity can reach are sampled in Ingeborg Walter's essay on Mr. E.'s dream of infanticide and Freud's interpretation of it. Walter traces the effects of the modernization process on a psychic level. For both E. and Freud have internalized the ordering principles of the laws and norms that enmeshed their lives. The process duplicated itself on multiple levels, such as Mr. E.'s criminalizing his own sexually exploitative attitude toward women of a certain social class, who were also stigmatized for allowing themselves to be so used, and at a more complex level creating an ordering system like psychoanalysis itself.

In sum the behaviors associated with crime allow us at one level to consider crime as a series of events that break and at times create the solidarities that bind society and groups together within societies. The discourses that proliferate around crime are rife with powerful representations of life itself. Thus, crime may be seen as involving both events and representations that mark out power and its social dynamics. In turn, such marking of power also defines individuals in a range of social roles as victims, accusers, criminals, judges, police, and executioners, as well as the perhaps too often overlooked categories of family, friends, neighbors, "innocent" bystanders, and the shadowy brokers of power. In very real, if seldom considered, ways, crime helps to mark out and sustain such relationships in a theater of power and authority. Such theaters of power interact with and are legitimated in part at least by a system of symbols generated in response to crimes, in large part because crimes test and measure values.

Perhaps the most important aspect of crime for the historian is the simple fact that it generates a wide diversity of documentation in virtually all record-keeping societies, a diversity that provides an unusual range of perspectives on the past. First, of course, a crime has to be declared or denounced. No matter what form it took, each denunciation can be read as expressing a vision of what at least some contemporaries considered to be criminally and culturally significant and threatening. Growing out of denunciations and often closely related to them are the administrative decisions that define a crime and assign it to the proper court, magistracy, or council. The documentation that records this process is often highly formulaic and repetitive, but, nonetheless, since it is concerned with evaluating the crime and locating its investigation in a hierarchy of administrative structures, it can be revealing of the political and social issues operating behind the scenes of a particular case.

Once a crime has been defined administratively and referred to the magistracy that will deal with it, the potential complexity of documentation increases exponentially. Investigation can produce masses of evidence: the depositions and testimony of those directly involved (witnesses, and often a string of neighbors, supporters, enemies, and authority figures); the questions asked of those same people; the questions and responses generated by torture; the collection of material evidence; the evaluation of legal and institutional issues by outside experts and members of the magistracy itself. The trial that grows out of this collection of evidence, while it tends to be crucial for those involved, may in fact produce less information of significance than the investigation. Still, the trial often has a ritual element that, by structuring information, can highlight deep issues that might be lost in the detail of depositions and testimony at the investigatory stage.

The sentencing stage offers a telling measure of how authorities evaluated a series of events; it would be unwise, however, to assert that the sentence in a case is merely a direct response to a specific type of crime. Frequently too many other factors are involved in deciding on a penalty for things to be so simple. Still, the serial nature of sentences can outline rough statistical parameters, while case-by-base analysis can bring out both the individual particularities of specific situations—particularities that may say little about crime per se but a great deal about the ordering structures and power dynamics of the society—and the more general factors that seem to color the evaluation of specific crimes. The appeal procedure is also revealing about the structures of social power and especially about the more informal power dynamics that can often short-circuit the official structures of power. Punishment in turn engenders its own documentation, from prison records to reports of public executions or ritualized penalties.

Finally, all these forms of historical documents generated by crime are paralleled by another range of documents: crime literature, which ranges across a rich spectrum from broadsheets and journalistic narrations to chronicle reports and novels to include even accounts of psychoanalysis concerned with crimes both real and imagined. In addition, in certain societies all this helps to create a vision and often a bureaucratic and practical reality that constitutes a criminal world and class, which in turn spawns its own controlling documentation. As this extensive list suggests, few historical events are likely to create as complex and layered a documentation as crime. Each level of documentation provides at the least a slightly different perspective on the issues involved.

Historians have frequently concentrated on the problems of such documentation and tended to overlook its possibilities. One widely shared concern has focused on the evident bias of the documents generated by crime. It could well be argued that every judicial document in a case is a tissue of lies: defendants reconstructing their past to make it as innocent sounding as possible; accusers recasting events to make the accused seem as guilty as possible; investigators working to fit individuals and events into preconceived notions of crime; witnesses shaping their testimony because of animosities, friendships, the desire to please the powerful, or the need to thwart them.

In the face of such an apparently endless range of possibilities, it might seem that reconstructing any sort of history from such documentation would be extremely problematic. However, lies can often tell more about the past than apparent truths. That is especially true in the types of documents generated by crime. The contingent events of the past described with honest intent often have the look and the impenetrability of the famous "one damn thing after another" that seems to dog history when it focuses too tightly on the individual and the local, as the historical analysis of crime often does. The lies or distortions that permeate crime documents can, however, shear away the contingent and get at what matters at least in the eyes of those creating the documents. Thus, for example, behind the many lies that constitute the documentation about the role of perpetuas in Oscar Di Simplicio's article, deeper truths can be discovered about the nature of clerical life and female roles in the parishes of early modern Siena.

Stated a different way and perhaps more simply: not just any lie will do in testifying about a crime. Usually lies must have the ring of credibility. Moreover, lies are normally invented to serve an end: they are most informative when examined as instrumental or teleological.

When Loriga discusses, for example, individuals who denounced others for attempting to use magic to kill the king and members of the royal family in Piedmont, it is clear that some of those accusations were patently false. Nevertheless, reconstructing a false past, while saying very little about ways of killing a king, tells very interesting things about attitudes toward the royal family, about ways of commanding attention and manipulating bureaucracies, and about the level of understanding which at least certain lower-class individuals had of the order and function of their society. In other words, the lies in the case tell important truths, truths that in many ways are more significant than the alleged truths of the crimes themselves.

Unfortunately, most often historians of crime discover in the criminal records not revealing lies but obscure biases, the significance of which is very difficult to unravel. The practical problem is how to identify and evaluate the bias or biases that create and permeate particular texts. Crime documentation brings this problem to the fore because with such obvious biases every text demands careful evaluation. The problematics of criminal texts have created a historiography (reflected well in the articles in this volume) which tends to treat texts with a close, deforming attention not unlike that called for by the newer forms of literary criticism.

One advantage, however, that the close reading of texts drawn from the criminal archives has over the close reading of other texts, such as literary ones, is the former's repetitive nature. For example, if investigators were trying to force a crime into a certain statutory mold, by looking at a series of such crimes one will begin to see how that bias helped to form cases and will get a clearer sense of the parameters and often the meaning that stand behind such bias. The stereotype of the witch and the way it was imposed during the sixteenth and seventeenth centuries on persons who attempted to heal and to hurt others reveal the process most clearly. According to Carlo Ginzburg's clever serial analysis, the workers of agrarian prophylactic magic, the *benandanti*, were slowly but relentlessly transformed into witches first by the investigations and trials run by the Inquisition and eventually by popular opinion. The transformative process can work at a much more humble level; in Di Simplicio's article on perpetuas, parishioners repeatedly showed concern with the "visibility" of the female servants of priests as a clue to the relationship between the priest and his servant: highly visible servants were often labeled concubines whether they were or not, and invisible concubines were often seen as properly modest servants. Such community perceptions reveal expectations about the way servants and women in general were expected to comport themselves. In fact, the structure of the bias in these cases is perhaps the best evidence Di Simplicio provides on the life and customs of priests and perpetuas in the period.

It would be difficult to overemphasize the heuristic potential in lies and bias. Nonetheless, as with most historical texts, along with potentialities come problems. Perhaps most notable is the fact that biases complicate the search for a text's meanings, revealing the artificiality of any attempt to record events in words and the very arbitrary notion of the event itself. Neither events, the words that attempt to represent them, nor the texts that attempt to capture them are in the end univocal. Events have a tendency to dissolve into an infinite regress of contingency, words into an infinite regress of representations, and texts into an infinite regress of both. Nevertheless, the very process of writing a text or series of texts about a reputed event limits the range of possible understandings and misunderstandings. The interpretive range is not infinite; thus even in a world of contingent truth, texts define a range of possibilities and some a more narrow range than others.

That range of readings is limited by a host of criteria, but for the historian the specificity of time and space is especially significant. At the most banally absurd level we cannot claim that a speech by Jefferson reveals the influence of John Kennedy or that Plato's thought was formed in reaction to nineteenth-century realists. Such criteria can and do dramatically reduce the possible readings of a text, and for texts generated by crime they are especially pertinent. If we take time and place to imply temporally specific cultural possibilities, then the range of possible readings is further reduced. Assuming that Renaissance representations of the Madonna breast-feeding the Christ Child, for example, reflect maternal affection—a reading of a picture which makes eminent sense today—may have made much less sense in the Renaissance or early modern period, when breast-feeding was normally done by lower-class nurses who were not the child's mother and had no necessary maternal feelings for the child. In that cultural context such representations may have said much more about Mary's humbleness and self-sacrifice before the son of God.

Perhaps the best example of this limiting of readings in this volume is the fate of the old vinegar lady in Fiume's article. Times had changed, and what had once been an excellent strategy to avoid serious punishment at the hands of authorities unwittingly played into a very different way of reading her crime because the authorities saw her deadly cures for unwanted spouses not as magic but as poisoning. If the old vinegar lady had stressed her faith in the magical qualities of her solutions to unwanted spouses, she might well have escaped punishment as a misguided eccentric, but by attempting to play on older forms for reading witchcraft in which the key to forgiveness was being willing to recognize one's magic as chicanery or misguided, she inadvertently "proved" to her judges that she knew that her "cures" were poisoning. The death of the old vinegar lady serves as a reminder that readings of events and texts have consequences.

The old vinegar lady died not simply because her reading was no longer the best reading of events but because her reading did not have the same power behind it as that of her judges. In fact, every reading will be limited to some extent by the parameters of power which create, condition, and enfold it. On the one hand, that makes texts often very interesting measures of power; on the other, it limits again the range of meanings that can be meaningfully given to them. For example, in a society with a strong sense of social hierarchy, the deference of witnesses in a crime investigation to their social superiors may well say more about their social values than about the role of those superiors as perpetrators or as repressors of the crime being investigated. The relative invisibility of certain of the women originally accused of being involved in the poisonings makes more sense if it is understood as a consequence of a social dynamic in which the powerful have the ability to protect their supporters and friends from prosecution. In turn, when one considers the resurrections and baptisms of babies described in Cavazza's article, the ability of the small sanctuary at Trava to avoid investigation by ecclesiastical authorities even after repeated complaints derives in large measure from the patronage of a powerful local noble family.

Charting the dynamics of power limits the possible readings and empowers certain ones over others. The resulting knowledge remains uncertain and contingent but nonetheless useful at several levels. Moreover, when judicial texts are repetitive or serial in nature, they may even have the potential to be predictive. One can hypothesize about relationships of power or relationships between cause and effect and attempt to predict the outcome of similar relationships in other texts. For example, if in adultery cases it appears that when a wife runs off with her lover the matter is treated more seriously than when a husband runs off with his lover, it is possible to construct and test a hypothesis that this is the consequence of attitudes about gender and use it to predict the results of other cases. Di Simplicio predicts that more publicly visible perpetuas will be more likely to be labeled concubines or prostitutes by local communities, and his predictions are borne out by his figures and presumably can be tested in other communities. Obviously, unlike predictions in science, the range of contingencies that could undermine the validity of such predictions is so great that one would not want to stake a great deal on them. Nevertheless, the ability to hypothesize about observable regularities again limits the range of possible readings.

The classic example of such limitations may well be the witch trials of the sixteenth and seventeenth centuries, in which it has been possible to observe in trial after trial how inquisitors with a certain program of questions and torture actually formed the responses of those accused to fit the inquisitors' vision of a witch. Such an observation is made possible by the serial nature of the texts of crime.

Finally, a text's range of reading may be limited, especially a text dealing with crime, when it is read as a form of microhistory. The possibilities of microhistory were discussed in Volume II of this series, *Microhistory and the Lost Peoples of Europe.* Each of the examples of history written from criminal records presented in this volume shares with microhistory a concern to trace names through a myriad of records. Names narrow the number of possible readings of texts: as they reveal the traces of networks and alliances; as they identify partially hidden protagonists reappearing in the background; as they highlight key figures and peripheral players. At the same time they also enrich the more limited number of readings that remain. For example, knowing the name of a judge or an investigating officer and watching his approach to a crime or a social group over several cases can make possible a very suggestive and powerful reading. Torre's masterful recounting of feuding in northwestern Italy shows how the ability to reconstruct groups and alliances that stand behind reported crimes narrows the number of possible interpretations while enriching those that remain. At times the proliferation of names can be daunting, but they literally circumscribe a world of conflict and in the process bring out deep connections that would otherwise remain hidden.

All these ways to limit the number of possible readings of texts generated in response to crime—that is, by placing a reading within the context of a specific time and place, within the parameters of the dynamics of power in that time and place, within the limits imposed by the serial nature of the documentation, and, when possible, within the context of a microhistory built around it—ironically seem actually to create more potential readings than more traditional ways of reading criminal texts, such as through the methods of criminology. When we see a murder as a crime of violence situated in a macro-theoretical system that explains criminal violence as a symptom of asocial malad-justment or pathology, our possible readings of that murder are rela-tively limited. However, when placed in the historical context of time, space, culture, and the dynamics of power, the possible limits on interpretation often seem to dissolve and the number of potential readings seems to multiply, even though new documents can also often eliminate some hypothetical interpretations as unlikely.

Texts, however, do much more than limit and empower readings of the past. As noted earlier, the documents created in response to a crime are also a form of literature, dramas in the theater of authority. Whether the players want to perform or not, a structure of jurispru-dence and control creates a special time and space in which deeds labeled criminal are replayed under the scrutiny of authority and power. Edoardo Grendi's suggestive article on counterfeiting provides a good example of how what seems a singular crime can, in fact, play different parts in various dramas of authority.

In a similar vein the texts of crime are themselves a series of narratives, as Natalie Zemon Davis has shown in *Fiction in the Archives*. Crime documents over and over again construct narratives that have a large fictional component and which are directed toward pleasing a certain audience. Both accusations and investigations try to force the details of an event into the mold of what was required or perceived to be required to designate a specific action as a crime. Testimonies might have the opposite goal of exculpation. Such narratives are fictions in that they consciously or unconsciously reconstruct the past with an eye to make it fit a perceived model rather than to reconstruct events. The task is always in some sense rhetorical, that is, to convince a jury, judge, or broader public that something criminal did or did not occur.

Many fictions are carefully constructed to ring true. They narrate events in ways that sound right at the time, and perhaps in the end, as noted above, that concern offers the best possible source for history. A narrative supplies at several levels a set of propositions about how events truly go together, in other words, about how life is lived. That is, obviously, one of the things that make reading narratives interesting and in turn one of the things that make reading them revealing for the historian. Even the most heavy-handed lies and the most innocent fantasies employ narrative schemes to create verisimilitude. Perhaps the best example of this is the revealing portrait of nineteenth-century bourgeois male values which Walter extracts from the mere dream of a crime that never was committed in Vienna.

Understanding how some texts are composed of simple lies or complex fantasies and dreams, how some are fictional narratives or moments in a theater of authority, how some narrow the range of readings of crime while they seem to increase their number, and how some are clearly biased makes the new history possible. Textual criticism in a historical context destructures the easy readings of past meanings, events, and representations, allowing the historian to face new ways of seeing, understanding, and enjoying the past. In the end all readings may be possible, but not all will allow one to see, understand, and enjoy at the same level. The texts of crime, however, because of their exceptional richness, are replete with possibilities for writing history that allows us to do all three or, to borrow from Robert Darnton, to write history that is fun to think.